ELGAR

AN EXTRAORDINARY LIFE

J. P. E. HARPER-SCOTT

First published in 2007
by The Associated Board of the Royal Schools of Music (Publishing) Limited
24 Portland Place, London W1B 1LU, United Kingdom

ISBN-13: 978 1 86096 770 2

AB 3288

A CIP catalogue for this book is available from The British Library.
Design and formatting by www.9thplanetdesign.com
Typeset by Hope Services, Abingdon.
Printed in England by Halstan & Co. Ltd, Amersham, Bucks.

Front cover
Caricature of Elgar conducting, by Edmond X. Kapp (1890–1978). By permission of Edmond X. Kapp / Lebrecht Music & Arts Photo Library.

Signature of Edward Elgar. By permission of the Lebrecht Music & Arts Photo Library.

for B, better without the moustache

Contents

Preface and acknowledgements

Like others in the series, this book is written for students and general readers with an interest in the life and music of its subject, in this case Edward Elgar. For those who want a one-stop source on the man and his music, it will provide a guide to current thinking on both. For those sufficiently interested in the subject to want to explore further, the footnotes and bibliography point to more specialized literature. I have attempted to focus these particularly on easily accessible works, such as books in print, rather than to the slightly more obscure material that can be found in academic journals. Nevertheless, those musty corners contain some of the most interesting of recent reflexions on Elgar, and I share several of these delights in the text for those who might not otherwise encounter them.

All future Elgar biographers owe a significant debt to Jerrold Northrop Moore, whose extensive researches, presented most impressively in *Edward Elgar: A Creative Life*,[1] will remain an important source. His editions of Elgar's letters are invaluable.[2] Other important life-and-works sources are by Michael Kennedy, Diana McVeagh, Percy M. Young, and Robert Anderson,[3] and any uncredited biographical details in what follows will almost certainly have been uncovered by these writers.[4]

I owe several people thanks for help in writing this book. My first go to Robin Barry who is responsible for the fact that it exists; judge his crime after reading it. I am also grateful to Sue Fairchild at the Elgar Birthplace Museum,

---

[1] Jerrold Northrop Moore, *Edward Elgar: A Creative Life* (Oxford: Oxford University Press, 1984).

[2] Edward Elgar, *Edward Elgar: Letters of a Lifetime*, ed. Jerrold Northrop Moore (Oxford: Clarendon Press, and New York: Oxford University Press, 1990); *Elgar and His Publishers: Letters of a Creative Life*, ed. Jerrold Northrop Moore (Oxford: Clarendon Press, and New York: Oxford University Press, 1987); and *The Windflower Letters: Correspondence with Alice Caroline Stuart Wortley and Her Family*, ed. Jerrold Northrop Moore (Oxford: Clarendon Press, and New York: Oxford University Press, 1989).

[3] Michael Kennedy, *Portrait of Elgar*, 3rd edn. (Oxford: Oxford University Press, 1987; orig. edn. 1968) and *The Life of Elgar* (Cambridge: Cambridge University Press, 2004); Diana M. McVeagh, *Edward Elgar: His Life and Music* (London: Dent, 1955; reprinted, Westport, CT: Hyperion Press, 1979); Percy M. Young, *Elgar, O.M.: A Study of a Musician*, 2nd edn. (London: Purnell Book Services, 1973; orig. edn. 1955); and Robert Anderson, *Elgar* (London: Dent, and New York: Schirmer, 1993).

[4] This book also often draws on work of my own published elsewhere. Most wickedly, this includes a joke that gets its third outing here.

for help with research trips and illustrations. Julian Rushton offered suggestions and support throughout the process of writing, selfless from the start, and Richard Ross also read sections and made very helpful comments. I am indebted to two anonymous readers for their intelligent criticisms, but my greatest thanks are owed to Elizabeth Eva Leach. She read the entire manuscript with a fierce captiousness that does her credit, and did much to improve my prose, as well as offering unfailing support and friendship throughout its composition.

I can't blame anyone for any remaining gaucheness or factual errors.

J. P. E. Harper-Scott

1. *Elgar composing for camera in his study at Plâs Gwyn, 1909.*

We are grateful to the following for the permission to reproduce photographs:

1. Photograph of Elgar composing in his study at Plâs Gwyn in 1909. Photographer unknown. By kind permission of the Raymond Monk Collection.

2. Photograph of Elgar in his study at Severn House, *c.*1915. Photographer unknown. By kind permission of J. P. E. Harper-Scott.

3. Photograph of the view along the Malvern Hills. By permission of James Osmond Photography, photographersdirect.com.

4. Painting, *c.*1900, of Elgar's birthplace, 'The Firs', at Lower Broadheath. By kind permission of the Raymond Monk Collection.

5. Photograph of Elgar with his mother, Ann Elgar, *c.*1859. Photographer unknown. By kind permission of the Raymond Monk Collection.

6. Photograph of Elgar Brothers music shop, Worcester, in 1904. Photographer unknown. By kind permission of the Raymond Monk Collection.

7. Programme cover for the first concert to feature a work by Elgar, *Sevillana*. By kind permission of the Raymond Monk Collection.

8. Photograph of Elgar's wind quintet, *c.*1878–9. Photographer unknown. By kind permission of the Raymond Monk Collection.

Page 24: Elgar's moustache style as illustrated in the *c.*1930 edition of *The Art and Craft of Hairdressing*, edited by Gilbert A. Foan and N. E. B. Wolters, published by The New Era Publishing Co. Ltd., London. By kind permission of the Chris Mullen Collection.

9. Photograph of Elgar and Alice (1848–1920) in Bavaria in 1892. Photographer unknown. By kind permission of the Raymond Monk Collection.

10. An ink-blot 'self-portrait' made from Elgar's signature. Courtesy of The Elgar Birthplace Museum.

11. One of Elgar's adverts for violin lessons. By kind permission of the Raymond Monk Collection.

12. The 'friends pictured within' the Variations, Op. 36, in variation order. Photographer(s) unknown. Courtesy of The Elgar Birthplace Museum.

13. One of a set of illustrations by Stella Langdale (1912–1950) for an early twentieth-century edition of Cardinal Newman's (1801–1890) 'The Dream of Gerontius', published by The Bodley Head. By permission of the Lebrecht Music & Arts Photo Library.

14. Book of words for the London premieres of 'To Women' and 'For the Fallen', containing August Jaeger's (1860–1909) 'analytical and descriptive notes' on *The Dream of Gerontius*. By kind permission of the Raymond Monk Collection.

15. Elgar's doodle of the Apostles. By kind permission of the Raymond Monk Collection.

16. Elgar's caricature of his daughter, Carice (1890–1970), ('Miss Elgar, The Censor'), 1915. By kind permission of the Raymond Monk Collection.

17. Photograph of Carice Elgar (1890–1970) holding her pet, Pietro d'Alba (Peter Rabbit), *c.*1909–10. Photographer unknown. By kind permission of the Raymond Monk Collection.

18. Photograph of Elgar practising chemistry in 'The Ark', his laboratory at Plâs Gwyn. Photographer unknown. Courtesy of The Elgar Birthplace Museum.

19. Photograph of Elgar timing a friend's billiards shot, probably at Severn House. Photographer unknown. By kind permission of the Raymond Monk Collection.

20. Facsimile of the opening of the Second Symphony, in short score. Courtesy of The Elgar Birthplace Museum.

21. Painting of Alice Stuart-Wortley (1862–1936), by her father, Sir John Everett Millais (1829–96). Photographed in 1967 by Sir Ralph Millais on behalf of Michael Kennedy. Photograph reproduced here by kind permission of Michael Kennedy.

22. Cover for the full score of the concert overture *Cockaigne*. By kind permission of the Raymond Monk Collection.

23. Programme cover for the play *The Starlight Express*, based on Algernon Blackwood's (1869–1951) novel *A Prisoner in Fairyland*, adapted by Violet Pearn, and with music by Elgar. By permission of Arthur Reynolds Collection / Lebrecht Music & Arts Photo Library.

24. A sentimental visualization of the Romantic Child, taken from a Victorian postcard. Photographer unknown. By kind permission of the Chris Mullen Collection.

25. Photograph of Elgar and companions eating aboard the HMS *Hildebrand*, on an Amazon cruise in 1923. Photographer unknown. By kind permission of the Raymond Monk Collection.

26. Photograph of Elgar conducting in 1933. Photographer unknown. By kind permission of the Raymond Monk Collection.

27. Photograph of Elgar boarding a plane for his first flight in 1933. Photographer unknown. Courtesy of The Elgar Birthplace Museum.

28. Photograph of Elgar at the Marconi studio in 1930. Photographer unknown. By kind permission of the Raymond Monk Collection.

29. Photograph of Elgar on his deathbed at Marl Bank, Worcester in 1933. Photographer unknown. By kind permission of the Raymond Monk Collection.

30. The old-style £20 note featuring Elgar and the West face of Worcester Cathedral (Bank of England, Series E revision, printed from 22 June 1999 to 12 March 2007). Reproduced by permission of the Bank of England. Photographed by Paul Mulcahy.

31. Sir Edward with poultry. Photographer unknown. Courtesy of The Elgar Birthplace Museum.

INTRODUCTION

Pompous circumstances

Not many people manage to filch a bit of Shakespeare and popularize it almost as their own invention, but in borrowing Othello's snappy farewell to 'The royal banner, and all quality, / pride, pomp and circumstance of glorious war!', Elgar did it.[1] It's a good phrase, and it was echoed immediately by Shakespeare's contemporaries Beaumont and Fletcher, and later by (among others) Sheridan, Dickens, and Twain, sometimes in contexts far removed from the original.[2] But when we use the phrase 'pomp and circumstance' today, we almost always have only one context in mind: Elgar's music, particularly as heard in 'Land of Hope and Glory' on the Last Night of the Proms.[3] Almost every modern use of the phrase is a conscious nod to Elgar and to the context we take its borrowing in his oeuvre to establish. That is, not the context of Twain's little boy making 'ding-dong-dong' noises by a river, but that of a contented ex-army type chuffing indulgently on a pipe whose smoke-whorls insinuate themselves into the bristles of his moustache, a flatulent man rolling port round his tongue and punctuating bloated silences with the occasional 'Bah!'.

Why do we think of Elgar this way? Is it his fault (the ex-army look he adopted as his personal image) or someone else's (for example, the fact that modern political parties of the right tend to use his music for

---

[1] Shakespeare, *Othello*, III. iii. 356–7; the quotation is taken from the third Arden edition, ed. E. A. J. Honigmann (London: Arden Shakespeare, 2001).

[2] Beaumont and Fletcher, *The Prophetess*, IV. vi. 72–4: 'farewell Pride and Pomp / And circumstance of glorious Majestie, / Farewell for ever', quoted in *Othello*, ed. Honigmann, p. 231; Sheridan, *The School for Scandal*, Epilogue, line 40: 'Farewell all quality of high renown, / Pride, pomp, and circumstance of glorious town!'. In Dickens's *Oliver Twist*, chapter 37, Mr Bumble is said – the second time in a page he is associated with the word 'pomp' – to 'read the paper with great show of pomp and circumstance'. In Twain, Ben Rogers, who enters the story of *Tom Sawyer*, chapter 2, '[im]personating a steamboat', becomes more ambitious by 'personating the Big Missouri' 'with laborious pomp and circumstance'.

[3] The other phenomenon that encourages people to wave the flag of St George – the prospect of a victory for the English football team in a major tournament – is probably more disturbing than the limited and musical (rather than tribal) enthusiasm of the Last Night, but nobody ever attaches the phrase 'pomp and circumstance' to it.

promotional material or in conferences)?[4] Or is it the evidence of his biography and reception – that as a friend of royalty (if he was one), heavily decorated in his lifetime and cemented into the musical Establishment (it seems), he must *necessarily* be viewed as a kind of musical Cecil Rhodes figure, an enthusiast for empire whose music is tainted by association with a part of Britain's past that we find it intensely shameful to think about? Maybe a mix of all of that.

Like all simplistic assessments it is an attractive one to accept uncritically as the truth. And Elgar himself does his modern reception few favours in this respect.[5] Figure 2 opposite shows him in typical gentlemanly pose, arms folded to preserve emotional distance, and weight on the back foot so that he can look slightly down his bent nose at us. The setting is the wood-panelled music room of Severn House, his residence in Hampstead, with splashes of heraldry and art to emphasize the social position that his smart suit and waistcoat (and the spats peeping out at the bottom) also proclaim. The fact that the candles on the wall behind him are unused, and that the furniture seems more decorative than practical, reinforces the sense that every detail of this image is fabricated tendentiously.

We are meant to be impressed by all this; whether it is in any sense a true representation of the man is immaterial. In any case, if he was the kind of man who *chose* to wear a mask of this kind, then perhaps that tells us something – though we shouldn't hastily decide what – about his character: a mask may after all be an exact copy of the face behind it, and reality might by sheer coincidence be exactly like our fabrication of it – as we see pungently expressed in several of Magritte's paintings, including either of those called *La condition humaine* (1933 and 1935).[6]

It was important to Elgar, living as he was at the height of Britain's political power and influence in the world, to be viewed as a man of the upper middle class (the imperial establishment of the day) by the people who mattered – that is, the ones his wife and her family respected, and who had the money to commission music from him or invite him to the best clubs.[7] That wasn't the only reason why he constructed this image, but it was an important part of his thinking, and the one that most impresses those who are wont to confirm their pre-existing intellectual

---

[4] He would approve of this. He wrote to the publisher Leslie Boosey on 17 April 1929 that its performance was 'all right . . . [for] the *conservatives* – don't let any blasted labour rogues or liberals use the tune!' (Elgar, *Elgar and his Publishers: Letters of a Creative Life*, p. 860).

[5] His other principal curse on all future critics was to propagate the ghastly notion of an 'enigma' behind his *Variations* – but we shall come to that in chapter 2.

[6] In these an artist's easel stands partly obscuring a window. At first we seem only to see a view through a window, but closer inspection reveals the edge of the artist's canvas and the easel supporting it. What we are mostly seeing is a *picture* of the view – but it is exactly the same as the view itself.

[7] To view the Britain of the turn of the nineteenth century as uncomplicatedly 'imperial' is another oversimplification, as we shall see in inter-chapter 1.

2. Elgar in his study at Severn House, c.1915.

prejudices by pigeonholing people according to type. And if at the same time we get to laugh at the wobbly old man who can now be seen on a British Film Institute DVD as he conducts an orchestra in 'Land of Hope and Glory' for the opening of EMI's Abbey Road studios in 1931 – well, so much the better.[8]

Our interpretation of Elgar as a jingoistic oddball rests overwhelmingly on knowledge of a few of his ceremonial pieces, and the vague sense that anyone who could compose such a gloomily nostalgic work as the Cello Concerto must have been depressed at the thought that the old imperial age was passing. This fact doesn't worry us, but it should. The evidence of the symphonies, the Violin Concerto, the concert overtures, *Falstaff*, the chamber music, songs, and most of the choral music, complicates the picture to such an extent that two readings of him begin to seem untenable. The first is the ill-informed reading of Elgar as a jingo. The second is the subtler bipolar reading of him as a man with a 'public' and a 'private' personality and compositional style – the former leading to 'Land of Hope' and *The Crown of India*, the latter to the deep emotional inwardness of the symphonic slow movements and *The Dream of Gerontius*. Elgar cannot be pigeonholed, either by those who wish to present him as an introverted romantic or by those who see only an extroverted figure of the Establishment. The chapters that follow will delineate some of the ways that we should begin to reform our impressions of him.

The first idea we ought to take on board is that although Elgar first came to public attention in the 1890s as a neo-romantic composer, by the time he wrote *In the South* in 1904, he had become a modernist (these terms, and others like them, will be defined and discussed later in the book). There are signs of this new stylistic direction in his music of the 1890s, but it took him longer than his contemporaries on the continent to settle on a recognizably modernist course. He never wrote twelve-note music, 'emancipated the dissonance', or rejected old forms and techniques, but in any case such a crudely limited definition of modernism has no place in intelligent criticism.

Modernism is not about horrid sounds and the abandonment of sonata form: philosophically it is a radical continuation of romanticism, and in some of its forms difficult to tell apart from it. In music it has much more to do with composers' comportment to their world, and their reflexions on the life of human beings in it, than a navel-gazing interest in the language of music. Elgar's modernism is less obvious, and less remarked-upon, than that of some of his contemporaries, but in the structures of his

---

[8] His awkward joke as he steps up to the podium – 'Play this as if you'd never heard it before' – raises not the slightest audible titter. The clip is available on the DVD *Ken Russell's Elgar*, released by the BFI in 2003, which also includes the famous drama-documentary made for the BBC series *Monitor* in 1962.

major orchestral works, and in the meanings suggested by his quickly evaporating climaxes and ambiguously presented endings (to name just two obvious places), we can find his modernism – which is of a colour in some ways more disturbing than Mahler's or Strauss's – shining out.

Music is infused with meaning, given by the age and social situation of its composition, and understood by us in ours. The great Idealist philosopher Immanuel Kant got it exactly, immaculately wrong when he said that appreciation of music was 'gustative' – that is, giving the same quality of pleasure as eating chocolate. We seek meaning everywhere in music, generally starting (because it is easier) with details of the composer's personality or personal circumstances at the time of composition. In Elgar's case, much of this interpretation is generated by his known neurotic tendencies – principally worries about health and about other people's opinions of him – and his involvement with empire (whichever side of the traditional arguments one comes down on). Meaning of the more purely musical sort is thought accessible only to those with special training, able to talk comfortably about augmented sixths and so on. But this is not so: by listening in the ordinary way (to themes, and what they seem to stand for or suggest), and with only a slightly altered attitude (so that attention is paid to the order in which they appear, and its significance), a wealth of meaning reveals itself. Later chapters will aid the development of this absorbing way of listening.

Back, finally, to the matter of Elgar's life. Much writing in recent years has focused on romantic or sexual involvements outside his marriage. His relationship with Alice Stuart-Wortley has long been acknowledged, but recent speculations have cast the net wider. His early engagement to Helen Weaver has been explored, as has the friendship with Vera Hockman in his last few years. More surprising, perhaps, has been carefully reasoned (and cautiously expressed) work by Byron Adams on the homosocial – possibly homoerotic – undercurrents of such works as *The Dream of Gerontius*, the *Variations*, and the Second Symphony.[9] These matters, and some others of great biographical interest (but not always of direct relevance to the music), will be addressed in this book in short 'inter-chapters', which offer moments for reflexion between the main chapters. Consider them arias, outside the narrative flow, but deepening the overall content. Other themes – his relation to empire, and his view of childhood – have a more direct bearing on the music, but over a wide span in his career, and are also best covered outside of the main chapters.

---

[9] This nest of homo-words, used elsewhere occasionally in this book, might need clarification. They all refer to same-sex relations: 'homosocial' when they're just friendly and to do with the passing of free time, 'homoerotic' when they involve erotic feelings but might not actually involve sexual acts, and 'homosexual' when there's a definite romantic or sexual element.

Elgar's was a complicated life, which has sustained a huge mass of biography. Indeed, the lives of few moustache-owners have been so thoroughly combed. A book of this length, which is an introduction to the music as well as the man, must inevitably present only a partial picture, tinted by the author's own interpretation. So its subtitle has a double meaning. As well as being just one of several 'lives' of Elgar, this is an 'extraordinary' one in the sense that it is a personal view – albeit one that is, I hope, reasonable. It is also unusual insofar as, when discussing particular works, I make no attempt to draw parallels with his life when to do so seems false. Artistic creation may spring in some sense from life, but it is not automatically autobiography, at least not if it is any good.

The story this book tells in brief is in certain respects well known, and in others misunderstood. A short list of commonly held beliefs concerning Elgar's life and career might read:

1. He was an imperialist.
2. He was not an imperialist.
3. He was a romantic composer.
4. His love of the English countryside means that his music is principally about that.
5. He disliked academic musicology.
6. Every work can be shown to relate to every other work, and all of them ultimately to a tune he wrote as a boy in Broadheath.
7. After his wife's death he could no longer compose.
8. He was a close friend of royalty.
9. He lost his faith.
10. He didn't want his Third Symphony to be completed.

Some elements in this list are exaggerations; others are at best unpersuasive. If not actually pernicious, the myth they help to compose is a figment of the collective imagination, an over-romanticized reading of an only partly romantic man's life. This myth should be challenged because it both distorts the truth and is less interesting than it. Time will alter it, but is unlikely to eradicate it altogether. It is not my intention to argue against the interpretations presented in the existing principal biographies of Elgar, or to run down the remarkable devotion of earlier researchers. Rather I mean to moderate some of their arguments in the light of more recent thinking, and hope to change a few minds in the process.

ONE

THE APPRENTICE YEARS (1857–89)

Broadheath

'The Firs' is a small cottage not far from the common that gives its name to the village of Lower Broadheath, just west of Worcester (see figure 4, overleaf). Edward William Elgar was born there on 2 June 1857 to Ann and William Elgar.[1] His sister Lucy, five at the time, recalled the day as an adult. 'The air was sweet with the perfume of flowers, bees were humming, and all the earth was lovely.'[2] It's an appealing image, and might be true (it was a June day in England, after all), but given that most five-year-old girls are likely to consider the birth day of a new baby brother somehow magical, it's entirely possible that Lucy's memory was elaborated by the passing of years. Would she have remembered if it had been raining or unusually cold?

The meteorological conditions might not seem to matter much, but there is a serious point here. Elgar is a composer with an especially clearly defined popular image, but many of the most delicious ideas we have of him should be judged with caution. His love of the English countryside, and desire somehow to infuse his music with it, cannot be disputed: as a man of 64 he told his friend Sidney Colvin, 'I am still at heart the dreamy child who used to be found in the reeds by Severn side with a sheet of paper trying to fix the sounds and longing for something very great'.[3] His spiritual closeness with nature is emphasized in many memorable scenes

---

[1] Basil Maine speculates that he might have been named 'after the sixteen-year-old Prince of Wales' (Basil Maine, *Elgar, His Life and Works*, 2 vols (London: G. Bell, 1933; reprinted, Bath: Chivers, 1973), vol. 1, p. 4.

[2] Quoted in Jerrold Northrop Moore, *Edward Elgar: A Creative Life* (Oxford: Oxford University Press, 1984), p. 8.

[3] Quoted in Michael Kennedy, *Portrait of Elgar*, 3rd edn. (Oxford: Clarendon Press, 1987; orig. edn. 1968), p. 15. Despite his travels in Europe and – to a limited extent – America, it is worth remarking that it remained largely the English countryside, or the Marches of Wales, that chiefly fascinated him.

3. View along the Malvern Hills.

4. A romanticized painting, c.1900, of Elgar's birthplace, 'The Firs', at Lower Broadheath, as it might have looked in 1850.

from Ken Russell's 1962 BBC film biography (for the documentary series *Monitor*), from the boy riding a pony on the Malvern Hills to the man riding his bicycle through the woods. But as agreeable as it is to imagine Elgar's Broadheath as an Eden in which the composer's character was fixed in the form of a vicar for nature, we should pause to consider the facts dispassionately. His parents moved to Broadheath only a year before Elgar's birth, possibly to escape the noise of ongoing restoration work at the east end of Worcester Cathedral, the site of their previous house.[4] And they moved back to Worcester, where they'd lived together since 1848 (and his mother since birth), eighteen months after Elgar was born; his older and younger siblings were all born in Worcester itself. He couldn't have formed an impression of Broadheath at an age when mother's (or wet nurse's) teat is a baby's only genuine interest, and although he visited it for holidays as a child (he said his father rented the cottage 'as a weekend sort of thing'), he never lived there again.[5]

Like many children, even those raised in inner cities, his older siblings adored their sometime childhood home in Broadheath, and his mother never lost a love of the country ideal that was certainly stronger than the vague, unfocused longing for a simpler kind of life felt by many in towns and cities. Elgar too remained fond of his later childhood memory of the place, sometimes referring to his suckling there as a time of special contentment. He made a public declaration of this affection by taking the title 'First Baronet of Broadheath' in 1931. But can we assume anything from this? The once Prime Minister Harold Wilson became 'Lord Wilson of Rievaulx' even though he was born and rooted in Huddersfield, West Yorkshire, over fifty miles from the idyllically located ruins of that abbey, and schooled even further to the west, on the Wirral. His connexion with Rievaulx might not extend beyond a feeling that, put after his surname, it sounded nice, and looked French and sophisticated. Perhaps something similar was true for Elgar: Broadheath has a toothsome, Anglo-Saxon feel to it. Of course Broadheath might sound and look nice *and* have meant something to him, but we cannot be certain of that.

The problem we face with Elgar's life, then, particularly in its early stages, is that much of the biographical material available to us is often silently shaded by hindsight, not least the hindsight of the people involved. To stress overmuch the Broadheath birthplace (now an attractive visitors' centre with well-maintained garden) fits the myth of Elgar as the child of nature, and with it the role of his mother in shaping his temperament, not least in the artistic direction. The result is to distract us from other, and equally fascinating, aspects of his personality, such as the consequences of his experiences as an Englishman growing up as the empire grew

---

[4] See Robert Anderson, *Elgar* (London: Dent, 1993), p. 3.

[5] Kennedy, *Portrait*, p. 18.

morbidly obese, and as a musician in a European musical world witnessing profound changes of style and technique. The Elgar who dreams of the little cottage outside Worcester, of the River Severn, and of the music-dripping air of a quiet country lane, is not a fabrication, but he is only part, and by no means the most interesting part, of the Elgar who was also one of the leading European composers of his generation, and who engaged with some of the most serious political, ethical, and existential questions of his time, in a musical language as richly modern and distinctive as that of his contemporaries Richard Strauss (1864–1949), Gustav Mahler (1860–1911), Jean Sibelius (1865–1957), Carl Nielsen (1865–1931), or Arnold Schoenberg (1874–1951). But this great European composer had modest beginnings.

Worcester

Elgar thought his surname had Scandinavian origins, coming from 'Ælfgar', 'fairy spear'.[6] The derivation could have been wrong ('Ælfgar' is actually Old English), though from his first biographer on it has been repeated.[7] It might just as easily be from the fifteenth-century word 'elger' (from Old English *œlgar*), meaning 'eel-spear'. At any rate, the stress in it should come on the first syllable, with the second being clipped so that it rhymes more with 'elder' than 'radar'. Elgar's father, William Henry Elgar (1821–1906), was a musician and tradesman, originally from Dover, who went to Worcester in 1841 to become a piano tuner, teacher, and church organist. He was also a good violinist, as his son would be after him. His first work in Worcester involved tuning pianos for local eminences, including those at Witney Court, twelve miles north-west of Worcester,[8] the seat of Lord Dudley and for three years home to the dowager Queen Adelaide.[9] Elgar's later love of the glib ceremony of court corresponds with his father's longing – common to the middle classes of all ages – for recognition (even if only financial) from social superiors.[10] He played piano or second violin in chamber groups, including the Worcester Glee Club (which Elgar himself would join, aged 13, in 1870). It was there that he met John Leicester, whose nephew Hubert Leicester would become one of Elgar's closest friends. Although William Elgar was not a Roman Catholic, Leicester put him up for the job of organist at St George's Roman Catholic church in Worcester, which he was offered in

---

[6] He should have said 'elf spear'.
[7] See Robert J. Buckley, *Sir Edward Elgar* (London: Bodley Head, 1905), p. 1.
[8] It was eviscerated by fire in 1937, but the ruin still stands with its extensive landscaped gardens.
[9] Diana McVeagh notes the symmetry in the fact that 'eighty years later his son was to tend the instruments of King George V'; *Edward Elgar: His Life and Music* (London: Dent, 1955), p. 1. She means he would become Master of the King's Musick.
[10] Michael Kennedy makes a similar point: Kennedy, *Portrait*, p. 19.

1842 and retained for 37 years before being replaced by his son. William Elgar had been lodging at the coffee-house of a Joseph and Esther Greening for a year; they then took him in as a lodger at the family home in Claines, three miles north of Worcester, where by 1848 he had fallen in love with and married Joseph's live-in sister Ann.[11]

The new couple soon moved to 2 College Precincts, then, after their brief time in Broadheath, to 1 Edgar Street (now 1 Severn Street) in 1859, back to 2 College Precincts in 1860, and finally to rooms above the family music shop, 'Elgar Brothers', at 10 High Street in 1863 (see figure 6, overleaf).[12] They had seven children. John Henry ('Harry', born 15 October 1848), Lucy Ann (29 May 1852), and Susannah Mary ('Pollie', 28 December 1854) were all born 'within the shadow of our dear, dear Cathedral'[13] in Worcester. After Edward, the only Broadheath child, came Frederick Joseph ('Joe', 28 August 1859), Francis Thomas ('Frank', 1 October 1861), and Helen Agnes ('Dot', 1 January 1864). There might have been an eighth child: a ledger entry, 'Mary died', is the only mention of another possible Elgar girl.[14]

Ann Elgar (née Greening, ?1822–1902) was 'a tall, fine woman with big features and splendid carriage, with a great personality and presence. Although she had practically no opportunities,[15] her love of reading was remarkable: she read every available book, and her great longing was to know more and more of the world of literature.'[16] She loved nature, and pressed wild flowers into scrapbooks, alongside notes on local history.[17] Her daughter remembered that in Broadheath 'she kept us from the contamination of the world as long as ever she could do so. It was too great a distance from the town for smuts to fly, and settle on our homely table-cloth! . . . She sought *natural* joy in her daily pin-pricks by taking long walks, and commun[ing] with Nature in its beauty'.[18] Because she didn't like William to walk alone to Worcester, she accompanied him to church every Sunday, and eventually took instruction to become a Roman

---

[11] Hubert Leicester remembered the domestic situation differently – that Esther had been a Miss Greening and that Ann was *her* sister – but both Diana McVeagh and Percy Young give a more cogent family history that suggests Ann was the husband's, not the wife's, sister. See McVeagh, *Elgar: Life and Music*, p. 2, and Percy M. Young, *Elgar O.M.: A Study of a Musician*, 2nd edn. (London: Purnell Book Services, 1973; orig. edn. 1956), p. 20.

[12] The building has been demolished, but a plaque on a hotel marks its approximate former location. Henry, Elgar's father's younger brother, was an employee, not a partner in the family business (Moore, *Creative Life*, p. 14).

[13] Lucy Pipe (Elgar's sister), quoted in Anderson, *Elgar*, p. 3.

[14] See ibid. She was born between Lucy and 'Pollie'.

[15] So far, so unlike Elgar's wife, who was squat and socially advantaged. But in the following ways the two women are more similar.

[16] Elgar's daughter Carice, quoted in Moore, *Creative Life*, p. 5.

[17] Young, *Elgar O.M.*, p. 28. Elgar pressed flowers too, later in life sending one as an annual gift to Alice Stuart-Wortley.

[18] Lucy Pipe, quoted in Moore, *Creative Life*, p. 7. Anderson gives '*material*' for '*natural*'; Robert Anderson, *Elgar and Chivalry* (Rickmansworth: Elgar Editions, 2002), p. 31.

5. *Elgar with his mother, Ann Elgar, c.1859 (the earliest known picture).*

6. *Elgar Brothers music shop, 10 High Street, Worcester, 1904.*

Catholic.[19] The children were all raised in this faith – as strong in her as it commonly is among neophytes – and in Elgar's youth it exercised a powerful hold, becoming one of the ways in which he defined himself as an 'outsider', and remaining an influence on his music for some time. At church he would have heard Mozart, Haydn, Beethoven, Hummel, Weber, Pergolesi, Handel, and Spohr.[20]

Ann Elgar's love of literature and of nature became Elgar's too, but she had an equally great influence on Elgar's older brother Harry, who by his early teens had already developed a keen interest in botany.[21] Tragically, he died of scarlet fever on 5 May 1864, aged only 15, and Elgar quite suddenly took on the mantle of eldest brother (and the nickname 'the Governor', which stuck until early adulthood), keeping watch particularly over his brother Joe, whose remarkable early musical talents led to his being called 'the Beethoven of the family'. But Joe too died, aged only seven, on 7 September 1866, of consumption.[22]

Elgar's debt to his mother, rather than his father, is stressed right from the first chapter of the first biography.[23] The theme has never gone away, and with good reason: Elgar *did* learn much from his mother's deep enthusiasm for literature,[24] and her fondness for the country doubtless helped mould him in that image. Elgar himself pointed to her influence often in later life. She also supported him in composition, which his father did not: Hubert Leicester (nephew of John) recalled that 'his father and uncle were merely amused and scoffed at these childish efforts – an attitude in which they persisted until E. had really made his way in the world'.[25] Yet his imprint on his son is still remarkable, and if William had not carped but played Leopold to Elgar's Mozart, we might be more interested in him.

---

[19] This was probably some time between the births of Lucy and Pollie: subsequent children were baptized as Catholics.

[20] This list is taken from John Butt, 'Roman Catholicism and Being Musically English: Elgar's Church and Organ Music', in Daniel M. Grimley and Julian Rushton (eds.), *The Cambridge Companion to Elgar* (Cambridge: Cambridge University Press, 2004), pp. 106–19, at p. 107.

[21] Her grandchildren inherited this trait, and in her seventies she joined in with their lessons (McVeagh, *Elgar: Life and Music*, p. 4).

[22] That is the end of the family's tragedy. The other son, Frank, survived into adulthood and became an oboist and conductor in Worcestershire. Lucy and Pollie married (the latter having six children: Elgar's living relatives come from her line), while Dot became a nun (he wrote a tiny organ piece, *For Dot's Nuns*, in 1906).

[23] Buckley, *Elgar*, p. 5. Although there is no evidence that father and son did not get along, there may have been a gulf between their personalities that led Elgar to bond more closely with his mother. William Elgar was 'breezy, cheerful, and downright', Ann 'romantic by temperament and poetic by nature' (McVeagh, *Elgar: Life and Music*, pp. 3–4). The latter personality could accommodate Elgar's tender sensitivity better. His mother wrote a couplet describing him: 'Nervous, sensitive & kind / Displays no vulgar frame of mind' (Kennedy, *Portrait*, p. 19).

[24] Which in her case extended to early attempts to write: Percy Young notes that 'an enigmatic quatrain composed at the age of nine point[s] to a sound tradition of scholarship in the parish church of Weston-under-Penyard [in the Forest of Dean] and also to some support for letters at home' (Young, *Elgar O.M.*, p. 20).

[25] Quoted in Michael Kennedy, *The Life of Elgar* (Cambridge: Cambridge University Press, 2004), pp. 11–12.

It wasn't just his son's music he scoffed at: religion – his bread and butter as church organist – got it in the neck too. He particularly disliked the 'absurd superstition and play-house mummery of the Papist; the cold and formal ceremonies of the Church of England; or the bigotry and rank hypocrisy of the Wesleyan'.[26] The provincial professional musical activity of father and son was broadly similar in shape, as was the trajectory of their religious faith (both men lost it in middle age). Nor was Elgar's mistrust of academic musicology, from which he consciously distanced himself, so very different from his father's instinctive reaction against the context in which he operated.

If his mother taught him to love Longfellow, God, nature, and dogs,[27] his father taught him not only to love Mozart but also how to make a living (and forget about God). The family's handyman, Ned Spiers, also had an effect on Elgar's development: he gave the boy his introduction to Shakespeare. Spiers 'had been stage carpenter with the touring companies . . . and quoted Shakespeare and speeches from all the repertory of the companies, and knew the whole of England, and was a wonderful companion – almost tutor to the [Elgar] children'.[28]

In a family environment well stocked with books (literature and music) and instruments, with music everywhere (his siblings were musicians too), and with a sturdy middle-class love of self-improvement, the circumstances were, if anything, even more propitious for the development of a composer than they would have been if Elgar had attended one of England's finest schools. His dedication as an autodidact was certainly extraordinary, and one of the chief wonders of his life; but his achievement is explicable, and the result of effort, not a miracle.

Education and early musical experience

As it was, Elgar began his education in 1863 (aged six) at the 'Middle Class School for Girls' run at 11 Britannia Square, Worcester, by Miss Caroline Walsh, a zealous Roman Catholic convert. Lucy and Pollie were already pupils there, and so, as Jerrold Northrop Moore notes, it is likely that the boy subconsciously and specifically associated both school and Catholicism with the female.[29] As he grew older, central features of Elgar's character and passions would be classed as 'feminine' (not to say

---

[26] Quoted in Moore, *Creative Life*, p. 6. He became a play-house mummer when he converted to Catholicism on his deathbed.

[27] Elgar recalled having read Longfellow with his mother when writing to her in 1892 (Young, *Elgar O.M.*, p. 35). Michael Kennedy owns a copy of *Hyperion* once owned by Elgar. In the margin Elgar has throughout noted textual differences from other editions, testifying to a remarkable level of familiarity with the work (Kennedy, *Portrait*, p. 19).

[28] A memory of Hubert Leicester's, quoted in Moore, *Creative Life*, p. 22. Spiers was so significant a figure for the family as to feature in a poem Ann Elgar wrote in the year the family moved to Broadheath (see Young, *Elgar O.M.*, pp. 28–9).

[29] Moore, *Creative Life*, p. 17.

'effeminate') by the social and musical culture of his day. Musicianship itself, especially of the luxurious Wagnerian sort, was considered essentially feminine or feminizing, as was personal sensitivity of the easily offended, heart-on-sleeve sort – a quality that abounded in Elgar. Catholicism too was a signifier of 'decadence' in later nineteenth-century England, and this concatenation of feminizing characteristics was liable to present Elgar with problems of personal image, both socially and sexually, as a grown man. These will be discussed in inter-chapter 1.[30]

Elgar was trained to be a stolid middle-class tradesman. This was made explicit when, after five years of schooling, he moved on to his last school, Littleton House, where it was said that 'Young gentlemen are prepared for Commercial pursuits by MR. REEVE'. This Francis Reeve inculcated a reading of the Bible that, as almost every commentator has remarked, would influence Elgar's conception of his oratorio *The Apostles* (see chapter 3). In an interview with his first biographer, Elgar said that 'Mr Reeve[,] addressing his pupils, once remarked: "The Apostles were poor men, at the time of their calling; perhaps before the descent of the Holy Ghost not cleverer than some of you here". This set me thinking, and the oratorio of 1903 is the result'.[31] He stayed at Mr Reeve's school until 1872. (In the year before Littleton House, he had been at Spetchley Park, another Catholic school, this time run by minor aristocracy: he spent his time there 'gaz[ing] from the school windows in rapt wonder at the great trees in the park swaying in the wind'.)[32]

A career in music was perhaps the natural route for him to pursue, given his father's occupation, and his paternal family's extensive musical ability. He began learning piano by improvising in the family shop in 1864, but soon further lessons were arranged with a brace of Victorian ladies: music theory with Miss Sarah Ricketts (a singer in the choir at St George's) and piano with Miss Pollie Tyler, a teacher at Miss Walsh's school. He was not so prodigious as Joe, but given the accessibility of instruments (not just pianos) in his father's shop, and the opportunity to join his father in the organ loft during church services (he didn't actually start playing for services until his middle teens), he was given ample scope

---

[30] These issues are explored in rich detail in Byron Adams, 'Elgar's Later Oratorios: Roman Catholicism, Decadence and the Wagnerian Dialectic of Shame and Grace', in Daniel M. Grimley and Julian Rushton (eds.), *The Cambridge Companion to Elgar* (Cambridge: Cambridge University Press, 2004), pp. 81–105. Elgar himself associated decadence with French, not German, composers, in his inaugural lecture as Professor of Music at Birmingham University; Edward Elgar, *A Future for English Music, and Other Lectures*, ed. Percy M. Young (London: Dobson, 1968), p. 51.

[31] Buckley, *Elgar*, p. 8.

[32] The music critic Ernest Newman's reminiscence, quoted in Anderson, *Elgar*, p. 4. Visiting Spetchley Park almost 50 years later, Elgar found a copy of his setting of Cardinal J. H. Newman's *The Dream of Gerontius*. By his setting of the words 'The sound is like the rushing of the wind – / The summer wind among the lofty pines', he wrote 'In Spetchley Park *1869*' (Moore, *Creative Life*, p. 41).

to explore his swift-developing enthusiasm for performance. The shop gave him privileged access to such works as Mozart's masses, Beethoven's piano sonatas, and his symphonies in piano reduction. 'I remember distinctly the day I was able to buy the Pastoral Symphony. I stuffed my pockets with bread and cheese and went into the fields to study it.'[33] The fields are the natural place to study a 'pastoral' symphony, perhaps, and in choosing to recall *that* incident, the adult Elgar was doubtless reinforcing his status as a nature-loving romantic.

By 1866 (aged eight or nine) he was musically literate enough, and interested enough in Bach, to spell out that composer's name in notation by writing a single semibreve at the junction of four interlocking staves, each with a different clef. A year later he wrote his first known tune. Recorded in a much later sketchbook by Elgar under the title 'Humoreske – a tune from Broadheath – 1867', this tune has become an especially powerful totem for Jerrold Northrop Moore, who regards it as the basis of Elgar's musical style and a ghostly presence in virtually every major work he wrote.[34] It is a very unremarkable tune, which rises and falls in the way most tonal music does. Although it is amusing for a moment to be heard in the work of a 50-year-old, it is best put out of mind swiftly thereafter. Certainly there can be no grounds for suggesting – as Moore does, and as is now commonly held – that it relates to the Malvern Hills or to Broadheath, unless every composer, great or small, for the last half millennium was raised in the same cottage Elgar was born in.[35]

In his last few years at school he began more seriously to teach himself music theory and history, plus the rudiments of composition and orchestration.[36] He began attending the Three Choirs Festival (the musical highlight of the year in the West Country: an annual rotation between Worcester, Gloucester, and Hereford cathedrals), and was inspired by a performance of Handel's *Messiah* there to take up the violin in 1869. By 1870, aged 13, he was playing in the Crown Hotel Glee Club as second violin (his father was first). Its repertoire – not purely vocal – ranged approximately from Handel to Mendelssohn, weighted towards the earlier end. It was there that he learnt to smoke properly, though he'd been puffing as an enthusiastic amateur for a couple of years already.[37]

---

[33] Elgar, quoted in Kennedy, *Portrait*, p. 23.

[34] See Moore, *Creative Life*, pp. 33–5 and *passim*.

[35] The same goes for Elgar's use of sequences, or for rising or falling melodies in general (the theme of the *Variations* isn't a musical sketch of those hills either). Here as much as anywhere we find the great Elgar Myth suffocating an interpretation of the music. A pity – though it would be nice if it were true.

[36] A list of music books surviving from Elgar's library is given in Peter Dennison, 'Elgar's Musical Apprenticeship', in Raymond Monk (ed.), *Elgar Studies* (Aldershot: Scolar, 1990), pp. 1–35, at p. 31. See below on some of his compositional exercises.

[37] Buckley says evocative things about the carcinogenic atmospheric conditions prevailing after the performance of 'Glorious Apollo', which traditionally opened Glee Club entertainments: Buckley, *Elgar*, p. 17.

At a relatively early age Elgar said that he and his siblings wrote a musical play built on simple oppositions of town and country, adults and children. According to the story, which has little supporting evidence, he was either 12 or 14; his banal 1867 tune was brought in for the scene with fairies and giants, and there was more music for moths and butterflies. The music was reused at the time of his fiftieth birthday in his *Wand of Youth* (the programme note for which is the source of this story), and the subject matter was doubtless remembered for his still later music for *The Starlight Express*.[38] In 1872 he first played organ for Mass, and wrote a song, 'The Language of Flowers', which he gave to his sister Lucy on her twentieth birthday. It is the earliest complete piece of his to survive, its music as anaemic as J. C. Percival's text. It wasn't an auspicious start, but a developing musical bent was evident. Upon leaving school he wanted to study music in Leipzig, and had learnt German for the purpose, but he would have to stifle his desire for almost a decade.[39]

The young professional

Straitened family means meant Elgar had to work, and for a time immediately after school it seemed that he might not have a musical career after all. Since Elgar was quiet, studious, and well-organized, his parents felt that a legal career might suit him, and he was apprenticed soon after his fifteenth birthday, on 26 June 1872, to the firm of solicitors in Worcester run by a family friend, William Allen.[40] The law couldn't contain him for long, and he remained only till the following year, but was later glad of the opportunity it had provided him to develop good working habits and clear handwriting.[41] (Readers of his occasionally impenetrable manuscripts might go boggle-eyed at the second thought.)

His musical career began in 1873 as assistant organist to his father at St George's Church, becoming full-time organist (1885–9) after his father's retirement.[42] He also helped in the shop. As the high quality of his playing and composing became widely known, conducting jobs were handed to him: he was engaged as conductor of the Worcester Amateur Instrumental Society in 1877, and in 1879 became both the conductor of the Glee Club and the musical director ('composer in ordinary') of the

---

[38] For an outline of the musical play, see Moore, *Creative Life*, pp. 46–8, and on *The Wand of Youth* and *The Starlight Express* see chapters 3 and 5 of this book.

[39] W. H. Reed, *Elgar*, 2nd edn. (London: Dent, 1943; orig. edn. 1939), pp. 10–11.

[40] Allen was a singer as well as law administrator, and sang Verdi's 'Di Provenza il mar' every time he visited the Elgars (Moore, *Creative Life*, p. 10).

[41] Young, *Elgar O.M.*, p. 37.

[42] When he took over he said to a friend in North Yorkshire, Dr Charles Buck (1851–1932), 'I am a full fledged organist now & – *hate* it . . . the choir is awful & no good to be done with them' (Anderson, *Elgar*, p. 15). Elgar holidayed in Buck's home in Settle in the early 1880s, and they remained friends for half a century. See William R. Mitchell, *Elgar in the Yorkshire Dales* (Giggleswick: W. R. Mitchell, 1987).

Worcester City and County Lunatic Asylum at Powick, where he was paid £30 a year for one day's service a week as conductor of the band, and extra for compositions. He began teaching violin in 1876, aged 19, and would continue to do so for 20 years. In later life he said teaching was like turning a millstone with a dislocated shoulder,[43] but at the time it was to prove useful, and not just financially.

The provincial musician's life that this catalogue of appointments evokes offered little money. He started to lodge with his sister Pollie upon her marriage to William Grafton in 1879, moving in with his other sister Lucy once she married Charles Pipe in 1882. (He was newly converted to Catholicism to placate the family: Elgar holidayed with Pipe in Paris in 1880.) The lack of money was compensated for by the many opportunities his work gave him to study, perform, and compose. Organists from Bach on have become inured to writing music at high speed and on demand, and Elgar's first composition after leaving Allen's solicitors in 1873 was a Credo based on themes from Beethoven's Fifth, Seventh, and Ninth symphonies, signed as a joke 'by Bernhard Pappenheim'.[44] He was never to balk at the idea of playing with other composers' music. At the first Three Choirs Festival he attended, in 1869, he was given an opportunity for perhaps his first musical 'jape' (a favourite word of Elgar's). Elgar Brothers were copying out the orchestral parts for a performance of *Messiah*, and Elgar secretly worked a little tune of his own into the music. 'The thing was an astonishing success', he said, 'and I heard that some people had never enjoyed Handel so much before!'[45] (He still got a clip round the ear for it.)

He wrote a *Salve regina* and a *Tantum ergo* for St George's, and arranged the overture to *The Flying Dutchman* for the Glee Club, all in 1876.[46] In 1878 he started to maintain sketchbooks, carefully numbered in a system he would maintain through his working life. As an exercise in composition and orchestration, at the time of the Worcester Festival in 1878 he used the skeleton of the first movement and minuet of Mozart's Symphony No. 40, musical systems ruled carefully with the exact same number of bars, as a prop for tunes of his own, modulations between them following the model. And as his mature composing style developed he engaged, like his modernist contemporaries Mahler, Strauss, Sibelius, and others, with the language and forms of past music in a creative

---

[43] Buckley, *Elgar*, p. 43.

[44] Moore, *Creative Life*, p. 62. John Butt provides an excellent overview of Elgar's organ music, and the implications of the fact that it was written by a Catholic (which is to say, someone distinctly outside the Establishment of his day), in John Butt, 'Roman Catholicism and Being Musically English: Elgar's Church and Organ Music', in Daniel M. Grimley and Julian Rushton (eds.), *The Cambridge Companion to Elgar* (Cambridge: Cambridge University Press, 2004), pp. 106–19. We shall return to this matter in the following inter-chapter.

[45] Moore, *Creative Life*, p. 43.

[46] He arranged the 'Entry of the Minstrels' from *Tannhäuser* for piano in 1883.

dialectic (an argumentative exploration of contrary viewpoints) that in part explains his music's special richness (see below, especially chapters 2 and 4).[47]

A wind quintet formed from the Worcester Instrumental Society[48] met for its first rehearsal in Elgar's father's shed, and Elgar wrote much 'Shed music' (or 'Harmony Music', as he also called it, from the German *Harmoniemusik*, meaning wind music) for this ensemble, as well as for the band at the Powick asylum, where doctors believed that the performance of ensemble music would have positive effects on the inmates. The music – mostly polkas and quadrilles – is in the style of Fauré's and Messager's highly recommendable humorous quadrilles on themes from Wagner, *Souvenirs de Bayreuth*: decidedly slight, but entertaining. Its composition was a useful practical aid in making best use of available resources – a skill taught consciously in conservatoires and universities but learnt equally effectively through necessity.

Advanced violin tuition came from Adolphe Pollitzer in London. Finances were so tight that in order to afford the lessons, Elgar claimed that he had to survive on two bags of nuts a day.[49] It soon became clear that his tone was too small for him to become a professional solo violinist, but Pollitzer was impressed by his composing ability and put him in touch with August Manns, the conductor of the Crystal Palace concerts at which London was given symphonic cycles by Schumann and Schubert, as well as music by Berlioz and Wagner. Elgar was given a rehearsal pass and devoted many long days travelling between Worcester and London to listen to as much music as he could there.

Helen and Alice

Romance took him to Germany in January 1883, when he went on holiday to Leipzig to visit Helen Weaver, the daughter of a Worcester shoe-shop owner, and therefore someone from his social milieu (they lived on the same street and must have known each other as children), who was studying abroad for a year. He heard Schumann,[50] Brahms, and Wagner, and by the summer he was engaged to Helen, and referring to her as *Braut* (German for 'bride') in letters.[51] Not for the first time, a woman's family was to interfere in a relationship. Her mother died

---

[47] He was aping Mozart again two years later, when he arranged his String Quartet in F, K. 547, as a *Gloria* for St George's.

[48] It included his brother Frank on oboe, his friend Hubert Leicester on flute, and Elgar himself on bassoon – an instrument he learnt so as to become a more marketable musician. Its combination of instruments was unusual: the normal combination was flute, oboe, clarinet, bassoon, and horn; Elgar's had two flutes and no horn (see page 23).

[49] McVeagh, *Elgar: Life and Music*, p. 8.

[50] Elgar said Schumann was 'my ideal!' in a letter to Buck (Moore, *Creative Life*, p. 97); he produced a piano transcription of the *Overture, Scherzo, and Finale* as a result of his trip.

[51] He would reuse this nickname for his real wife.

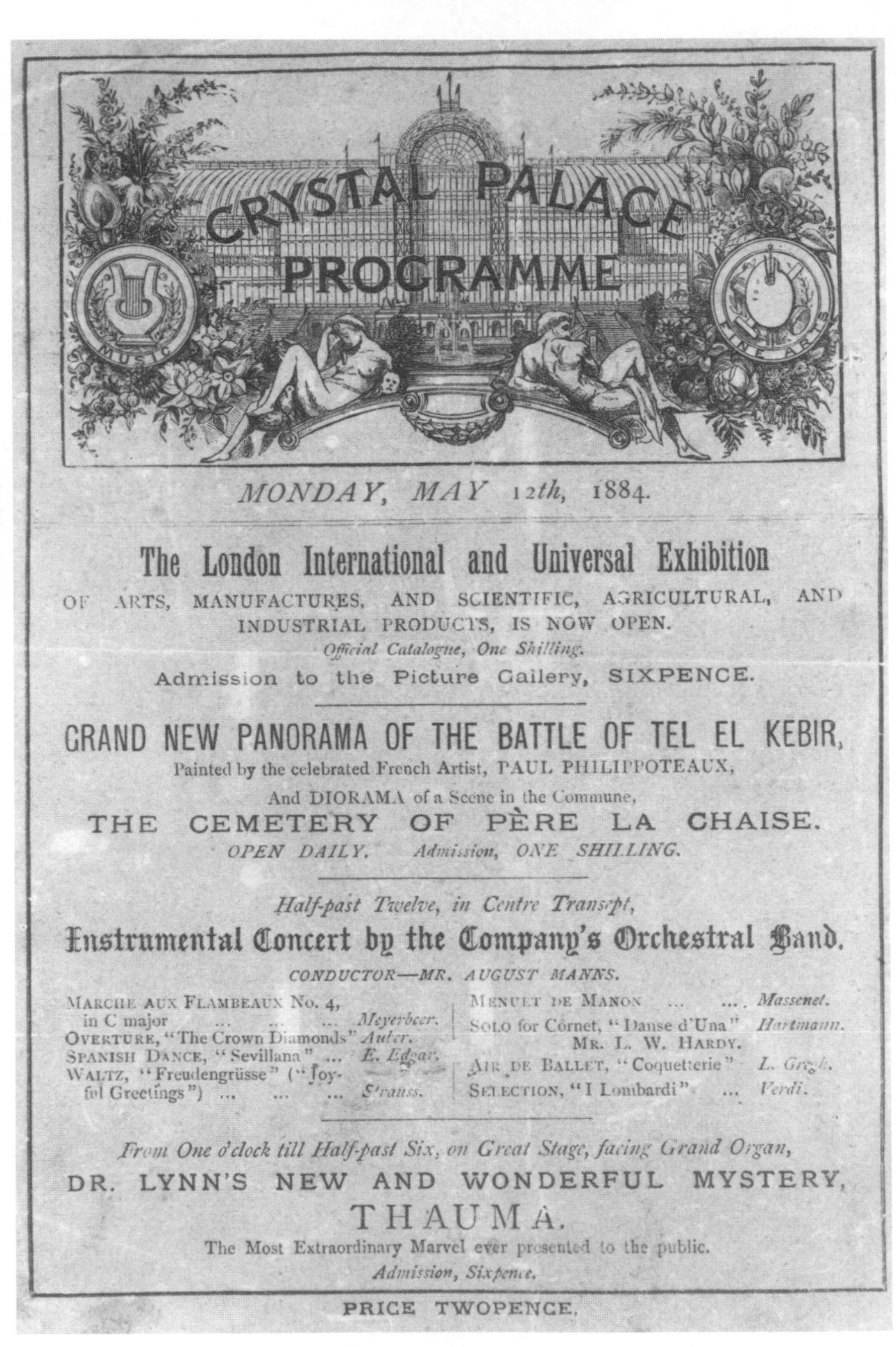

CRYSTAL PALACE PROGRAMME

MUSIC

FINE ARTS

MONDAY, MAY 12th, 1884.

The London International and Universal Exhibition

OF ARTS, MANUFACTURES, AND SCIENTIFIC, AGRICULTURAL, AND INDUSTRIAL PRODUCTS, IS NOW OPEN.

Official Catalogue, One Shilling.

Admission to the Picture Gallery, SIXPENCE.

GRAND NEW PANORAMA OF THE BATTLE OF TEL EL KEBIR,

Painted by the celebrated French Artist, PAUL PHILIPPOTEAUX,

And DIORAMA of a Scene in the Commune,

THE CEMETERY OF PÈRE LA CHAISE.

OPEN DAILY. Admission, ONE SHILLING.

Half-past Twelve, in Centre Transept,

Instrumental Concert by the Company's Orchestral Band.

CONDUCTOR—MR. AUGUST MANNS.

MARCHE AUX FLAMBEAUX No. 4, in C major ... ... *Meyerbeer.*
OVERTURE, "The Crown Diamonds" *Auber.*
SPANISH DANCE, "Sevillana" ... *E. Edgar.*
WALTZ, "Freudengrüsse" ("Joyful Greetings") ... ... *Strauss.*
MENUET DE MANON ... ... *Massenet.*
SOLO for Cornet, "Danse d'Una" *Hartmann.*
MR. L. W. HARDY.
AIR DE BALLET, "Coquetterie" *L. Gregh.*
SELECTION, "I Lombardi" ... *Verdi.*

From One o'clock till Half-past Six, on Great Stage, facing Grand Organ,

DR. LYNN'S NEW AND WONDERFUL MYSTERY,

THAUMA.

The Most Extraordinary Marvel ever presented to the public.

Admission, Sixpence.

PRICE TWOPENCE.

7. *The cover of the programme for the first concert to feature a work by Elgar,* Sevillana.

towards the end of 1883 and she cut short her studies in Leipzig; her remaining, Protestant, family found Elgar too serious and too Catholic, and the engagement was broken off in Spring 1884.[52] He distracted himself that summer in two ways. Musically, Dvořák's visit to Worcester for the Three Choirs Festival was an enormous thrill for the aspiring provincial composer. The Czech conducted his Sixth Symphony and *Stabat Mater*, and Elgar played in the orchestra. He found Dvořák's musical style engrossing, and never lost his enthusiasm for it. The second form of distraction came through meeting on holiday a mysterious Scotch woman whose initials were also 'E.E.'[53] Nevertheless the failure of his engagement had scorched his pride, leaving a mark that lingered for years. It is possible that he also proposed marriage to Gertrude Walker, an actress and local secretary of the British Shakespeare Society, three years later in 1887. If he did propose, she rejected.[54]

What ultimately provided consolation were the twin facts that his music began to be performed and appreciated and – a couple of years later – that he found a woman who could replace all others (once Gertrude was out of the picture) in his affections. William Stockley gave Elgar's short *Intermezzo moresque* at his concert series in Birmingham, and in May 1884 Manns conducted the first London performance of a work by Elgar, the orchestral miniature *Sevillana* (see figure 8, opposite).[55] The new woman in Elgar's life was a student who wanted to learn piano accompaniment, the better to socialize with musical friends; a note in Elgar's diary for 1886 reads 'Miss Roberts. 1st lesson. Oct. 6th'.[56]

Caroline Alice Roberts (1848–1920), who was always known by her second name, was the daughter of the grandly decorated Major General Sir Henry Gee Roberts KCB[57] who, according to the *Dictionary of National Biography*, killed around a thousand men in the Indian Mutiny (during which Elgar was born).[58] In other words, he was 'the right sort'. Both of Alice's siblings (two brothers) followed their father into the empire. She was born in India into the privileged imperial class. Moore describes her, with typical chivalrousness, as 'a short woman in her late

---

[52] A family in New South Wales believes it is descended from an illegitimate child of Elgar and Helen Weaver, but even the writer who explodes this bombshell doesn't believe for a minute that it could be true. See Michael Greening, *A Family Story: The Greenings and Some of Their Relatives (Including the Elgars)* (Leicester: Matador, 2006), pp. 60–71.

[53] See Moore, *Creative Life*, p. 107.

[54] See Robert Anderson, 'Gertrude Walker: An Elgarian Friendship', *Musical Times*, 125 (1984), pp. 698–700. On his relationship with Helen, 'E.E.', Gertrude, and the other women (and men) with whom he was passionately close, see further inter-chapter 3.

[55] Perhaps it was confidence woken by this breakthrough that caused him to resign from his Powick position in October that year. There is no other obvious explanation.

[56] Moore, *Creative Life*, p. 115.

[57] Knight Commander of the Order of the Bath. Genuinely an honour.

[58] 'Roberts, Sir Henry Gee', in Sidney Lee (ed.), *Dictionary of National Biography* (London: Smith, Elder & Co., 1896).

thirties . . . Her features tended more to character than conventional beauty: a high forehead, china-blue eyes under arched brows, a prominent nose, and firm lips were set off with abundant light-brown hair swept up and plaited in the fashion of the day'.[59] Some people today might describe her as dumpy, plain-looking, and with a frumpy hairdo. But Elgar felt deep affection (if not passion) for this woman who was nine years his senior (commentators have picked up on the potential Freudian significance of the age difference, especially given her mothering tendencies). He wrote the popular, deliciously sweet miniature *Salut d'amour* as an engagement present for her.[60] They were married at the Brompton Oratory, London, on 8 May 1889. As would not have been the case with Helen Weaver, Elgar was marrying above his station, and Alice's aunt snobbishly disinherited her for marrying 'trade'.[61] This financial loss would blight their early years together.

The new Mrs Elgar fancied herself a novelist and poet.[62] A kind of proto-feminism evident in an early poem, 'Question and Answer' – in which she argues that woman's imaginative impulse is more truly alive than man's prosaic striving – seems to have faded away in her resolve to support a spouse with a more evident creative genius.[63] Her support for and encouragement of Elgar was lifelong, tireless, and at least partly selfless, although there is no doubt that she also wanted him to succeed in order to prove her family wrong and bring her back to the social world she 'belonged' to. On the occasion of the announcement of Elgar's knighthood their young daughter Carice said, 'I am so glad for Mother's sake that Father has been knighted. You see – it puts her back where she was'.[64] She was 14 at the time, and a child of that age would be unlikely to make such a statement without behind-doors muttering beforehand. And Elgar said he only accepted the honour 'out of a sense of gratitude to his wife, to whom these outward signs of esteem meant a great deal'.[65]

The Elgars honeymooned on the Isle of Wight. Returning home certain of his manhood at last, Elgar promptly resigned from every job he held in Worcester, and moved with his new wife to London, to rebegin his life.

---

[59] Moore, *Creative Life*, p. 115.

[60] It would be nice were it still the case for us, as Ernest Newman thought it was in 1906, that 'the horny-handed proletarian who never enters a concert-room has it sung or played to him every day by his little daughter'; Ernest Newman, *Elgar*, 3rd edn. (London: Bodley Head, 1922; orig. edn. 1906), p. 5.

[61] McVeagh, *Elgar: Life and Music*, p. 14.

[62] She wrote poetry all her life, some of it inspiring Elgar to write music (the first was 'The Wind at Dawn' in 1888), but most of her writing was done before she met Elgar. Her published novels, *Isabel Trevithoe* (in blank verse, 1878) and the two-volume *Marchcroft Manor* (1882) together amount to about eight inches of bookshelf space, and Robert Anderson has summarized their plots for those who haven't the stomach to read them: Anderson, *Elgar and Chivalry*, pp. 41–51.

[63] The poem is quoted in ibid., p. 40.

[64] See Rosa Burley and Frank Carruthers, *Edward Elgar: The Record of a Friendship* (London: Barrie and Jenkins, 1972), p. 174.

[65] Kennedy, *Portrait*, p. 16.

(Alice was resolved to move to London, where she felt a woman of her stature belonged.) Their first house was in Marloe Road in Kensington, a good base for concert-going: he heard Brahms's Third Symphony, and Wagner's *Die Meistersinger* three times. The lease ran for only a few months, and so after spending the summer in Alice's old house in Malvern they moved into 'Oaklands' on Fountain Road (now Fountain Drive), the much more substantial home of William Raikes in Upper Norwood, near the Crystal Palace. Without Raikes's favourable rates (they were relatives on Alice's mother's side, and the only ones who remained friendly after the marriage) they could not have afforded it. Elgar attended many rehearsals and concerts (hearing Brahms's Second Symphony twice) and London performances of his own *Salut d'amour* and 'Queen Mary's Song' (after Tennyson), and he began work on larger projects: the *Vesper Voluntaries* for organ and his most ambitious work to date, *The Black Knight*, a cantata based on Longfellow. Before the end of the year, he received a commission from the committee of the Worcester Festival for an overture to be performed there in 1890. With his first important commission, he had arrived as a composer. But London was to bring him misery before glory.

8. The wind quintet c.1878–9: back row, William Leicester, Elgar, Hubert Leicester; front row, Frank Exton, Frank Elgar.

An extraordinary moustache

Fig. 119

Wearing the moustache

One of the great poetic observers of the First World War, Siegfried Sassoon, first encountered Elgar by chance at the Three Choirs Festival of 1920. 'Could this possibly be the man who composed that glorious work [*The Apostles*] – this smartly-dressed "military"-looking grey-haired man, with the carefully trimmed moustache and curved nose?'[1] Sassoon developed a prickly impression, finding him

> a very self-centred and inconsiderate man . . . always pretending and disguising his feelings . . . He prides himself on his conventional appearance. I have often heard him use the phrase a 'Great Gentleman'. It is his sublimity of encomium . . . No doubt he sublimates himself as a G.G. – the Duc d'Elgar.[2]

By 1924 he had a more moderated view. Sassoon was in the circle of Frank Schuster, one of Elgar's closest friends and supporters, and saw Elgar at Schuster's home, The Hut. After an evening of music-making there he said

> It was splendid to see him glowing with delight in the music, and made me forget (and makes me regret now)

---

[1] Diary entry, quoted in Anderson, *Elgar*, p. 149.
[2] Quoted in Kennedy, *Portrait*, p. 305.

> the 'other Elgar' who is just a type of 'club bore'. At lunch, regaling us with long-winded anecdotes (about himself), he was a different man. The real Elgar was left in the music-room.[3]

As a homosexual in early-twentieth-century Britain, Sassoon had reason to be sensitive to outward appearances. Mask-wearing led him into marriage in 1933. Although the nature of their sexuality was not the same – Sassoon had many failed homosexual relationships, Elgar none of any kind – their struggle to create an obfuscatory self-image *was*, so Sassoon's analysis is interesting.

This 'other Elgar' was also perceived by Osbert Sitwell, who thought that in 'his grey moustache, grey hair, grey top hat and frock-coat [Elgar] looked every inch a personification of Colonel Bogey'.[4] Elgar's first biographer Robert Buckley breaks the 'other Elgar' down into five differently shaded characters, all public, posed, unreal. The fifth, dressed in black at a Three Choirs Festival, 'gives the impression of a distinguished colonel home for a year's holiday, and at present attending a funeral'.[5] Published at the height of Elgar's fame, this reading must have been sanctioned by Elgar himself.

Aside from their easy dismissiveness, these accounts are united by their insight that Elgar looked like a military type, a country gent – anything but a sensitive artist. This is crucial, and the only really important thing about Elgar's image. He lived most of his life in the country (or at least the provinces), wore spats and tweeds whenever he could manage it, and had a moustache so mesmerizingly big that it looked like a living thing, parasitic on his stiff upper lip and threatening to overwhelm his personality. He has always been considered an *echt*-English, *echt*-Edwardian composer, and we don't need to pay much attention to his efforts as personal image-manipulator to realize that he always wanted us to.

We won't be fooled; we are expert in spotting ulterior motives. In adopting the deportment of a gruff old buffer, affecting to have little knowledge of musical process, or even to care much about it (his affected philistinism was an irritation to others in

---

[3] Quoted in Anderson, *Elgar*, p. 155.

[4] Osbert Sitwell, *Laughter in the Next Room* (Boston: Little, Brown, 1948, and London: Macmillan, 1949), p. 196. Kenneth J. Alford's popular march, *Colonel Bogey*, which created the term, was written in 1913. 'Bogey' is a golfing term meaning one over par, and the tune was suggested by his partner's habit of whistling a descending minor third rather than shouting 'fore'. The golfing association is not inappropriate for Elgar.

[5] Buckley, *Elgar*, p. 38.

his last years, though doubtless a defensive response to his loss of status in the musical world), he was distancing himself from an art-form and way of life that reeked – to the contemporary mind – of effeminacy, loucheness, and (gasp!) un-Britishness. He told his violin pupil Mary Beatrice Alder that 'great musicians are things to be ashamed of'.[6] Papists were too, and he suppressed his Roman Catholicism, which was also bound up with this effeminacy (though possibly still important to him personally). His chosen mask of moustache, tweed, and bluster gave him a clearly recognizable air at the turn of a century awash with such characters. He was not just a wannabe squire. He was a wannabe imperialist. And that causes problems for his admirers in a post-colonial world.

De-imperializing the moustache

We are quite sure that we understand the late-nineteenth-century British view of their Empire. Everyone was for it; the spicy whiff and savour of it percolated through society, so that every personality was sodden with it, bound to it, in love with it. Academics tend to put it more grandly than that, and say that it was the 'dominant ideology' of the age.

We tend to find little attractive about that empire at its height. A poll in the *Daily Telegraph* in 1997 confirmed that latterday Britons, particularly those under 50 years old, on the whole don't know that General Gordon died in Khartoum, and General Wolfe in Quebec, or even that Rudyard Kipling wrote *Gunga Din*, or that George III (familiar from the cinema as Nigel Hawthorne in a night-shirt, calling his member 'England') was the king who lost the American colonies.[7] Yet a surprising proportion of the population still feels that it knows enough about empire to be sure that it is a shameful episode in our history, not just politically but socially (which is worse).

One reason for the confidence of our understanding is our knowledge of modern America, and its disastrous trifling with Vietnam (and other more recent conflicts). We see, largely because our mass media allows easy access to what, for short, we can call facts, how empires build – consciously or unconsciously, the effect is the same – and how their ideologies affect the rulers and the ruled. Modern Americans know all about their informal empire

[6] 'Memories of a Pupil', in *An Elgar Companion*, ed. Christopher Redwood (Ashbourne, Derbyshire: Sequoia, 1982), p. 148.
[7] See Jeffrey Richards, *Imperialism and Music: Britain, 1876–1953* (Manchester: Manchester University Press, 2001), p. 1.

and those in the Blue States (the ones that vote Democrat), where the appeal of macho posturing abroad is tempered by liberal–intellectual rumination on moral and practical questions, feel a strong sense of collective guilt about it.

The basic pattern is that more powerful countries exert authority on less powerful ones, by a mixture of cultural and military means, in a systematic manner that follows an appallingly crude logic: (a) our way is right; (b) we can help others by imposing our way on them; (c) they'll be happy with it in the end.[8] What America has done in Vietnam or (at the time of writing) is doing in Iraq, we know (even if we don't know about *Gunga Din*) that the British once did in India, and in slices of Africa.

There is therefore a tidiness to our picture of empire, and a tacit pride in the ethical credibility of our post-colonial guilt, that both reassures us that we know our recent ancestors were as intellectually involved with the British Empire as we currently are with the American, and also causes us to worry when we are stirred by the *Pomp and Circumstance* marches or the musically attractive closing pages of *Caractacus*. And in lieu of confessing our proto-imperialist sins to a priest, we broadcast them in newsprint, to general nodding and back-patting.

But empire is a serious matter, and serious scholars have had to address the issue in their appraisal of Elgar's music: for here is a composer born during the Indian Mutiny (hardly his fault, but still a fact), whose attempt to construct himself as a masculine figure of the Establishment – not to mention his writing of works with titles such as *Imperial March* and *The Pageant of Empire* – has the inevitable effect of associating him with the deeply masculine-gendered ideology of empire in the late-nineteenth and early twentieth centuries.

Among Elgar's biographers, Kennedy side-steps the question by saying the real Elgar is the 'private', not the 'public' one, while Moore pretends that his imperialism is really nature-worship.[9] Jeffrey Richards, by contrast, finds Elgar's imperialism joyful. It is a mystic imperialism of hope and promise; however foolish it might seem to us, the idea behind it was that through its efforts the British Empire could civilize the globe, and lift

---

[8] For a more nuanced presentation of this argument, and the ways that the ideology can be argued to seep into and control the culture of the ruling nation, the most influential study is still Edward W. Said, *Orientalism* (London: Routledge & Kegan Paul, and New York: Pantheon, 1978).

[9] See Kennedy, *Portrait* and Moore, *Creative Life*; also Jerrold Northrop Moore, *Elgar: Child of Dreams* (London: Faber and Faber, 2004).

billions out of poverty and ignorance.[10] But this picture of Elgar as a boundless optimist sits uncomfortably with the known facts of his highly neurotic character.

What underlines all these readings is the assumption that because he lived between 1857 and 1934, when imperialism was the 'dominant ideology', he *must* have been an imperialist. The airborne disease could not be avoided. What therefore scuppers them all is the fact that this is almost certainly a distortion of history. There was no single, clearly defined entity called 'Britain', in which everyone knew and cared about empire. Experience of empire varied enormously according to class and geographic background.[11]

In the upper- and upper-middle-classes in London in the second half of the nineteenth century (when Elgar was growing up and becoming a man), empire was a fact of life. Fathers worked for the Indian Civil Service, and sons were trained to follow their steps. Houses were filled with artefacts brought back from the colonies. Alice filled a room in Severn House with some brought back by her father (one of Elgar's first actions following her death was to hand them all over to the Victoria and Albert Museum).

In the lower-middle classes and below, by contrast, and even more so in the provinces (like Worcester; and Elgar had a lower-middle-class upbringing above a music shop), empire was an irrelevance, even if it was known about at all. School geography lessons focused on maps of the Holy Land if they ever dealt with places overseas – the famous red-bespeckled maps of empire didn't appear in British schools until the 1880s at the earliest,[12] long after Elgar had pulled off his last pair of short trousers – while history lessons focused on kings and queens at home. The historian John Seeley's famous suggestion that Britain obtained its empire 'in a fit of absence of mind' was a negative judgement: as a pro-imperialist he felt aggrieved that the masses hadn't known it was growing, and that their ignorance was about to result in its loss.[13]

The higher classes ruled the empire and needed to know about it; it wasn't *necessary* to involve the lower classes in the enterprise until the end of the nineteenth century, when a propaganda

---

[10] See Richards, *Imperialism and Music*, pp. 44–87.

[11] The summary which follows is drawn from Bernard Porter, *The Absent-Minded Imperialists: Empire, Society, and Culture in Britain* (Oxford: Oxford University Press, 2004).

[12] Ibid., p. 66.

[13] Ibid., p. 169.

9. Elgar and Alice in Bavaria, 1892.

10. An ink-blot 'self-portrait' made from Elgar's signature, folded before the ink dried, with the exraordinary moustache then added.

campaign was started in an attempt to hold the empire together. Social changes threatened to deepen rifts in society, so stirring up interest in empire was an attempt at a 'social adhesive'.[14] The empire sold then was the kind Richards says Elgar approved of: a mystical one full of benevolent promise. The best way to hoodwink the masses is always to present them with a sugary concoction.

Elgar married a woman whose upper-middle-class breeding in a family that served in the empire made her strongly pro-imperial. Her family's scornful attitude towards Elgar would have been coloured by his status as an outsider from the *imperial* class. Part of his reasoning in adopting the image of an imperialist, therefore, was surely to justify his wife's faith in him in the face of her obdurate and despicable family. But it was also calculated to bring him closer to Alice – we might say that for him imperialism acted as a *marital* adhesive.

There can be no doubt that he genuinely became an imperialist. The question is *on what level* he became one. Kennedy says on the public level, Moore says on none, and Richards says in a deeply heartfelt manner, as a mystic visionary for empire. The truth is probably more prosaic. He liked empire in the way most English people like tennis. On the *very* rare occasions that he was given the chance to write something roughly patriotic, or with an imperial subject, he was happy to produce. Yet the feeling in this music is no more essentially a part of his whole character than the squawked encouragement in the 1990s for the home-grown Tim Henman ('Come on, Tim!') is of a merely seasonally interested Wimbledon audience. He found it all superficially attractive. We might find that stupid, but we cannot judge him on the basis of a profoundly expressed opinion, in the way we can Cecil Rhodes or Warren Hastings, because none exists.

Elgar was a man of great intellect and magisterial powers of musical composition. Had he felt deeply about empire he would have produced at least one masterpiece inspired by it – a setting of Kipling, perhaps – and certainly rather more than *The Crown of India*, *The Banner of St George*, a couple of marches, and the final chorus of *Caractacus*. The fact that he did not speaks volumes. The cultivated moustache that hid a deeply emotional, sensitive, homosocial, and above all musical man was only the main visual symbol of an imperialism that was always only uxorious and tweed-deep.

---

[14] Ibid., p. 168.

TWO

NEO-ROMANTICISM IN THE PROVINCES (1890–1903)

Neo-romanticism: a definition

In 1889, the year Elgar married Alice and moved to London, there were two significant premieres in Europe: Mahler's First Symphony and Strauss's tone-poem *Don Juan*. It was the dawning of musical modernism. Roughly from then till 1914 composers in the European classical tradition would concern themselves with revising the Beethovenian symphonic archetype in the light of Wagnerian harmony and structure, and developing the various models of sonata form (for it was never a single copybook design of exposition, development, and recapitulation).

But in 1889 Elgar was not quite ready to join the vanguard. He had written some decent music before his marriage to Alice, much of it light but useful for developing his personal style of counterpoint and orchestration, as well as his sense of form and rudimentary musical process. As yet, though, he hadn't sufficient fire in his belly to set the English musical scene alight. He was just on the point of digesting Wagner, whom he'd begun to inhale in great ecstatic gulps. In the 1890s the whole of Europe – not just its musicians but all its artists – would be obsessed with Wagner. His final music drama, *Parsifal*, oozing with incense and lust, was a fetishistic favourite of the Decadent poets and authors, including the notorious (to that age) Oscar Wilde (1854–1900). Alongside the spectacular ritual and indulgent piety of certain brands of Roman Catholicism, Wagner was taken up as a means of exploring the sybaritic decay of the *fin de siècle*, a joy in the putrefaction of the world order. Maybe Elgar was attracted to the effete luxuriousness that could be imputed to Wagner, and to Catholic writers such as Cardinal John Henry Newman (1801–90). Or maybe he was attracted to the musical potential of the chromaticism that was an essential component of Wagner's musical language, and the deep (if cloying) spirituality of Newman's poetry at a time when Catholic faith still meant much to him. Either way, he certainly entered a recognizable musical world. He did so later than some of his contemporaries on the continent, but with equal vim.

In the first half of the nineteenth century it was impossible to throw a half-brick in Europe without striking a romantic of some description. E. T. A. Hoffmann and others considered romantic music (or Beethoven's: it amounts to the same thing) as something that invokes a sense of awe in the face of the majesty of the self and an 'indefinite longing' for the infinite.[1] The same was true of the other arts, which tended to aspire to the special expressive potential of the non-representational, and therefore the highest, art – music. After the European revolutions of 1848, however, the other arts left music alone, turning instead to realism and impressionism. Music has its realist and impressionist masterpieces, of course, but for the most part music of the later-nineteenth century was 'romantic in an unromantic age, dominated by positivism and realism. Music, *the* romantic art . . . stood for an alternative world'.[2] This was neo-romanticism.

It was this world that Elgar entered into after his marriage. Though his style would continue to develop, and take a more markedly modernist turn around 1904, certain details of Wagnerian technique, such as his chromatic slipping between chords a third apart, were not set aside but used to construct vast symphonic forms. While he was perfecting his technique he steered clear of the complex symphonic forms that were fascinating Mahler and Sibelius, and worked instead in the more traditional English forms of oratorio and cantata, changing them out of recognition in the process.

A chivalrous beginning and retreat

When their term at 'Oaklands' ran out, the Elgars moved from Norwood back to more expensive Kensington, this time to 51 Avonmore Road on a three-year lease. It was a smaller house, and not cheap: in March 1890 they had to pawn Alice's pearls. It was perhaps this stress that led to the start of his lifelong health troubles, particularly with his eyes, throat, and head, which began to bother him now. (These worries generally came to nothing: he was an inveterate hypochondriac.) There was good news too: on 14 August 1890 the Elgars' only child, a daughter named Carice Irene, was born.[3] Her birth prevented Alice from attending the premiere of the

---

[1] In this, music was following the philosophy of Beethoven's near-exact contemporary Hegel (1770–1831).

[2] Carl Dahlhaus, *Between Romanticism and Modernism: Four Studies in the Music of the Later Nineteenth Century*, trans. Mary Whittall and Arnold Whittall (Berkeley: University of California Press, 1980; orig. edn. 1974), p. 5.

[3] Her first name was a portmanteau of Caroline Alice, Mrs Elgar's forenames.

only work Elgar was to write in London until 1912, the overture *Froissart*, which had been commissioned for the Worcester Festival of 1890.

In *Froissart*, Op. 19, Elgar found his feet, and began to show evidence of an individual musical personality. He learnt of Jehan Froissart (*c.*1337–*c.*1410)[4] through reading Sir Walter Scott (1771–1832), whose works are dappled with paeans to Froissart's historical romances.[5] These chronicles might make tedious historical reading were it not for their great poetry. Typical of the age, inspiration for the voice in the poem springs from his unfulfilled and unfulfillable love for an unattainable woman. The tradition is deeply misogynistic and solipsistic, insofar as the actual human reality of the woman is more or less irrelevant: it is the thought of love and – being honest – the unsated longing for carnal fulfilment that is the lover's real interest. Although there is often a secondary focus on another male, the only important character in the poetry is the lover himself; the woman is just a trope, an image, a focus for the words, but not the thoughts or feelings. This model appealed strongly in the nineteenth century to the romantic mind, which tended to give this role of cipher to the whole of nature, as well as women. Elgar was entranced by the tradition of chivalry, and an inheritor of the romantic subjectivity of the nineteenth-century composer. Given his situation in an age and country that viewed women as fragile ornaments and objects of tender worship, this is not surprising. Later, he would to some extent mirror the role of a medieval court poet in his relationship with Alice Stuart-Wortley, a married woman of relatively high birth, and an inspiration for much of his most important music.

Perhaps it took something that got right into his marrow like this to motivate Elgar to serious musical effort. *Froissart*, to which he appended in the score a line from Keats, 'When chivalry lifted up her lance on high', was his first significant work. Its subject matter and musical language begin a neo-romantic phase in Elgar's work, and the start of his mature compositional development. Though marred in places by unconvincing structural decisions, the overture is still satisfying to hear, with a high quality of invention throughout. It makes use of a relatively simple sonata-form design – the unimaginativeness of this is one of its slight disappointments – and introduces music in a melodic mode that Elgar would make his own, the noble or chivalrous sound of the *Pomp and Circumstance* marches and much else.

---

[4] Froissart's first name is generally spelt 'Jean', to harmonize with modern French, but an acrostic in his poem *Le paradis d'amours* suggests that 'Jehan' was his own spelling. I am grateful to Elizabeth Eva Leach for pointing this out, and for discussion about Froissart.

[5] It is sometimes said that *Old Mortality* was the work that inspired Elgar to name his overture, but since he knew Scott almost as well as he knew Longfellow and Shakespeare, it really could have come from anywhere. His copy of Froissart's chronicles is held at the Elgar Birthplace. See Anderson, *Elgar and Chivalry*, pp. 76–96.

The premiere was conducted by Elgar, and was well – if patronizingly – received by the critics. A *Musical Times* correspondent said 'The Overture is of course chivalric in style, and, perhaps, more commendable for what it tries to say than for the manner of its expression. There is upon it, what surprises no one – the mark of youth and inexperience; but it shows that with further thought and study, Mr. Elgar will do good work'.[6] That reads like the comical underestimation of a headmaster's report – a favourite staple of biographers made smug by hindsight – but is fair enough.

The work was also significant for marking the start of a new direction in the publication of his music. Elgar's earlier music had gone to various publishers. The Romance in E minor for violin and piano, Op. 1 (published 1885), and *Salut d'amour*, Op. 12, had gone to Schott; others went to John Beare, Stanley Lucas, G. Metzler, Alphonse Cary, and Orsborn and Tuckwood. *Froissart*, though, was sent to Novello, which was at the time the leading publisher of choral music (the biggest market) in Britain.[7] Elgar had already had a song, 'My Love Dwelt in a Northern Land', published by the firm, but an orchestral overture of almost fifteen minutes duration was altogether a different prospect. They agreed to engrave the string parts and copy the wind, which helped with performances, and though this wasn't ideal, a relationship was begun that would sustain Elgar's composition perhaps as much as his wife's efforts at home, and in the figure of August Jaeger, his contact at Novello, would give him one of his greatest musical confidants, guides, and inspirations.

This was all a few years in the future. At the end of 1890 the warm afterglow of *Froissart*'s reception couldn't begin to counteract the frigid cold of the London winter in a house the Elgars could not afford to heat. He also hated the black London fogs.[8] And one orchestral work alone could not pay the bills. For several months he had been reverse-commuting to Worcester once a week to give violin lessons (see figure 11, opposite), some of it at the Mount School for girls, where the 25-year-old headmistress Miss Rosa Burley (1866–1951) would become a great friend, one of those who would later write a book about him.[9] She found him sometimes difficult to deal with, remarking on his mercurial character, and tendency to speak ill of Malvern while having himself a pronounced Worcestershire twang.[10]

---

[6] *Musical Times*, October 1890, quoted in Young, *Elgar O.M.*, p. 65.

[7] The information here is drawn from Robert Anderson, 'Elgar and His Publishers', in Grimley and Rushton (eds.), *The Cambridge Companion to Elgar*, pp. 24–31, a lively and at times prickly account of Elgar's relationship with Novello by an author who had experienced difficulties with them himself as the co-ordinating editor of the Elgar Complete Edition.

[8] 'Yesterday all day & to-day until two o'clock we have been in a sort of yellow darkness: I groped my way to church this morning & returned in an hour's time a weird & blackened thing with a great & giddy headache' (quoted in Moore, *Creative Life*, p. 155).

[9] Burley and Carruthers, *Record of a Friendship*. She also went to Bavaria with the Elgars in 1893.

[10] Ibid., pp. 28 and 37. Often her writing is bitingly sarcastic, particularly on the subject of Mrs Elgar, who appears in Burley's hands to be a grumpy little snob resentful of the fact that her husband couldn't afford to keep her in the very highest comfort and style.

Mr. Edward Elgar,

Violinist,

(Pupil of Herr A. Pollitzer, London).

BEGS to announce that he visits Malvern and neighbourhood to give Violin Lessons, advanced and elementary. Also Lessons in Accompaniment and Ensemble playing.

For Terms, &c., address 4, Field Terrace, Worcester.

11. One of Elgar's adverts for violin lessons.

Nevertheless, she took up violin lessons with him herself. Soon after, as an investment, he bought an expensive violin by the eighteenth-century Neapolitan maker Niccolo Gagliano.

In the worst of the winter the Elgars made the sensible decision to move back to the country. On 20 June 1891 they took a house in Alexandra Road, Malvern, which previous owners had propitiously called 'Forli' after Melozzo da Forli (1438–94), Renaissance painter of musical angels. They would not live again in London until 1912.

Choral music: Longfellow and the digestion of Wagner

Part of the British ruling class's domestic policy in the nineteenth century was to opiate the masses with music. A sight-singing solfège system (in Britain called 'tonic sol-fa') was devised in the 1830s by Sarah Glover, a Norwich school teacher; it worked by avoiding 'difficult' traditional notation. By mid-century the lower classes could use the method to sing Handel's *Messiah* and Mendelssohn's *Elijah* (which to the British were more or less the only pieces in the canon). Its use waned after the First World War.[11] Growing and living in this system, any composer in Elgar's position, with an eye on gaining national recognition and a lucrative publishing contract, was bound to write oratorios and cantatas – big choral–orchestral pieces with religious or secular texts. Alexander Mackenzie, Frederic Cowen, Hubert Parry, and Charles Villiers Stanford were all at it in the 1880s and 90s, and this is what Elgar spent his eight years at 'Forli' doing.

The house had an attractive situation, on its own road, swaddled by good gardens, and with a view of the Worcestershire Beacon (the highest of the Malvern Hills, in its last few years before a toposcope, identifying nearby hills, was installed there for Victoria's Diamond Jubilee in 1897). Elgar gave an interview there to Buckley, his biographer, making one of his most quoted remarks.

> He paused and walked out into the sunshine. 'My idea', he continued, 'is that there is music in the air, music all around us, the world is full of it and – (here he raised his hands, and made a rapid gesture of capture) – and – you – simply – simply – take as much as you require!'[12]

---

[11] For more on the historical development and significance of solfège in Britain, see Charles Edward McGuire, *Elgar's Oratorios: The Creation of an Epic Narrative* (Aldershot: Ashgate, 2002), pp. 3–9, and Bernarr Rainbow, 'Tonic Sol-Fa', in Stanley Sadie and John Tyrrell (eds.), *The New Grove Dictionary of Music and Musicians*, 2nd edn. (London: Macmillan, and New York: Grove, 2001).

[12] Buckley, *Elgar*, p. 32.

An oddly effusive remark – perhaps he'd got too much sun on the top of his head – but typical of the man. The out-of-doors was his element, and he wrote his music in a tent in the garden. It had a flag on top which, when raised, announced both his regal presence and the fact that he Must Not Be Disturbed.[13]

The first substantial music completed there was *The Black Knight*, Op. 25, a 'sort of Symphony in four divisions',[14] for chorus (no soloists) and orchestra, which he had begun in London. It is an impressive piece drawn ultimately from the poem 'Der schwarze Ritter' by Ludwig Uhland (1787–1862), as distilled through Longfellow's 1839 novel *Hyperion: A Romance*.

Henry Wadsworth Longfellow (1807–82) was by profession an academic – a professor of modern languages at Harvard. The translations of old poetic legends that pepper the novel came directly from his teaching, and this one was probably improvised (which would explain its awkwardness).[15] The brief story of *The Black Knight* concerns the great thirteenth-century king of Scotland, Alexander III, whose three children died within a few years of each other, placing the succession in doubt. Alexander remarried, but a few months later fell from his horse and died. Uhland makes the tragedy macabre by drawing on a legend that Death himself, in the form of a shadowy figure at the wedding feast, had caused Alexander's fall.

In the first movement of Elgar's work, the Black Knight (Death) enters during a tournament at the castle, with the music in 'a fluent euphonious chivalric idiom out of Weber and Mendelssohn with touches of early Wagner and a muscular Brahmsian warmth'[16] – that is, Elgar on top early form. In the second movement the strange figure is asked for his 'name and scutcheon', and declares himself 'a Prince of mighty sway', at which the music takes on a darker tone. He joins in a joust and wounds the king's son. In the third movement, music presaging the mature pastoralism of the interludes in *Falstaff* (1913) prefaces a dance of death, 'weird and dark', in which the king's daughter's flowers fall dead from her hands. These two disturbing blows lead to the obvious outcome: in the fourth movement, son and daughter die in the king's arms, and his despairing outburst, 'Take me, too, the joyless father!' ('six bars of full-fat pomp and

---

[13] Monty Python's interview with the composer Arthur 'Two Sheds' Jackson ('And did you compose your symphony – *in* the shed?') is not far from the eccentric truth here, though Jackson probably wasn't modelled on Elgar.

[14] Letter to Jaeger, 1 March 1898, quoted in Elgar, *Elgar and His Publishers*, ed. Moore, p. 67.

[15] On Longfellow, *Hyperion*, and Elgar's *Black Knight*, see Anderson, *Elgar and Chivalry*, pp. 97–105. Elgar made a habit of setting poor texts to music. Vera Hockman – see further, chapter 6 and inter-chapter 3 – recalled Elgar saying that 'it is better to set the best second-rate poetry to music, for the most immortal verse *is* music already' (quoted in Moore, *Creative Life*, p. 280).

[16] Robin Holloway, 'The Early Choral Works', in Grimley and Rushton (eds.), *The Cambridge Companion to Elgar*, pp. 63–80, at p. 64.

circumstance'),[17] is countered by the knight's chilling closing line, 'Roses in the Spring I gather!'

Elgar wrote nothing quite like this again. The tale's presentation in *Hyperion* makes the moral clear, because the novel is about forgetting sorrow through travel, and this is merely one example in it of profound loss. There is little succour, though, in the closing pages of Elgar's version, which has no concluding message of hope. It is an ambitious work, with thematic recall in the finale suggesting the early stirrings of a serious symphonic ambition. In different ways Elgar would adapt this hopeless narrative or philosophical model throughout his life. The work was completed in vocal score in time to be sent to Novello on 30 September 1892; once publication was accepted it was orchestrated by 26 January and premiered in Worcester on 18 April 1893. It was received well there, but two years later fared poorly in London.

While composing *The Black Knight* he had gone with Alice on the first of a succession of Bavarian summer holidays. He went six times: four times in a row from 1892 to 1895 (he learnt German again before his 1893 trip), then again in 1897 and 1902. Wagner was on the menu: Elgar heard all the mature operas and music dramas, plus the early *Die Feen* ('The Fairies'). He was given a score of *Tristan und Isolde* (in many ways Wagner's most important work) on his thirty-sixth birthday, 2 June 1893. Opposite the first page of the Prelude he wrote a pithy summary: 'This Book contains the Height, – the Depth, – the Breadth, – the Sweetness, – the Sorrow, – the Best and the whole of the Best of This world and the Next'.[18]

Study of Wagner, which had begun more than a decade earlier, now took off with heightened seriousness. Score study proceeded alongside activity such as arranging the Good Friday music from *Parsifal* for Worcester High School in 1894 (his third and last Wagner arrangement). The fascination led to a definite shift of emphasis in the early 1890s. He still wrote delicious 'lighter' music, though. The popular and not inconsequential Serenade for Strings in E minor, Op. 20, and the *Spanish Serenade*, Op. 23, (a setting for two sopranos, violin, and piano, of Longfellow), both came in 1892. He collaborated with his wife (who wrote the text) on *Scenes from the Bavarian Highlands*, Op. 27, six trivial choral songs written on German folk tunes (with piano, 1895; orchestrated and arranged as *Bavarian Dances*, 1896), and also wrote an Organ Sonata in G, Op. 28, and a *Sursum corda*, Op. 11 (brass, organ, strings, timpani) for Hugh Blair (1864–1932), assistant organist at Worcester Cathedral and an important promoter of *The Black Knight* and (later) *The Light of Life*. But now his mind was bent to more substantial works.

---

[17] Ibid., p. 66. Holloway's essay should be read as much for the delightful turning of every phrase as for its insights into the early choral works.
[18] This vocal score is held at the Birthplace.

A simple understanding of Wagner's art as the sustaining of an 'unending melody' by the systematic use of leitmotivs led Elgar to experiment with the technique.[19] *The Light of Life*, Op. 29 (1894–6), was his first half-hearted attempt. He collaborated with the Anglican priest Edward Capel-Cure (1860–1949), making changes to the libretto while holidaying in Bavaria in 1895. The text is a disappointing soup of emulsified Bible verses telling the story of Christ's healing of the blind man in John 9: 1–34. An oratorio in the form then traditional in Britain, it has a number of purely didactic movements, intended to inculcate Christian doctrine.[20] Today they sound like rants, and Elgar's music for them shows no sign that he was gripped. Some of the best music is in the opening 'Meditation', probably an attempt at a Wagnerian prelude (something he would take to new heights in his *Dream of Gerontius*). One theme, representing the Blind Man, is introduced in the 'Meditation' and recurs three times more, in the second, fourth, and ninth movements. Its last and most dramatic appearance corresponds with the Blind Man's narrative of his cure: 'A man that is called Jesus made clay, and anointed mine eyes, and said unto me, "Go to the pool of Siloam, and wash": I went and washed, and I received sight'. With the purging of his infirmity the identifying theme disappears from the music.[21]

The Light of Life had been a Worcester Festival commission for 1896; it was premiered on 8 September. The *Worcestershire Echo* described it as 'the best English work that had been produced . . . for certainly twenty years', and the metropolitan press was similarly respectful. The *Sunday Times* said 'the young Malvern teacher has uncommon talent. He knows his Wagner well – sometimes, perhaps, a trifle too well . . . But his sense of proportion and tone colour, and his knowledge of effect are quite exceptional'.[22] It was not Elgar's only festival commission that year. The superbly named conductor Swinnerton Heap (1847–1900) had given *The Black Knight* in Walsall, near Birmingham, in 1894, and was sufficiently enthused by it to ask Elgar for a bigger work for his 1896 North Staffordshire Festival.[23]

Elgar turned again, and for the last time in a major work, to Longfellow, this time to a 'Saga of King Olaf' he had found in a collection in Burley's Mount School (true to his self-teaching impulse, he continued to consume as many books as he could lay his hands on). Written in tandem with

---

[19] Leitmotivs are reminiscence themes (literally 'leading motives') – little snatches of music that are associated with certain ideas. Wagner never used the term, which was concocted by an enemy, Heinrich Dorn, to suggest that motives were necessary to lead one through the mess of his music – but the word stuck.

[20] See McGuire, *Elgar's Oratorios*, pp. 92–3.

[21] See ibid., pp. 106–9.

[22] Both quoted in Moore, *Creative Life*, p. 215.

[23] Good news for now: more money and exposure. But Heap's sudden death from pneumonia, aged 53, would scupper the premiere of *Gerontius* six years later.

The Light of Life, it was an even grander project which, because it tapped into Northern myth, brought him still closer in spirit to Wagner. He asked a Malvern neighbour, H. A. ('Harry') Acworth (1848–1933), to trim Longfellow's text. The result is *Scenes from the Saga of King Olaf*, Op. 30, a cantata for chorus, three soloists, and orchestra, in eight named scenes bookended by a Prologue and Epilogue. At an hour and a half in length, it was his most substantial work to date.

Longfellow narrates his saga in the traditional bardic fashion (familiar from *Beowulf* or Chrétien), namely through disjointed episodes. Some are bawdy or gory; Elgar bowdlerized them, making Longfellow's pagan Olaf a hearty Christian soul. Like *Buffy the Vampire Slayer*, this is what one might call, coining a phrase, 'action theology'. (Religion was still important to Elgar, and Alice herself was admitted to the Roman Catholic Church on 21 July 1894, a few weeks after Elgar began work on *Olaf*.) The story is not simple, but Elgar's newly assured motivic technique increases coherence. After an introduction worked around a magnificent 'Saga' motive, the god Thor issues an open challenge to battle, which Olaf accepts, setting sail. Olaf defeats the pagan Ironbeard, though a counterpoint of motives associated respectively with the old and new religious systems seems to suggest that pagans and Christians can peacefully coexist.[24] Blood spilt, the narrative turns to honeyed love scenes with three women. First is Gudrun, his enemy's daughter – a bad marriage that ends on the wedding night when she rather uncivilly brings a dagger to bed with her. Next, Sigrid, 'the haughty Queen of Svithiod' (the ancient name of Sweden), who earns a sweet ballad for women's voices – but he insults her by saying that he won't marry 'a heathen dame', and that in any case she looks neither beautiful nor young. After a scuffle in which she 'dash[es] his glove on the oaken floor' (a high insult), he slaps her none too manfully on the cheek and flees, chased by her menacing last line, 'I am one can watch and wait'. His third woman, Thyri, 'the sister of Svend the Dane', is introduced to a lilting waltz for women's voices that leads into a duet with Olaf. A choral recitative announces that Sigrid the Haughty has married Thyri's brother, the king of the Danes, and persuaded him to fight Olaf at sea. Our hero dies, and in the epilogue Elgar returns to the superb music of the opening, 'That with its cadence, wild and sweet, / Makes the Saga more complete'. The reception of its first performance at Hanley, Stoke on Trent, on 30 October 1896 was flattering. *The Times* said that it was 'a work of high importance', and another critic said that Elgar was 'the greatest English genius since Henry Purcell'.[25]

---

[24] Holloway, 'The Early Choral Works', p. 72.
[25] Quoted in Kennedy, *Portrait*, p. 59 and Moore, *Creative Life*, p. 217.

Novello commissioned two shorter works from the new genius to mark Queen Victoria's Diamond Jubilee the following year: a nationalistic cantata, *The Banner of St George*, Op. 33 (not remotely his best music), and the immediately popular *Imperial March*, Op. 32, which was premiered at the Crystal Palace on 19 April, and within the year performed at 'Queen's Hall, a Royal Garden Party, a State Concert [the official Covent Garden performance for the Diamond Jubilee], the Albert Hall, and the Three Choirs Festival'.[26] It has a title that makes some bristle, but nowadays organists slip it unobtrusively into church services where its stately, processional tread fits well. It is another excellent early essay in his best ceremonial style. Together these two works made his name at last among a wider public, and the obscure Worcestershire music teacher and part-time composer became, overnight, a (very minor) national figure. Yet, infuriatingly, good works such as *Froissart* and the Serenade for Strings were still hardly ever being performed. He was not yet remotely a fixture of the popular concert series; the public continued to prefer mediocrities.

Recognition from nation and 'Moss-head'

Elgar holidayed in Bavaria again in 1897, hearing Wagner's *Tristan* and Mozart's *Don Giovanni* in Munich, conducted by Richard Strauss. During the summer he worked on a small piece for the Hereford Festival, a *Te Deum and Benedictus*, Op. 34, for chorus, organ, and orchestra. It had been suggested by, and was subsequently dedicated to, George Robertson Sinclair (1863–1917), who had been appointed cathedral organist at Hereford in 1889. He was to become 'G.R.S.' in Elgar's 1899 orchestral *Variations* in which friends would be given their own movements, their identities shown by initials. G.R.S. had a bulldog, Dan, which inspired Elgar to write a separate series of portraits in music. He called these 'the Moods of Dan'. Several would crop up in unexpected places in later works, and the dog too would feature in the *Variations*. In late October, while conducting a performance of *Bavarian Highlands* in London, he gave Novello a short violin piece which he wanted to call *Evensong*; they preferred *Chanson de nuit* (Op. 15, No. 1), and upset him by offering 10 guineas for the copyright, when he foresaw (and was proved right) that it would be as popular and lucrative for them as *Salut d'amour*.

Friendships soon to be immortalized in music were either made or strengthened in 1897. Arthur Troyte Griffith, the architect of All Saints' Church in Malvern (consecrated 1903), joined Elgar in kite-flying in June.[27] In the autumn Alice noised-abroad a potential return to London, which led to a countervailing attempt to persuade Elgar to stay in the provinces by the creation of a new performing outlet for him, the County of Worcester

---

[26] Anderson, *Elgar*, p. 35.

[27] On Elgar's various leisure pursuits, see inter-chapter 2.

Choral and Orchestra Association (COWCOA; Elgar liked the initials). He became friends with one of the secretaries, Winifred Norbury (1861–1938; 'W.N.' to be). Some people were friends without becoming variationees. One was Nicholas Kilburn (1843–1923), a Cambridge and Durham graduate (an iron merchant but also a Doctor of Music) whom Elgar met at the Three Choirs Festival in 1897. He lived in Bishop Auckland, County Durham, where he promoted Elgar's choral music among local amateur groups, earning a later dedication. Ivor Atkins (1869–1953), organist of Worcester Cathedral, gained a regular Friday-evening slot with the Elgars. More names would follow, but one of the most significant at this time was the one nicknamed 'Nimrod' in the *Variations*.

August Johannes Jaeger (1860–1909) was probably the most important musical figure of Elgar's life. He was German by birth but had come to England aged 18. He worked for Novello from 1890 but became closely involved with Elgar in 1896, becoming a firm supporter and perceptive critic from then until his death. His most familiar nickname, 'Nimrod', is a linguistic joke: 'Jaeger' is German for 'hunter', and Nimrod was called 'the mighty hunter before Jehovah' in the Bible. Elgar gave him many more nicknames in letters, some of them so deeply affectionate as to invite speculation on their significance:

> 'Jaerodnimger', 'Jägerer', 'Corporal Nym', 'Jägerissimus', 'Jay' (with drawing of the appropriate bird), 'Demon (?)', 'Grosvenor', 'Jaggs', 'Jaybird', 'Moss-head', 'Pig', 'Augustus darling', 'Lieber Augustin', 'Shylock', 'Jagpot', 'Jaggernaut', 'Glorious Moss', 'Jag', 'Skittles', 'Jaguar', 'Jagbird', 'Heart Friend', 'Nim', 'Minrod'.[28]

Jaeger called Elgar 'my dear Elgarlein' (an affectionate German diminutive, 'my dear little Elgar') and 'Dearie E.E.', and signed off 'Ever yours', or with 'Much love to you'. Lovers play with nicknames to a similarly incredible extent, and sign off with words like 'Ever deary Moss / with love / Yrs / Edward', but if there was a deeper love between these two, there is no evidence it was physical.[29] What is certain is that Elgar felt Jaeger warranted the most passionately romantic of all the *Variations*.

Before that work would give him an international reputation, however, Elgar had to write something for the 1898 Leeds Festival. He proposed a symphony – a further sign of his developing interest in the genre – but the committee insisted, predictably, on a cantata. The result was *Caractacus*, Op. 35, for four soloists, chorus, and orchestra: an even larger work than

---

[28] Anderson, 'Elgar and His Publishers', p. 27.
[29] Quotations all in Elgar, *Elgar and His Publishers*, pp. 534–6, 543, 547. See inter-chapter 3 for more on Elgar's loves.

Olaf, more satisfactory as a narrative and with equally high musical standards. Harry Acworth was re-engaged, and produced a libretto which in its imperial overtones revealed him as a typical former Indian Civil Servant. The story concerns the king of the Catuvellauni, who in AD 51 made an unsuccessful attempt to defend the ancient country against the Romans from his base on Herefordshire Beacon. The Romans capture the defeated Britons and take them in captivity to Rome, where through strength of rhetoric Caractacus persuades them to have mercy and set their captives free.

Acworth's text for what would become the 'big sing' at the end of the cantata is a song of praise to empire, suggesting that two thousand years after Caractacus's defeat the Roman empire would have been washed away by the British, the greatest empire the world had seen, and one which, the librettist suggests, would never fail. Jaeger balked when he saw it in June 1898, and Elgar barked by return of post. 'Any nation but ours is allowed to war whoop as much as they like but I feel we are too strong to need it – I *did* suggest we should dabble in patriotism in the Finale, when lo! the *worder* (that's good!)[30] instead of merely paddling his feet goes & gets naked & wallows in it'. There is room to think here that Elgar felt the final text a little disgusting (not seemly paddling, but lewd, naked immersion in patriotism),[31] but he wrote in a different tone in July: 'never mind: England for the English is all I say – hands off! there's nothing apologetic about me'. 'Nothing tactful either', Michael Kennedy notes.[32]

The music is as ambiguous on the matter as these letters. The closing scene recalls material from the Arch Druid's prophecy before the battle the Romans win over Caractacus. The Arch Druid had prophesied victory for the Britons, and it is possible that by recalling the old music at the point of presenting a text vaunting empire, Elgar is making the point that its majesty is as hollow as the Arch Druid's words. But for the imperial historian Jeffrey Richards, the thematic recall means simply that the Arch Druid's words would *eventually* be proven true, and that two thousand years later, Britain would be the victor. That sounds like cold comfort for a bloody annihilation, but it's possible. At any rate, the music is glorious, tainted by empire or not, and the delicate 'Woodland Interlude' in the cantata's third scene shows the brand of patriotism Elgar was most deeply interested in: a patriotism of green lanes, little rivers, and hills one can get up and down in an afternoon. He told Jaeger 'I made old

---

[30] Elgar loved word-play of this sort, here marking his pleasure in his creation of 'worder' in the act of writing. He also called *Caractacus* 'correct-a-cuss'. Doubtless the list of names given to Jaeger above was another example of this admirable indulgence.

[31] It should be remembered that patriotism – which is what Elgar had suggested – is not the same as imperialism. See above, inter-chapter 1.

[32] First two quotations Moore, *Creative Life*, p. 239, the third Kennedy, *The Life of Elgar*, p. 58.

Caractacus stop as if broken down on p. 168 & choke & say "woodlands" again because I am so madly devoted to my woods'.[33] Elgar was too ignorant of politics and too ill-trained by his background to think very deeply about empire, though he unquestionably found its showy display and the (rather abstract) idea of Britain's majesty attractive.

The work was dedicated, with permission, to the Queen, a year after her jubilee, and the year of Elgar's parents' own fiftieth wedding anniversary.[34] It was first performed at the Leeds Festival on 5 October 1898 with the same trio of singers that had performed *Olaf*: Medora Henson, Edward Lloyd (who had also sung the Blind Man in *Light of Life*), and Andrew Black. The reception was cooler than for its predecessor, but still very favourable. The *Court Journal* got excited by the closing chorus, saying stiffly that 'Mr. Elgar has not inaptly been dubbed "the Rudyard Kipling of the musicians"' (that is, equally fervently imperialist),[35] and the *Manchester Guardian* wished that a composer of such evident talent would turn away from the tired British cantata tradition. 'Such is the vigour and resource of his music that one regrets to hear it thrown away upon manufactured verse.'[36] His first biographer, a member of this generation, said that '"Caractacus" did not touch the masses, was not played upon the barrel organs'[37] (despite the catchy closing chorus, and the possibly pro-imperial sentiment we are led to believe was so pervasive), but the Leeds Festival of 1898 cemented Elgar's reputation among the concert-going public at least. And with his next work he would both turn away from the choral tradition and towards a more symphonic mode, and become a composer of international fame.

Orkestry and incense: the first English progressivist

Elgar toyed during October 1898 with the idea of writing a symphony for the Worcester Festival in 1899 on the subject of General Gordon, who had died during a siege in Khartoum in 1885, capturing the popular imagination in Britain. The notion was scrapped for practical reasons ('I have to earn money somehow & it's no *good* trying this sort of thing even for a "living wage"'),[38] but sketches for it were reused in *Gerontius* a year later. It seemed to awake the symphonic urge in Elgar.

The evening after a day of teaching at the Mount on 21 October has come down to us as a mythical creation narrative, with Elgar's words

---

33 Kennedy, *Portrait*, p. 65.

34 His father was still tuning pianos, including his son's, in his late 70s. He wasn't well enough to attend the premiere, but looked through the score and wrote encouragingly (Young, *Elgar O.M.*, p. 82).

35 Moore, *Creative Life*, p. 244.

36 McVeagh, *Elgar: Life and Music*, p. 24.

37 Buckley, *Elgar*, p. 54.

38 Letter to Jaeger, Moore, *Creative Life*, p. 247.

remembered (or, more probably, imaginatively recreated) many years later.

> 'After a long day's fiddle teaching in Malvern, I came home very tired. Dinner being over, my dear wife said to me, "Edward, you look like a good cigar", and having lighted it, I sat down at the piano . . .'
>
> . . .
>
> 'In a little while, soothed and feeling rested, I began to play, and suddenly my wife interrupted by saying:
> "Edward, that's a good tune."
> I awoke from the dream. "Eh! tune, what tune!"
> And she said, [“]Play it again, I like that tune."
> I played and strummed, and played, and then she exclaimed:
> "That's the tune."'[39]

The tune was the theme of what would become the *Variations on an Original Theme*, Op. 36, which goes by the unfortunate name 'Enigma'. It 'stands at the portal of our perception of English symphonism. Yet this is no symphony'.[40] For several reasons, most of them concerning Germans, but also because it was his first masterpiece, the first of his works to be published in full score, and one of the most important works of his career, it is worth dwelling on it at length.

The idea of producing a series of orchestral variations on this new theme came to Elgar at the highest speed. There were earlier models for such a set by Parry (*Symphonic Variations*, 1897), as well as Brahms (*Variations on a Theme of Haydn*, Op. 56, 1873) and Dvořák (*Symphonic Variations*, 1877). Only Parry's was written on an original theme; further examples by Stanford (1898), Wood, Gatty, and Hurlstone (1899) use pre-existing themes.[41] Elgar gave his set a personal twist by deciding to fashion each variation after defining characteristics of some of his friends (by no means all of them close friends; and some good friends, like Kilburn, didn't get a variation). He wrote to Jaeger only three days after he is said to have stumbled across the theme.

---

[39] Assembled from two sources by Moore, who makes a brave but unbelievable defence of their authenticity (ibid.). He magnifies the day's status as a great turning point for Elgar by prefacing this narrative with one of the composer's many despairing letters: 'E.E. having achieved the summit (or somewhat) of his amb[itio]n, retires into private life & bids adieu (or a diable [to the devil]) to a munificent public' (ibid.).

[40] Julian Rushton, *Elgar: 'Enigma' Variations* (Cambridge: Cambridge University Press, 1999), p. 3. See pp. 11–12 for a careful dissection of this genesis narrative. It is not certain that Elgar made up the theme while improvising on the piano, and it was probably – like most tunes in his life – in his head for a while before this date.

[41] See Rushton, *'Enigma' Variations*, p. 19.

> I've sketched a set of Variations (orkestry) on an original theme: the Variations have amused me because I've labelled 'em with the nicknames of particular friends – you are Nimrod. That is to say I've written the variations each one to represent the mood of the 'party' – I've liked to imagine the 'party' writing the var: him (or her) self & have written what I think they wd. have written – if they were asses enough to compose – it's a quaint idee & the result is amusing to those behind the scenes & won't affect the hearer who 'nose nuffin'. what think you?[42]

Jaeger thought well of it, and by 21 February 1899 Elgar had sent a full score of the work to Novello, having begun the orchestration only 13 days previously. It was at this point, and not before, that the word 'Enigma' was added by Jaeger (on Elgar's instruction) above the theme: the 'enigma' was no part of the original conception.

Aside from Jaeger, all but one of the men chosen for the set receive musical caricatures: Hew Steuart-Powell (1851–19??, 'H.D.S.-P.') and Troyte Griffith ('Troyte') have their pianistic techniques parodied; William Baker (1858–1935, 'W.M.B.'), a Gloucestershire squire and friend of Alice's, who often invited them to his home, Hasfield Court, is portrayed slamming the door as he leaves the room; the laugh of Richard Penrose Arnold (1855–19??), son of the poet Matthew Arnold, is recorded musically for posterity; and George Sinclair ('G.R.S.') has a variation concerned mostly with the descent of his dog Dan into the River Wye. Basil Nevinson (1853–1908, 'B.G.N.'), whose London home Elgar sometimes used for short visits, and with whom Elgar played chamber music, was of sufficient talent on the cello to warrant a deeply expressive cello variation, though at a significantly lower voltage than 'Nimrod'.

The female variations excite curiosity. Mrs Elgar's variation ('C.A.E.') is by far the most subdued of them all; perhaps his tenderness for her was privately shown. Dora Penny (1874–1964, 'Dorabella') was the first younger woman that Alice allowed Elgar to develop a fascination for. This tolerance makes Alice a deeply admirable woman, and balances her at least partly selfish desire to make her husband a success. Elgar required this tolerance, though; he wrote to Jaeger in 1898, 'Oh these boys: if only they knew that a woman's not worth a damn who won't put up with everything except ineptitude and crime'.[43] 'Everything' is a big word. Dora met Elgar in 1895, aged twenty-one, and soon earned her nickname from Mozart's *Così fan tutte*.[44] Her stammer is captured in the music; the

---

[42] Letter of 24 October 1898, quoted in Moore, *Creative Life*, p. 253. He signed off 'Much love & sunshine to you'.

[43] Quoted in ibid., p. 351.

[44] Her book, Mrs Richard Powell, *Edward Elgar: Memories of a Variation* (London: Remploy, 1979; orig. edn. 1937), is 'more enchanting than accurate' (Anderson, *Elgar*, p. 462).

C·A·E: C·Alice Elgar.

H·D·S·P: H·D·Steuart Powell.

R·B·T: R·B·Townshend.

W·M·B: W·M·Baker.

R·P·A: R·P·Arnold.

Ysobel: Isabel Fitton.

Troyte: Troyte Griffith.

W·N: Winifred Norbury.

Nimrod: A·J·Jaeger.

Dorabella: Dora Penny (Powell).

G·R·S: G·R·Sinclair.

B·G·N: Basil Nevinson.

∗∗∗ Lady Mary Lygon.

E·D·U: Edward Elgar.

12. *The 'friends pictured within' the Variations, Op. 36, in variation order.*

variation, marked 'Intermezzo', barely references the theme. 'Ysobel' is another caricature, this time of Isabel Fitton (1868–1936), one of Elgar's pupils, whose viola exercise is included in her variation. Winifred Norbury (1861–1938, 'W.N.') lived in the country with her sister Florence, close by Birchwood Lodge, which Elgar had begun to use as a retreat (and from where he signed off the *Variations*). Her gently pastoral variation is a portrait of her house. The variation marked '***' was originally marked 'L.M.L.' for Lady Mary Lygon (1869–1927; later Lady Mary Trefusis), who had founded a composing competition at Madresfield Court in 1896 and was a committee member of the Worcestershire Philharmonic Society, founded in 1897. Elgar said later that the quotation in her variation (another intermezzo, since it avoids the theme) of Mendelssohn's *Calm Sea and Prosperous Voyage* was inserted because she was at sea at the time. Although this story is often repeated, it isn't true: she visited Elgar on the day the full score was completed, and didn't sail to Australia for two months, when she accompanied her brother, Lord Beauchamp, who was to become governor of New South Wales.[45] Evelyn Waugh based the Flyte family from *Brideshead Revisited* on the Lygons.[46]

In the period before the premiere Elgar busied himself with everyday activities. He composed a violin and piano piece, a companion for *Chanson de nuit*, calling it *Chanson de matin*. He also contributed a madrigal, 'To her beneath whose steadfast star', to a collection of choral songs arranged for Queen Victoria's eightieth birthday by Sir Walter Parratt (1841–1924), the Master of the Queen's Musick (Elgar called it a 'Partrigal').[47] That was performed for the queen on her birthday, 24 May. He also moved house. Perhaps sensing success around the corner, Alice had found a much larger house south of Great Malvern, with spectacular views of Worcestershire. Elgar formed an anagram of E[dward], A[lice], and C[arice] ELGAR to form 'Craeg Lea'. They moved in March 1899. Lady Mary Lygon (still not at sea) came to tea, and he sought her permission to dedicate *Three Characteristic Pieces*, an arrangement of an 1883 Suite in D, to her. He conducted the London premiere of *Caractacus* on 20 April, and after the concert Dora Penny returned to 'Craeg Lea' with the Elgars. She wanted to know the identity of 'E.D.U.' in the final variation of Op. 36. These were no initials but a playful way of writing 'Edoo', Alice's pet name for Elgar. The finale, the work's most substantial and proto-symphonic movement, is a self-portrait.

The score had been sent to Hans Richter (1843–1916),[48] the conductor of the first *Ring* cycle in Bayreuth in 1876 and an important interpreter of

---

45 Rushton, *'Enigma' Variations*, p. 53.

46 Byron Adams, 'The "Dark Saying" of the Enigma: Homoeroticism and the Elgarian Paradox', *19th-Century Music*, 23 (2000), pp. 218–35, at p. 222.

47 Moore, *Creative Life*, p. 266.

48 It wasn't carried to him under Parry's eager arm in the rain, as one myth has it. It was simply sent to his agent, Vert, and Richter accepted it without knowing anything about the composer. McVeagh, *Elgar: Life and Music*, p. 27.

Wagner,[49] Brahms, and Bruckner. A high-culture celebrity, he started a series of regular Richter Concerts in London in 1879, and the *Variations* were intended for the 1899 concert on 19 June. Their reception was, for the first time in Elgar's life, unreservedly enthusiastic. The newly knighted Sir Hubert Parry (1848–1918; his knighthood came in 1898) deemed the work 'first rate. Quite brilliantly clever and genuine orchestral music', one critic said that on the evidence of the *Variations* (with their several movements for women) Elgar was 'in the best sense a "feminist" in music', and Elgar's mother wrote to say 'I feel that he is some great historic person – I cannot claim a little bit of him now he belongs to the big world'.[50]

'E.D.U.' was much shorter in its first performance than we now know it. It recapitulated 'C.A.E.' but not 'Nimrod'. The extension came at the instigation of Jaeger, who said that both he and Richter found the conclusion unsatisfactory (although he was very deeply impressed by the whole). It was the first of several critical improvements Jaeger was to suggest in Elgar's music. Though always resistant at first, Elgar saw sense each time. The extended finale was first heard in a performance, conducted by Elgar, on 13 September.

The work's first century of reception was dominated by attempts to unsnarl its supposed riddle. The idea of an 'enigma', imagined (as we've seen) at a late stage in the work's development, and almost certainly inserted into the programme note by a composer uncertain of the work's 'purely musical' value,[51] served the work well as an advert in its early years. It gave it mystique. Elgar eventually tired of attempted solutions, and probably regretted having said anything at all. Although human nature guarantees that attempts to solve it will never end until the Ark of the Covenant and the Holy Grail are on permanent display in the British Museum, they all somehow fail to convince. It is easy to carp, since the riddle cannot be answered now its perpetrator is dead, but the evidence supporting all the 'solutions' is weak. Suggested musical counterpoints fit so poorly with the theme as to do disservice to Elgar's contrapuntal ability; most literary connexions suffer from code-breakers' distortion (or flat misunderstanding) of the source quotation, and are in general too abstruse to sit well with Elgar's suggestion that Dora Penny, 'of all people', should know it; and biographical readings mystify in their fantasy. That said, many people find them amusing, and I suppose there are worse vices.[52]

---

[49] He copied the score of *Meistersinger* at Triebschen, while Wagner was orchestrating it in 1866.
[50] Anderson, *Elgar*, p. 41, Moore, *Creative Life*, p. 271, and Young, *Elgar O.M.*, p. 105.
[51] Vaughan Williams suffered from the same insecurity throughout his life. It is notable that most of his symphonies bear vaguely programmatic titles.
[52] See Rushton, *'Enigma' Variations*, pp. 64–78 for a discussion of the main 'solutions' up to 1999.

More interesting for us, and more significant for Elgar's development as a composer, is the tentative use made in it of a structural device that would become critical to his symphonic music. Although each variation is a self-contained unit, each also depends for its effect, like the romantic 'fragments' in works such as Schumann's song-cycle *Dichterliebe*, on its placement next to the ones before or after it. Some of the variations run into each other very obviously. The best example of this is the meltingly beautiful Schubertian slide between the third-related keys of 'W.N.' (G major) and 'Nimrod' (E flat major), which holds onto the same melodic G across the bar (at once the first note in the scale of W.N.'s G and the third note in Nimrod's E flat: the effect of such a 'pun' on a note is almost always magical). Other variations have no such obvious link, but Elgar exploits the resources of the tonal system to subtly leave the musical structure 'open' at the ends of many of the movements, with the result that multi-movement structures are formed by groups of variations.[53] In the *Variations* this kind of structure is not important – if we don't listen to the individual variations as character sketches we are missing the point and the joy of the piece. But it was a useful structural experiment for the composer, and an important stage in his development as a symphonist.

A visit to Sinclair's in the aftermath of the premiere led to another tune for the bulldog, 'Dan triumphant (after a fight)'. It would open the overture *In the South* a few years later. Elgar made an important new friend while preparing a concert.[54] Alfred Rodewald (1861–1903) was an amateur conductor and founder of the Liverpool Orchestral Society, and became a promoter and financial supporter. He was a friend of Richter's (who had taught him conducting), and knew many other musicians; through him Elgar met Britain's leading music critic, Ernest Newman. An even more important new friend was Frank Schuster (1852–1927), a patron of the arts who became one of Elgar's closest homosexual friends.[55] He often offered the Elgars hospitality at The Hut on the Thames in Maidenhead (where Elgar wrote much of the First Symphony, the Violin Concerto, and *Falstaff*) and in Westminster.

Also that summer Elgar wrote an orchestral song cycle for Clara Butt, a popular music-hall singer (created Dame in 1920). *Sea Pictures*, Op. 37, has a hotch-potch jumble of five poems, one of the best of them by Alice

---

[53] There are four coherent multi-movement units in the work, governed by tonality and voice-leading. The first runs to the end of 'R.B.T.', the second from 'W.M.B.' to 'Dorabella', the third is 'G.R.S.', and the fourth runs from the start of 'B.G.N.' to the end of the work. The proper demonstration of this would require the use of a system of analysis drawn from the work of Heinrich Schenker (1868–1935). Its inclusion would probably double the length of the present book.

[54] It was a summer of many performances: the *Imperial March*, *Variations*, Serenade for strings, and extracts from *The Light of Life*, *Olaf*, and *Caractacus* were all heard in a single concert.

[55] His sister Adela sent Oscar Wilde £1,000 – a huge sum – during his imprisonment at Reading Gaol (Adams, 'The "Dark Saying"', at p. 227).

(a memory of a trip to Capri, set in 1897 as 'Love alone will stay'). One of the songs, 'Sabbath Morning at Sea', is made of old music from 1883; it is the weakest of the set. The cycle was given at the Norwich Festival in October 1899, and at a command performance for Victoria at Balmoral on 20 October. A row with Novello led to it being published by Boosey.[56]

A more substantial commission came for the 1900 Birmingham Festival. Elgar entertained two ideas, and both would eventually bear fruit. The first was a setting of Cardinal Newman's *Dream of Gerontius* (in September Elgar started to spend time with Father Richard Bellasis, a priest at the Birmingham Oratory that Newman had founded in 1848); the second was for an oratorio based on the teaching of the apostles. The latter was early favourite, and he wrote some music for it (an idea for Judas going later into *Gerontius*), but when the prospect of producing a text on such a scale unnerved him, he resigned the commission. Then G. H. Johnstone, representing the Festival committee, convinced him instead to turn to *Gerontius*, and offered to negotiate publication of the resulting piece with Novello. An acceptance letter came from the chairman, Alfred Littleton, on 23 January 1900. Elgar would earn £200 plus 'a fair proportion' of any subsequent sales.[57]

Elgar had known Newman's pungently Catholic poem since at least 1889, when Fr Knight, S. J., had given him a copy as a wedding present. It deals with the 'four last things' of Christian theology: death, judgement, heaven, and hell. It follows a worldly man, Gerontius (the name roughly means 'old man'), from death-bed to the throne of judgement. On earth, a priest and assistants pray for his soul; in the afterlife, he is instructed in the doctrines of purgatory, heaven, and hell, and after being alternately taunted by demonic voices and enchanted by angelic choirs, he sees God 'for one moment', and commits himself to purgatory (for a while), with the words 'Take me away!'.

Between them, *Gerontius* and the *Variations* were to crystallize his reputation as the leading composer of his generation. Although Elgar was still teaching violin at the Mount when he started work on *Gerontius*, Richter was continuing to promote the *Variations* in concert performances. Elgar's world was changing.

In writing *The Dream of Gerontius*, Op. 38, Elgar radically trimmed the fat from Newman's flaccid poem, reducing it from 900 to 435 lines. The resulting oratorio (the generic title fits well enough, though Elgar resisted it) for three soloists, chorus, and orchestra falls into two parts, the second almost twice the length of the first; Gerontius's death precedes the interval. Jaeger read the score in manuscript before performance and was astonished by its quality, which he saw would put Elgar in the first

[56] See Moore, *Creative Life*, pp. 288–9.
[57] Ibid., p. 298.

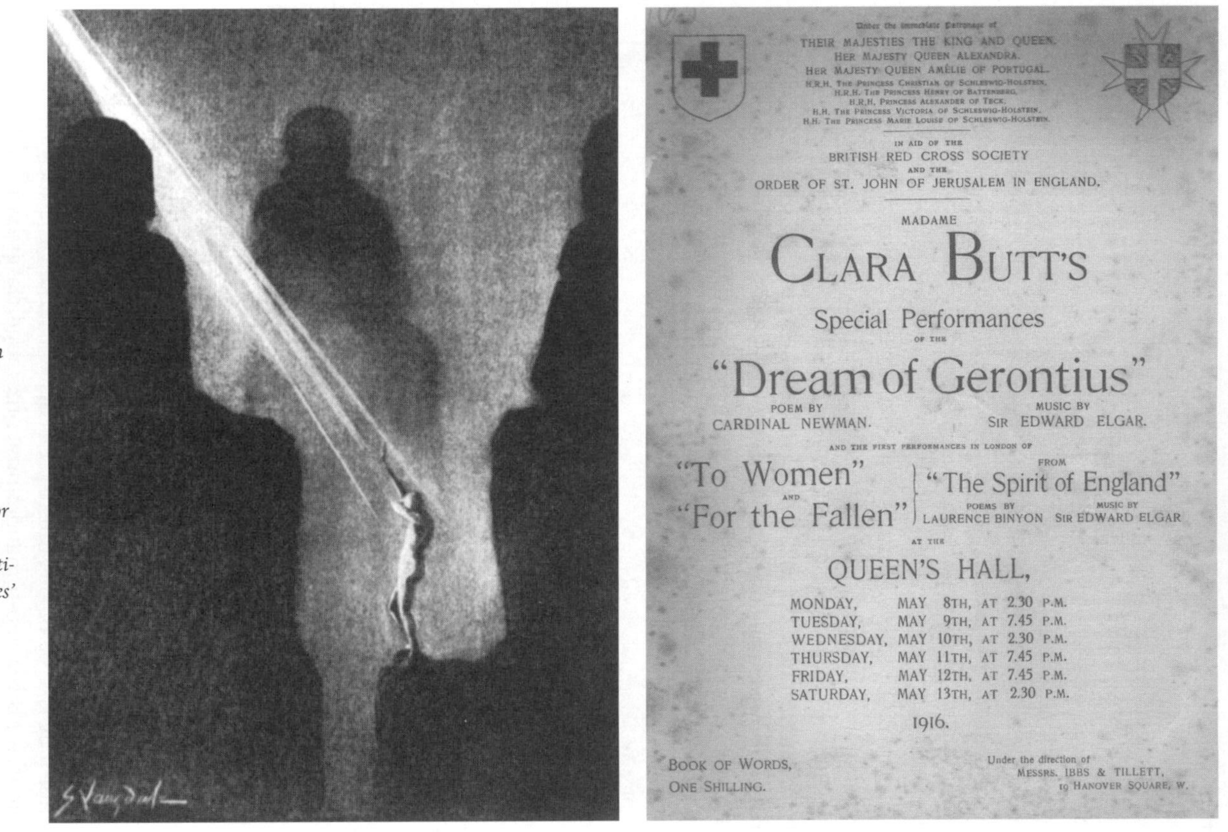
Under the immediate Patronage of
THEIR MAJESTIES THE KING AND QUEEN.
HER MAJESTY QUEEN ALEXANDRA.
HER MAJESTY QUEEN AMÉLIE OF PORTUGAL.
H.R.H. THE PRINCESS CHRISTIAN OF SCHLESWIG-HOLSTEIN.
H.R.H. THE PRINCESS HENRY OF BATTENBERG.
H.R.H. PRINCESS ALEXANDER OF TECK.
H.H. THE PRINCESS VICTORIA OF SCHLESWIG-HOLSTEIN.
H.H. THE PRINCESS MARIE LOUISE OF SCHLESWIG-HOLSTEIN.

IN AID OF THE
BRITISH RED CROSS SOCIETY
AND THE
ORDER OF ST. JOHN OF JERUSALEM IN ENGLAND.

MADAME
CLARA BUTT'S
Special Performances
OF THE
"Dream of Gerontius"
POEM BY CARDINAL NEWMAN.
MUSIC BY SIR EDWARD ELGAR.

AND THE FIRST PERFORMANCES IN LONDON OF
"To Women" AND "For the Fallen"
FROM "The Spirit of England"
POEMS BY LAURENCE BINYON
MUSIC BY SIR EDWARD ELGAR

AT THE
QUEEN'S HALL,

MONDAY, MAY 8TH, AT 2.30 P.M.
TUESDAY, MAY 9TH, AT 7.45 P.M.
WEDNESDAY, MAY 10TH, AT 2.30 P.M.
THURSDAY, MAY 11TH, AT 7.45 P.M.
FRIDAY, MAY 12TH, AT 7.45 P.M.
SATURDAY, MAY 13TH, AT 2.30 P.M.

1916.

BOOK OF WORDS,
ONE SHILLING.

Under the direction of
MESSRS. IBBS & TILLETT,
19 HANOVER SQUARE, W.

13. One of a set of illustrations by Stella Langdale for an early twentieth-century edition of Cardinal Newman's 'The Dream of Gerontius'.

14. Book of words for the London premieres of 'To Women' and 'For the Fallen', containing August Jaeger's 'analytical and descriptive notes' on The Dream of Gerontius.

rank of European composers. His main criticism was the moment at which the Soul receives his judgement from God, when, after a grand orchestral climax, at the top of which (Elgar wrote in the score) '"for one moment" must every instrument exert its fullest force', the tenor sings 'Take me away!' in a whining tone that Jaeger didn't like. Elgar was resistant to the idea of change, but the German spurred him on with a heady comparison. 'Wagner would have made that the *climax* of *expression* in the work . . . Wagner *always revelled* in seemingly *"Impossible"* situations & this one would have brought forth his most splendid powers'.[58] One more letter in this manner, three days later, was enough: the work's climax was rewritten and its most effective moment produced. The work was completed on 3 August.

For 1900 the musical tone was a little old-fashioned, still neo-romantic at a time when Europe was exploring early modernism, but Elgar's command of structure was magisterial, at least the equal of his contemporaries Mahler and Strauss. *Gerontius*'s use of leitmotiv, which Jaeger analysed in a booklet published by Novello,[59] was less thoroughgoing than *Olaf*'s, but only because Elgar had begun to go beyond aping Wagner in that slightly superficial manner. Having learnt the power of Wagner's tonal structures, where many hours of music can by careful stages 'compose out' a single, richly satisfying tonal design, he could now create a structure which makes its effect both conceptually (a level central to musical appreciation, as to all modes of human expression) and at a more-or-less inexplicable emotional level.

The multi-movement structuring of the *Variations* was taken to new lengths: the D of 'judgement' (major or minor depending on whether it is good or bad) which frames both part I and the whole work, enfolds a second, intricately designed structure in flat keys (for Gerontius's declaration of faith and the prayers around his bed, and the Angel that accompanies the Soul before his encounter with God), and a pure C major for the chorus of Angelicals who sing 'Praise to the Holiest'. Both through the text, which leaves the Soul in Purgatory with the promise of eventual salvation – expected but not shown to be fulfilled – and through the musical design, whose return to the work's opening key is tentative, not conquering, Elgar makes a point that would characterize the modernist phase to come. There is no guarantee of victory, only hope for it (this note of pessimism recalls *The Black Knight*). In *Gerontius*, the pinnacle of his neo-romantic music, the hope leaves little room for doubt; the later music would be soaked with uncertainty.

Problems blighted the premiere in Birmingham on 3 October. Novello couldn't get chorus parts ready in good time for the rehearsals for what

---

[58] Letter of 27 June 1900, quoted in ibid., p. 319.
[59] A. J. Jaeger, *The Dream of Gerontius: Analytical and Descriptive Notes* (London: Novello, 1900).

was a difficult work. Swinnerton Heap, who was to have trained the choir, died unexpectedly of pneumonia on 11 June; his replacement Stockley returned from retirement to do his (insufficient) best. Richter, with highest faith in the work's quality, presided over a travesty. 'But it was not Richter's fault', wrote Vaughan Williams, who was at the premiere, 'that the semi-chorus consisted of second-rate professionals from Birmingham and district, that the choir got hopelessly flat . . . that Plunket Greene [the Angel of the Agony] lost his voice, that Marie Brema [the Angel] had none to lose, and that Edward Lloyd [Gerontius] sang it like a Stainer anthem in the correct tenor attitude with one foot slightly withdrawn'.[60]

Elgar was aghast, and blamed the obvious suspect: 'I always said God was against art & I still believe it. anything obscene or trivial is blessed in this world & has no reward . . . I have allowed my heart to open once – it is now shut against every religious feeling & every soft, gentle impulse *for ever*'.[61] He was to compose for another 33 years, among his works two further substantial oratorios totalling around three hours of religious music, but it shows his customary anguished reaction to setback. Critics in any case saw through the poor performance. *The Daily Telegraph* didn't like the 'unhealthy' (which is to say luxurious, effete, even homosexual) Wagnerian language of the music, but generously noted that 'a man when armed with technical skill, and able to put *a healthy restraint* upon himself, may go far and do much',[62] but other critics considered it a signal work, the finest yet written by a British composer. Suddenly, German critics were interested. Otto Lessmann (1844–1918) said that 'the "coming man" has already arisen in the English musical world . . . the composer of the only considerable, sacred choral work, "The Dream of Gerontius".'[63] German critics like Lessmann sensed in Elgar the post-Wagnerian spirit that could spread to Britain the redemptive project of contemporary German art – the idea that artistic generation could regenerate the body politic. Despite the failings of the premiere, Elgar had reached the height of his critical reception. He would hold onto his position for a decade.

Stanford, professor at Cambridge, had suggested after the *Variations* that the University make Elgar an honorary Doctor of Music (Mus.D.). The formal invitation finally came in November 1900. Elgar's first instinct was to refuse – the official excuse was that he was too poor to buy the pretty

---

[60] Michael Kennedy, *The Works of Ralph Vaughan Williams*, 2nd edn. (London: Oxford University Press, 1980; orig. edn. 1964), p. 389.

[61] A letter to Jaeger, quoted in Moore, *Creative Life*, p. 334.

[62] Quoted in ibid., pp. 332–3, emphasis mine. This issue is explored most interestingly in Adams, 'Elgar's Later Oratorios'.

[63] 'Occasional Notes', *The Musical Times and Singing Class Circular*, 42 (1901), p. 20. On German reception, see Aidan J. Thomson, 'Elgar and Chivalry', *19th-Century Music*, 28 (2005), pp. 254–75 and 'Elgar in German Criticism', in Grimley and Rushton (eds.), *The Cambridge Companion to Elgar*, pp. 204–13.

cream damask and cherry satin robes[64] – but he accepted, and was given the honour on St Cecilia's Day, 22 November. He wrote proudly to his sister Dot, in tones that would please a Catholic nun: 'You must not think this is a 2½d. thing like the Archbp of Canterbury's degree but it's a great thing: it has of late only been given to Joachim, Tschaikowsky, Max Bruch & a few others'.[65] Elgar criticized the Public Orator's Latin at the ceremony. He took no pleasure in the title, which hid his proud self-training ('Why the divule you call me doctor I don't know!'), but took the honour, predictably, for Alice's sake.[66]

In many ways the four years following the premiere of *Gerontius* were a time of consolidation. The work didn't pay much (it took two years for a second full performance to be mounted in Britain, and he had more or less given up teaching; once more they had a winter without fires), and his main compositional energy was directed towards the second religious work he had been considering in 1899, *The Apostles*, which would appear in 1903. While revising *Froissart* he began a second concert overture, *Cockaigne* (a humorous name for London, though it originally indicated 'an imaginary country, the abode of luxury and idleness') (see figure 22, page 116).[67] Some of its structural features qualify it for inclusion among the modernist works from *In the South* onwards (we shall hear more of this in the next chapter). Again, the score was published by Boosey. The overture was premiered in 1901, as were two orchestral marches, conducted by Rodewald, *Pomp and Circumstance* 1 and 2. The first had 'a tune that comes once in a lifetime', 'a tune that will knock 'em – knock 'em flat'.[68] He spoke to Rodewald about his dream of writing a symphony (the 'Gordon' idea was not yet put to bed), and was offered generous financial support. Still the project did not take flight.

Queen Victoria's death in January 1901 gave Elgar an opportunity to write a *Coronation Ode* for the new King Edward VII, who would become a notable supporter. He decided to use the trio tune from the first *Pomp and Circumstance* march for the triumphant finale, and the well-connected librettist Arthur Benson (1862–1925), son of the Archbishop of Canterbury and Fellow and Master at Magdalene College, Cambridge, wrote the lines 'Land of Hope and Glory, / Mother of the Free' to fit it. It was popularized by Clara Butt in an orchestral song version of 1902 for which Benson supplied more viciously imperialist words ('Wider still and wider . . .': the original text exhorts the monarch to keep 'Truth and Right and Freedom' at the centre of his regal credo).

---

64 These were eventually bought for him by Parry, Richter, Granville Bantock, and Henry Wood.
65 Moore, *Creative Life*, p. 337.
66 McVeagh, *Elgar: Life and Music*, p. 34.
67 *Oxford English Dictionary*, s.v. 'Cockaigne'.
68 Quoted in Moore, *Creative Life*, pp. 339 and 348.

Elgar spent the summer of 1901 once more at Birchwood, this time without a major project to consume him. Since Alice wasn't interested in cycling, he did it with Rosa Burley. Then he went on holiday with her to Cardiganshire, where he had an idea for an important 'Welsh tune' that would form part of his *Introduction and Allegro*. In August he was approached by the Irish writer George Moore (1852–1933), who wanted him to write instrumental music for the play *Diarmuid and Grania* that he had co-written with W. B. Yeats and was being produced by the Irish Literary Theatre company (forerunner of the Abbey Theatre) in Dublin. Elgar wrote a little incidental music and a fine funeral march, largely for financial reasons, modernizing the spelling to *Grania and Diarmid*. He was egged on to write a Grania opera, but didn't, perhaps because he wasn't interested or because he knew that Hamish MacCunn's 1897 opera on the subject was already in repertory (and would remain so until the First World War). The music was first heard with the play at the Gaiety Theatre, Dublin, on 21 October, and Elgar arranged the funeral march for separate publication. A short *Allegro (Concert Solo)*, 'Concerto without orchestra', was written for the pianist Fanny Davies, to be played at a 'Purcell to Elgar' concert she was planning. He completed this novelty piece in time for the concert at St James's Hall on 2 December.

In a letter of 1 December 1901 he was commissioned to write a work for the 1903 Birmingham Festival. Ernest Newman, echoing the sentiments of one critic of *Caractacus*, wished that Elgar would turn away from the British choral-music tradition and write something that would be considered more worthwhile by the contemporary musical world. No hope of this yet: Elgar pressed on with another huge choral–orchestral work with six soloists, *The Apostles*, the first part of an intended trilogy on the early Church.

Composition of these 'GIGANTIC WORX'[69] was interrupted briefly by a pair of two short orchestral pieces under the title *Dream Children* (on which, see inter-chapter 4), and for his last Bavarian holiday in 1902. There he met the conductor Julius Buths (1851–1920), who had conducted *Gerontius* twice in Düsseldorf with his own German translation, once at the end of the previous year, and again on 20 May 1902. Buths and Strauss presented Elgar with a copy of Beethoven's death-mask, and at an after-dinner speech at the Essen Festival, Strauss toasted 'the welfare and success of the first English progressivist, Meister Edward Elgar'.[70] This was another sign of Elgar's reception as a modernist – but for the time being he was resting on his laurels. The death of his mother on 2 September 1902 after a swift decline in health might have stirred up faith enough for a few years more effort on the oratorio project. He could

[69] Letter to Ivor Atkins, quoted in ibid., p. 372.
[70] Ibid., p. 369.

cope with life without her partly, no doubt, because in Alice he had found a wife to mother him.

After a bowdlerized *Gerontius* at Worcester Cathedral on 11 September (the Church of England didn't like its prayers to saints or to Mary, so the text was altered), Elgar spent the autumn with Rodewald conducting more concerts near Chester. Newman was also a guest at 'Craeg Lea'. After symbolically installing the new king in the diadem with the premiere of the *Coronation Ode* in Sheffield on 2 October 1902, Elgar made the acquaintance of a woman who would gradually take over his life, Alice Stuart-Wortley (1862–1936). She was the daughter of the painter John Everett Millais, and wife of Charles Stuart-Wortley, the MP for Sheffield. Her mother Euphemia Gray had previously been married to John Ruskin.[71]

1903 began as a year of *Gerontius* performances; Elgar conducted one for Nicholas Kilburn in Middlesbrough on 22 April, and it was given at the new (Catholic) Westminster Cathedral on 6 June – its first London performance. It was also suggested that Covent Garden hold an Elgar Festival in 1904; *Gerontius* would fill the first evening, *Apostles* the second, and orchestral works, including a new one, would compose the third. He planned to write a symphony in E flat, which he would dedicate to Richter. On 3 April, he was elected a member of the Athenaeum Club, smoking shop of bishops and judges, under Rule II, which allowed commoners to join: Sir Walter Scott, Dickens, and Kipling had got in that way too. As before with the Cambridge doctorate, he worried about the cost of membership, but he managed to pay the fee with advance royalties from some songs.[72] Later in the month he went to Morecambe for a performance on 30 April of *The Banner of St George* and a new part song, 'Weary Wind of the West', and was also invited to adjudicate at the Morecambe Festival. He met and stayed with the organizer, Canon Charles Vincent Gorton (1854–1912), whom he would ask for advice on oratorio librettos for the next few years.

Elgar had to surrender Birchwood Lodge when his tenancy expired, and there was a significant departure from his life too. Although a trip to Liverpool to see Rodewald was planned for November, Rodewald contracted influenza early in the month, and within a few days was paralysed and unconscious. Elgar fretfully took the train to Liverpool but arrived only an hour or two after his friend died. He wrote three despairing letters to Jaeger. 'He was the dearest, kindest, *best* friend I ever had . . . I am utterly broken up.' Finding Rodewald dead he said 'I broke down & went out – *and it was night to me* . . . I know I walked for miles in strange ways . . . then I went to my room & wept for hours . . . I thank

---

[71] Her significance will be discussed further in chapter 3.

[72] Kennedy, *Portrait*, p. 152.

heaven we all had that bit of time together in Wales: you know a little of what he was'.[73] Michael Kennedy finds Elgar's reaction theatrical, and Diana McVeagh compares it to Tennyson's after the death of his passionately close friend Arthur Hallam.[74] Like Elgar, she says, Tennyson had suffered an artistic setback, the failure of his *Poems* soon before. In Elgar's case, she says the artistic failure was the premiere of *Gerontius*. This doesn't quite convince, since that work had clearly taken off by 1903, and been very warmly received in Germany in 1902. But a reading suggesting that Elgar had latently homosexual feelings for Rodewald (whose death was memorialized in the Second Symphony's Larghetto, sketches for which were written within a few months of the event) won't wash either, for the simple reason that Elgar poured out his heart to Jaeger, another man he could be supposed to have been potentially sexually interested in, and notes specifically in his letter that the men's time together as a trio was especially precious. Either Elgar yearned at some subconscious level for gay threesomes, or else the men were all just very close friends. An alternative and subtler reading is Byron Adams's, which argues that Elgar was playing along with an established discourse that was homoerotic (a closeness to the same sex which dabbles in erotic thoughts but not acts) but not actually homosexual (a closeness to the same sex which includes or aspires towards sexual acts) – an effete panting and wailing that was a familiar part of the Decadent movement. In any case, Elgar certainly seemed to expect the death of 'Rodey' to move Jaeger just as intensely as it did him. Given Rodewald's considerable financial support of Elgar, however, money was also surely a factor in his misery.[75]

The rest of 1903 was consumed by the composition of *The Apostles*, Op. 49, for which Elgar wrote his own libretto, drawn from the King James Bible. It sets the Beatitudes and then, following Bach's Passions in a very individual way, deals with traditional Christian interests like death and resurrection, as well as some fairly unexpected things, like the mental anguish of Judas. This biblical focus, and his critical reading of Church doctrine, makes Elgar's oratorio project an essentially Protestant work[76] – a move towards the Establishment through its Church, but also a critical turn away from the conservative religion of his converted mother, which (perhaps) eventually led to a complete loss of faith.

In the oratorio, Judas and Mary Magdalene, not Christ, are the central characters so far as the music is concerned. Both require divine

---

[73] Quoted in ibid., p. 159.

[74] Diana M. McVeagh, '"A Man's Attitude to Life"', in Raymond Monk (ed.), *Edward Elgar: Music and Literature* (Aldershot: Scolar, 1993), pp. 1–9, at pp. 4–9.

[75] But on a possible homosexual component of this grief see Adams, 'The "Dark Saying"', especially pp. 220–21.

[76] I owe this insight to Julian Rushton, 'Elgar, Empire, and Kingdom', the A. T. Shaw lecture given at the Annual General Meeting of the Elgar Society, Worcester, 2006. Published in the *Elgar Society Journal*, 14/6 (2006), pp. 15–26.

forgiveness, and they respond in opposite ways to the possibility (Mary accepting, Judas denying and so damning himself).[77] The work's structure has been criticized as clunky, with too much emphasis on the local level of character portraits – in that sense making it a step backwards from *Gerontius* and the *Variations* – and the leitmotiv system returns in its crudest manner. Notwithstanding, there is much in the oratorio to recommend a hearing, particularly scenes 3 and 4, the scenes of greatest human interest with Magdalene and Judas. Newman was right to note an essential difference between this work and *Gerontius*. 'In the latter the human element is predominant, the religious secondary; in the former, the human element at times almost disappears, and a frankly religious and didactic purpose[78] flies out at us from the score'.[79] Critical reaction to the premiere on 14 October was very warm – it was the highlight of the musical year – but not unmixed. To those who disliked the genre, the knowledge that this was to be only the first part of a huge trilogy of works disappointed. In the mind of Newman and others like him, Elgar *had* to stop writing oratorios. It would take the massive effort of struggling through the next in the trilogy (ideas for which had already been sketched) to bring him round to their way of thinking.

On 21 November the Elgars left London for Italy. They found a house at Alassio on the Gulf of Genoa, near the French border. Carice, who as usual (for short trips as well as long) had been left at home with Rosa Burley, arrived on 21 December. Elgar enjoyed the food but disliked the wintry weather, and could not compose. When the weather changed, he moved into another stage of his compositional development.

---

[77] See Charles Edward McGuire, 'Elgar, Judas, and the Theology of Betrayal', *19th-Century Music*, 23 (2000), pp. 236–72.

[78] A throw-back to the unsatisfactory *Light of Life*.

[79] Newman, *Elgar*, pp. 81–2. He thought the opening of Part II 'the most unsatisfactory piece of work ever put together by Elgar . . . In this prelude . . . the musical interest diminishes to vanishing point' (p. 102).

In his spare time

In his hobbies and interests as well as in his composition Elgar showed himself a lively and imaginative, if not always dedicated, explorer. The range of his modes of relaxation is large, and while some are to be expected of the middle-class intellectual (reading; sports like golf, horses, bowls, and billiards), and others are no surprise in the same social class (heraldry; word-play and cryptography), some are genuinely unusual (chemistry, and microscope work). Less pleasant to the modern mind, but an important part of his constructed self-image as a country squire, were shooting and hunting. 'There's no music like the baying of hounds', he said.[1]

Elgar's miniature laboratory – which he dubbed 'the Ark' – at his new home, 'Plâs Gwyn', received much use in the 1900s (see page 78, figure 18). One of many textbooks Elgar bought to teach himself the rudiments of the science was John Attfield's *Chemistry: General, Medical, and Pharmaceutical* (1869), which begins with recommended apparatus and types of chemicals before running to several hundred pages of numbered questions and experiments. Early ones Elgar has marked and presumably conducted include preparing mercuric iodide by precipitation. Later in the book the questions and experiments will interest only the very dedicated. '869. What is the average composition of healthy urine? 870. Give the tests for urea . . . 873. Sketch out a plan for the chemical examination of urinary sediments. 874. A deposit is insoluble in the supernatant urine or in acetic acid; of what substances may it consist?'[2] It is probably as well that the hobby fizzled out.[3]

At the height of his enthusiasm he told Schuster he had made something useful in 'the Ark'. 'I am resuming chemistry & made soap yesterday between fits of scoring (not scouring!) the [First] symphony. I have been vainly trying to persuade Carice to wash

[1] Anderson, *Elgar*, p. 42. This sentiment was voiced as early as the fourteenth century, when John I of Portugal said that 'even Guillaume de Machaut cannot create such harmonies and melody as do hounds when they are running true'; Elizabeth Eva Leach, *Sung Birds: Music, Poetry, and Nature in the Later Middle Ages* (Ithaca, NY: Cornell University Press, 2007), p. 220.

[2] John Attfield, *Chemistry: General, Medical, and Pharmaceutical*, 6th edn. (London: Van Voorst, 1875), p. 441.

[3] It recrudesced in 1917 when he decided to massacre some wasps and (he had a sleepless night worrying) passing children with some cyanide. See W. H. Reed, *Elgar as I Knew Him* (London: Gollancz, 1973; orig. edn. 1936), pp. 58–61. No children were killed. But neither were all the wasps.

with it – strange how little encouragement I get!'[4] This was perhaps understandable, given his reputation for irresponsibility. He once attempted to prepare a chemical 'jape' that would produce a small explosion by spreading a phosphoric paste onto blotting paper. He produced too much paste, left it unattended in a water butt (thinking it would be safe), and returned to the house. The thing exploded with the noise of 'all the percussion in all the orchestras on earth', blowing up the water-butt and flooding the drive. Elgar denied all knowledge to his next-door neighbour, who ran out of house expecting the apocalypse.[5]

Perhaps his labelling of a theme in the First Symphony as having 'a nice sub-acid feeling' had a chemical meaning: the *Oxford English Dictionary* defines 'sub-acid' as 'containing less than the normal proportion of acid'. He was not chary of using chemical terms to describe people. In his Birmingham lecture on 'Critics' in 1905, George Bernard Shaw's writing is described as having 'a substratum of *practical matter*, or to put it chemically to volatile and pellucid fluid, held in solution, matter which was precipitated into obvious solid fact by the introduction of the reader's *own common sense*. His imitators give us the watery fluid without the useful *precipitate*'.[6]

Chemistry blended into microscope work. W. H. Reed complains about its effects on billiards, a respectable middle-class game. 'I never once succeeded in getting Sir Edward to *finish* a game. We would get as far as 30 or 40, or perhaps even 50; but he always switched off to the study of diatoms [unicellular algae] . . . I have seen three beautiful microscopes at once on that billiard-table, with slides, condensers, and everything complete, strewn all over it'.[7] But billiards – or a strange version of it bordering almost on snooker – was still a consuming interest. He would have known that love of the game united him with Mozart; but the Austrian would probably have beaten him.[8]

Technology in general intrigued Elgar. He was as up-to-date with the gramophone as he could be. Aside from his own career as a recording artist (of which we shall learn more in chapter 6) he was also an avid collector. He had a device for controlling the gramophone's volume, operated by a button on his armchair,

---

[4] Anderson, *Elgar*, p. 86.
[5] Reed, *Elgar as I Knew Him*, pp. 39–40.
[6] Elgar, *Future*, p. 185.
[7] Reed, *Elgar as I Knew Him*, p. 50.
[8] See Julian Rushton, *Mozart: An Extraordinary Life* (London: Associated Board of the Royal Schools of Music, 2005), p. 74.

that could swing densely orchestrated bits of Berlioz or Wagner from whispering *ppp* to blasting *fff*.

Another important technology of his age was the bicycle. His fascination with this (he called his Sunbeam 'Mr Phoebus', after the Greek sun god) dwindled when cars took over the roads. While it lasted, and because Alice was no cyclist, it provided him with time, among other things, to dally with women like Rosa Burley while exploring the countryside, so uniting two favourite pastimes. He was a keen walker – mostly with male companions – both in Britain and on the Continent. Golf and bowls were other social activities. Kite-flying was also social but in addition gave him further scope for technological experiment. Buckley said that it was Elgar's dream to invent a kite that would 'break in and bridle the innate *diablerie* of the fiery untamed kite in a state of nature . . . Nothing came of it except the fall of his neighbour's spouting'.[9] With kites came another children's favourite, the boomerang. Reed reports of one day when an unusually heavy and long boomerang, flung enthusiastically by Elgar over the River Wye in an attempt to hone his skills, chased their sprinting forms across a meadow, threatening to decapitate them.[10]

Not all of Elgar's pastimes were so physical. His interest in literature, of course, bridged the private and musical spheres and is discussed elsewhere, as is his casual interest in doodling and sketching (see figures opposite).[11] His passing interest in heraldry too found its place in the chivalrous idiom of his music, particularly in the earliest phase, but had other outgrowths. For instance, it informed the inscription on Alice's headstone, 'Fortiter et fide' ('bold and faithful'). Yet more broadly than in literature or heraldic inscriptions, words themselves held enormous fascination for Elgar, and made him one of the wittiest of all composer letter-writers.

The names given to 'Nimrod' (starting with that one: others are given in chapter 2) attest to his fondness for wordplay, and a pair of letters he wrote to F. G. Edwards is especially delicious. Elgar began, as people interested in words do, with a speculation into semantic history – in this case of Potters Bar, a town in Hertfordshire.

---

[9] Buckley, *Elgar*, p. 35.

[10] Reed, *Elgar as I Knew Him*, p. 39.

[11] See Brian Trowell, 'Elgar's Use of Literature', in Raymond Monk (ed.), *Edward Elgar: Music and Literature* (Aldershot: Scolar, 1993), pp. 182–326, and chapters 2–5 of this book, *passim*.

15. Elgar's doodle of the Apostles, with word games at the top.

16. Elgar's caricature of his daughter, Carice ('Miss Elgar, The Censor'), 1915, with a frivolous quotation from King Lear*.*

> Who was Potter & why did he possess a Bar? . . . This is my theme: I cannot conceive that Potter kept a tavern; the occupation is too common to be identified in this public way.
>
> Potter surely did not levy toll at a private 'pike': a sort of sedentary highwayman? the thing is not possible[.]
>
> I conceive Potter as a philosopher: high & serene musing on & clarifying problems far beyond human knowledge; I see him brought face to face with some impenetrable riddle before which the mighty intellect – even that of Potter – quailed, paled & failed.
>
> Surely this was Potter's Bar.

Edwards suggested that it might be for soap or music that Potter was remembered, and Elgar twitted gently by return of post.

> I *am* aware that soap & music are given to the world in bars; surely you will not contend that Potter was a musical composer because he has left one bar? . . . we say Bach's Mass, or Beethoven's Violin Concerto; those great men having left behind them one only of the compositions named – always in the possessive case. But Potters Bar! produce the bar & we can judge its musical value.
>
> I hold it were trifling on your part to suggest that Potter, whom I assume to have been a man of intellect, made soap: even if he did condescend to soap he must necessarily have made more than one bar. I wish you would treat Potter seriously. . .[12]

An attendant interest was cryptography. Buckley reports that Elgar enjoyed working on ciphers on railway journeys (putting Elgar into the class of people who take books of crosswords or sudoku with them on trains), even proudly solving 'one by John Holt Schooling who defied the world to unravel his mystery'.[13]

A cipher or cryptogram is simply a way of encoding a message. Morse code is one form; email 'smileys' are, effectively, another. No doubt Elgar would have used the latter with pleasure. Emails and instant messaging software would have made his relationships with women much easier and more satisfying, too. He had collected Schooling's cryptograms, published in the *Pall Mall*

---

[12] Quoted in Anderson, *Elgar*, pp. 85–6.
[13] Buckley, *Elgar*, p. 41.

Gazette, from January to May 1896; Schooling's collection of historical examples ran from the beginning of the seventeenth century to the present.

It is possible, though not likely, that he had a cryptographic challenge in mind with his own 'enigma'. To this Eric Sams (1926–2004), music's resident code-breaker, produced an ingenious (and unbelieveable) solution.[14] At any rate, Elgar produced a cryptogram based on a Russian-nihilist numerical square (learnt from Schooling) for Alice Stuart-Wortley in 1915. A letter to Dorabella in 1897 makes extensive use of odd symbols as part of a substitution code, which he reused in 1924, perhaps to entertain a child, to spell out 'Marco Elgar' – the name of his spaniel.[15]

The dogs with which he passed his final years – Alice wouldn't allow them in the house while she was alive – were not the only kind of animals he loved. In chapter 3 we shall learn the depth of his love for a rabbit, and as we shall see in chapter 5, at the outbreak of war, horses seemed almost more important to him than human beings. He was a keen race-goer all his life. On the date of the first performance of *The Apostles* he noted that Grey Tick had won the Cesarewitch (a handicap race at Newmarket, named after Tsar Alexander II of Russia). To disguise his identity with bookmakers he used false names such as 'Elhamboy', 'Alectryon', 'Elmusic', 'Elbow', 'Elsie', and 'Siromoris'; the last is a palindrome (more wordplay) based on his two best honours, the knighthood ('Sir') and the Order of Merit ('OM'). He was delighted to hear that an 'Elgar Plate' would be held at the Worcester Races in 1935.[16] Sad for him that he would miss it: he died a few weeks after hearing the news.

---

[14] For the record, he suggests that the tune of *Auld Lang Syne* is encoded in the theme of the *Variations*, and therefore (which makes his 'solution' stand out from the pack) can be discovered throughout the composition. Julian Rushton notes that 'the short interval between conception and the commitment implied by mentioning the existence of the Variations to Jaeger makes elaborate precompositional calculation unlikely' (Rushton, *'Enigma' Variations*, p. 70). See Eric Sams, 'Variations on an Original Theme (Enigma)', *Musical Times,* 111 (1970), pp. 258–62, and 'Elgar's Enigmas: A Past Script and a Post Script', *Musical Times,* 111 (1970), pp. 692–4.

[15] See Eric Sams, 'Elgar's Cipher Letter to Dorabella', *The Musical Times,* 111 (1970), pp. 151–4 and Anderson, *Elgar*, p. 156.

[16] Anderson, *Elgar*, pp. 61, 173, 175.

THREE

MODERNISM AND LAUREATESHIP: A DIVIDED SELF (1904–13)

The character of musical modernism

The years 1904–1913 saw Elgar at the height of his considerable fame in Britain and overseas, and at the forefront of the fledgling modernism of musical composition in Europe. In these years not only 'accessible' (often slightly inaccurately called 'late-romantic'), but also 'inaccessible' composers were writing in styles that, however varied, were recognizably approaching the same musical questions (of form, technique, language) as each other. These questions, and the reasons for their formation, can be expressed simply. Romanticism had raised art, and particularly music, to the level of the divine. It was a way of speaking otherwise ineffable 'truth'. Modernism swallowed this philosophy whole, and pushed an existing preoccupation to its logical climax by focusing the greatest energy on musical form. The implication is that if music is a carrier of 'truth', then its organization and the manner of its presentation *counts*, not just to oddballs who like that sort of thing, but to the future of the human race. *Meaning*, which had exploded onto the critical scene at least a century earlier, became a watchword. 'Non-musical' texts and images were routinely associated with music in the romantic period, but now the significance of the art form was deemed so great that even if it meant nothing but *itself*, it remained important – and perhaps became more so, again sticking to the romantic principles of the previous century.

In this period, then, composers wrote gigantic works; the eccentric firebrand musicologist Richard Taruskin accurately but unattractively calls this the period of 'maximalism'. Whatever else such works may be, they are all highly elaborate explorations of form, meaning, and (for modernists are no less mystical than romantics) questions of what it is to be human. As we have seen, Elgar entered this period late. From its rough beginnings in 1889, through the first rupture in 1908, when Schoenberg first abandoned tonality, to the second important break of 1914, there came a torrent of remarkable works. Strauss wrote all his tone-poems and four of the century's greatest operas: *Salome*, *Elektra*, *Der Rosenkavalier*, and *Ariadne auf Naxos* (the range of these is enormous). Mahler wrote everything on which his reputation stands: nine completed symphonies and *Das Lied von der Erde* ('The Song of the Earth'), before dying tragically early in 1911. Sibelius wrote his first four symphonies, the last of which in this period (1912) was a morbid death-knell for the early modernist movement. Nielsen wrote his first three symphonies and the Violin Concerto. Puccini produced his greatest operas: *Manon Lescaut*, *La bohème*, *Tosca*, *Madama Butterfly*, and (slightly less notable) *La fanciulla del West* ('The Girl of the Golden West'). Debussy contributed the opera *Pelléas et Melisande* and the orchestral works *Prélude à l'après-midi d'un faune* ('Prelude to the Afternoon of a Faun'), *Nocturnes*, *La mer* ('The Sea'), and *Images*. Among the 'inaccessibles', Schoenberg, musically not unlike Elgar in this period, wrote *Verklärte Nacht* ('Transfigured Night'), two string quartets, the first, ravishing Chamber Symphony, and one of the largest of all musical works, orchestrally, the song-cycle *Gurrelieder* ('Songs of Gurre'), which was premiered years after its completion, in the same year as Elgar's *Falstaff*. Stravinsky wrote an early Symphony in E flat (premiered in the same year as Elgar's First) and *The Firebird*. In the influential concerts in St Petersburg organized by an early supporter, the Ukrainian Aleksandr Ziloti (1863–1945), Stravinsky could have heard music by Debussy, Rachmaninoff, Sibelius, Scriabin, and Elgar (*Cockaigne*, *Variations*, *In the South*, *Introduction and Allegro*, and the First Symphony).

To the extent that they were all artists, and therefore sages of one kind or another (according to the modernist philosophy), all fulfilled the role of Nietzsche's 'Overman' (*Übermensch*), the seer who stands above the herd (the rest of us) and brings it to enlightenment.[1] Perhaps because he was generally regarded as the finest musician to have come from Britain in a few centuries, Elgar became, if anything, *more* than that. That he was a great artist was taken for granted; but in the way he was called upon to stand as a figurehead for new universities and artistic endeavours (both in Britain and America), the focus for festivals, and became perhaps the most decorated musician of any age, we can wonder whether this very hottest of hot properties was also considered a kind of lucky rabbit's foot for the intellectual and musical classes. People and institutions wanted him around in the hope that it might do them some good.

Fame and, crucially, wealth, freed him from a routine life of teaching, or composing only to commission (most of the time; there remained short

---

[1] Strauss's tone-poem *Also sprach Zarathustra* sprang directly from this philosophy. Although Nietzsche's *Übermensch* was once routinely translated 'Superman', scholars have preferred 'Overman' in recent decades.

periods of financial need when he had to write potboilers – normally when Alice decided they needed to move house), or otherwise being restricted in his compositional options. It does not follow that his fame locked him into the function of a musical laureate, a composer whose every phrase or theme pinned his colours more firmly to the flag. Not a bit of it: the context for Elgar's modernist music is the one just outlined, not the public accident of an accumulation of medals and outfits. At last Elgar was free to write what he wanted; he lived a musical life that traced to some extent the general crude motion in recent music history from tightly controlled output (often in churches or courts) to greater individual freedom, and works that existed for their own sakes.

The tale of his years at the summit is therefore best told in separate parts, giving this part of the book a different structure from the rest. First, in this chapter, the life-outside-music: his recognition, foreign travel, domestic life, and his time as Professor of Music. Relatively minor works are covered here, at the time of their writing, but discussion of major compositions is reserved for the next chapter, which is exclusively concerned with the music. This structure fairly reflects the way that his major works in these years both stood out from his everyday life and were not essentially bound up with it.

Elgar, Overman

He was mere weeks short of becoming Elgar, Overman while on holiday in a rainy Italy. On 3 January 1904 the sun came out, and Elgar composed a tune while visiting Moglio, near Alassio. On the same day he wrote to Jaeger to say that 'this visit has been, is, artistically, a complete *failure* & I can do nothing', and that he was planning a concert overture, not a symphony, for the Elgar Festival at Covent Garden.[2] *In the South*, Op. 50, the final name of the resulting work, retained the key of E flat, the same as two significant precedents, Beethoven's Symphony No. 3, 'Eroica' ('Heroic') and Strauss's *Ein Heldenleben* ('A Hero's Life'). It was Elgar's heroic arrival as a modernist. The tune which opened it was one he'd written for the bulldog, 'Dan triumphant (after a fight)'; it is as vigorously masculine as the opening of Strauss's *Don Juan*, perhaps the first modernist work. It was premiered on 16 March 1904.

On 21 January Elgar had received a letter inviting him to dine with the king and the Prince of Wales at Marlborough House on 3 February. He left Italy early. It would be the start of a cordial relationship, if one given too much weight in some biographies.

Elgar probably thought he was closer to King Edward VII than he was. Their catalogue of involvements is limited, and having access to a diarist

---

[2] Quoted in Moore, *Edward Elgar: A Creative Life*, p. 425.

so assiduous and so attentive to status as Alice, one may be sure that every second of his time with royalty is accounted for. His introduction to the king was propitious. It came at the first royal performance of the *Coronation Ode*, Op. 44, on 24 June 1903, when he was told that his music had soothed the king in a recent illness. Seven months later he dined with the king and the Prince of Wales at Marlborough House, though as part of a larger party,[3] and in the same week the king attended the first two nights of the Covent Garden Elgar Festival, and Queen Alexandra all three. In June that year Elgar's knighthood was announced in the king's birthday honours list, and he dined with the Prince of Wales on 14 July. He was at Buckingham Palace again on 18 March 1905; the king had a cold, so again the Prince of Wales entertained him.[4] The king and queen were present at the granting of his honorary doctorate at Aberdeen. He dined again with the king on 18 February 1909. Around the beginning of 1910 he said that he would dedicate the Second Symphony to him 'so that dear kind man will have my best music'.[5] By 6 May Alice was noting in her diary the news of Edward VII's last illness, which would kill him the next day: 'Oh! our own King', she wrote with high melodrama. One can almost see the hangdog look of the socially ambitious woman keen to be associated with the monarch whom she grieves as if he were a brother.

That Edward VII admired Elgar's music is not in question, but the essential truth is that he admired it more or less from afar. He spoke well of it to whomever he could, and Elgar was grateful for that. Meanwhile Elgar admired the king in turn, as did many of his subjects. Edward VII was one of the more cultivated royals of recent centuries, displaying definite evidence of brain activity. He established himself in his long service as Prince of Wales as a favourite of the bohemian and artistic classes. He was directly involved in the planning of the Royal Albert Hall and the Royal College of Music, supported Sunday opening of the British Museum as one of its trustees, and as the first heir to the throne ever to sit on a royal commission (for the housing of the working classes), he 'visit[ed] East End slums incognito'.[6]

On the very few occasions that Elgar and Edward VII met one can imagine a bit of polite English coughing as they exchanged stilted pleasantries amid large groups. Their relation with each other was almost entirely through their respective reputations and activities. There is nothing wrong with that, and indeed few people earn the respect, and once or

---

[3] See Young, *Elgar O.M.*, pp. 113–14.
[4] See Elgar, *Elgar and His Publishers*, p. 614.
[5] See Moore, *Creative Life*, p. 574.
[6] H. C. G. Matthew, 'Edward VII (1841–1910)', in H. C. G. Matthew and Brian Howard Harrison (eds.), *Oxford Dictionary of National Biography*, vol. 17 (Oxford: Oxford University Press, 2004); available online at www.oxforddnb.com.

twice the use of the fish knife, of a monarch; but it is a mistake to imagine that their association was closer than has just been outlined. At the same time, Alice's and Elgar's desire to make as much of their contact as possible is understandable. Yet in her disapproval of George V, the next king, who could not concentrate all the way through a piece of music, Alice seemed to suggest by contrast that Edward VII had been a close personal friend whose good example was being destroyed by the new upstart.[7] That can only properly be regarded as snooty and dishonest.

The knighthood was not the only honour to come Elgar's way during his modernist years. The first tribute was a musical one, the Elgar Festival at Covent Garden that had been mooted just before Rodewald's death. By bringing together *Gerontius* and *The Apostles* with *In the South*, it marked the boundary between the provincial obscurity and neo-romanticism of the 1890s and the fame and modernism of the 1900s. It was virtually unprecedented for a living English composer to be accorded such an honour.

Already 'Dr Elgar' from Cambridge, his second honorary doctorate came from Durham, on 22 June 1904; Leeds followed on 6 October. There the award was both a token of esteem for the composer and also a rabbit's-foot moment, because the ceremony was the one that founded the University of Leeds; Edward VII granted the necessary degree-awarding charter. Five other composers, including Parry and Stanford, were also given degrees, and there was talk of installing Elgar as the first professor of music. There were two more doctorates in 1905, first in Oxford on 7 February (at Parry's instigation: he was professor there), then at Yale on 28 June. The Aberdeen degree granted in the presence of the king and queen came on 26 September 1906, the result of agitation from Charles Sanford Terry (1864–1936), professor of history there. Elgar and he became fast friends, and Terry proof-read some of Elgar's scores. He also became very close to Carice.[8]

Two of Elgar's honorary degrees came from America, and he made four increasingly frustrating trips there, in 1905, 1906, 1907, and 1911 (when he also went to Canada). His first impressions were favourable – New York's harbour and river impressed him – but he had arrived in the full humidity of an East-Coast American summer, and complained about it in letters ('We sit in pyjamas bathed in perspiration from morning till night').[9] During the six-day voyage he met Mrs Julia Worthington, with

---

[7] See Young, *Elgar O.M.*, p. 181.

[8] See Alison I. Shiel, 'Charles Sanford Terry in the Elgar Diaries', *Elgar Society Journal,* 12 (2002), pp. 193–201. He took her on country trips and into London to entertain her. She called him 'uncle' (ibid., p. 195), which was perhaps a reflexion of the fact that he showed her more obvious affection than either of her parents, who tended to leave her behind whenever they did anything interesting.

[9] Letter to Littleton, 24 June 1905, quoted in Moore, *Creative Life*, p. 462.

whom he developed a very warm friendship.[10] He was met on arrival in New York, on 15 June 1905, by Samuel Simons Sanford (1849–1910), Professor of Applied Music (that is, performance) at Yale, where he would receive his degree. (Sanford had been in Worcester to hear the premiere of the *Variations*, and was introduced to Elgar by Schuster at the Gloucester Festival of 1904.) The journey to New Haven came next day, and although the Elgars were hosted in great luxury, the trip was not a happy one. At the degree ceremony the trio tune from the first *Pomp and Circumstance* march was played on the organ. Moore speculates that this might have been the first time it accompanied an American graduation.[11] At the end of his trip he was enticed by an offer of £1,500 to return the following year to conduct at the Cincinatti Festival. The prospect galled him 'but my pocket gapes aloud'. He made no secret of his views on American national music, telling a newspaper reporter 'Your national anthem is even worse than England's . . . There is "Yankee Doodle", which has words that are stark idiocy, while the music would set the teeth of a buzz-saw on edge'.[12]

On his return in April 1906 he was met in New York not only by Sanford but also a gaggle of reporters and photographers. He described the flat landscape en route to Cincinatti: 'Most uninteresting country . . . Clearings & little wooden houses & hideous towns'. The natives at his hotel appalled too, as Alice wrote: 'Girls & ladies come & play Bridge in the afternoon & shriek & make a wretched noise . . . noisy rowdy sounding people, man whistling loudly, most exasperating . . . We went down & E. expressed himself forcibly about the noise &c, we were disgusted.'[13]

More serious sadness came from the news that his father had died on 29 April. The Elgars were treated to dinner at the mansion of Andrew Carnegie, who hoped that Elgar would return next year to receive an honorary degree at the opening of his new Carnegie Institute at Pittsburgh (now called the Carnegie Museums of Pittsburgh). Alice set down her thoughts in characteristic prose. 'Fine large house but *very* dull – a very commonplace dinner & ugly dinner table'.[14] These things mattered to her.

So did being called 'Mrs' Elgar, a title to which her ambition never reconciled her, but her misery ended soon after the Elgar Festival,[15] where Elgar had been making representation to the prime minister, the

---

[10] Few letters between the two survive, so it is more difficult to gauge the depth of their involvement than it is with Alice Stuart-Wortley. Yet there is evidence – thin, but difficult to dismiss entirely – that she influenced the composition of the Violin Concerto (see below).

[11] Moore, *Creative Life*, p. 462.

[12] Both quotations ibid., p. 463.

[13] Ibid., pp. 495–6 and 497.

[14] Ibid., p. 498.

[15] A sketch in Elgar's hand in the British Library, BL 58008, f.35*v*, shows a tune from *Cockaigne* with text above: 'I will *not* be called Mrs E!' (such a form of address would not befit a major-general's daughter). Below the final bass note is 'oh!' – a feeble man's response. It is reproduced in Diana M. McVeagh, 'Mrs Edward Elgar', *Musical Times*, 125 (1984), pp. 76–8.

Conservative Arthur Balfour, about musical copyright.[16] The knighthood was announced on 24 June 1904. On 26 November Sir Edward Elgar then accepted the invitation to become the first Professor of Music at Birmingham, though he was never a lover of his academic title.

He had by now moved house. Alice thought 'Craeg Lea' too small for a knight of the realm, and found a larger home, 'Plâs Gwyn' ('White House' in Welsh), 'a miniature mansion in German Imperial style', on the edge of Hereford'.[17] They moved in on 1 July 1904, three days before the knighthood was conferred. It had an attractive veranda on two sides, and views of the Wye Valley, but to Rosa Burley 'it looked . . . the sort of house that might be chosen by a prosperous and aesthetically not very exacting merchant rather than a suitable home for a sensitive and highly strung artist'.[18] She might have overstated the case. Though, as evidenced by a letter to Richter in August, it took him two months to find the heart to compose after the move, he eventually wrote some of his best music there.

Elgar used Plâs Gwyn as a base for most of his last important travels. All of the American ones started and ended there, as did several trips to Italy, one of them (1907–8) very significant musically. His first continental trip as a knight was with Schuster, a brief one to Cologne, Mainz, Berlin, and Rotterdam in November and December 1904 to hear performances of *In the South* and *The Apostles*. Alice and Carice stayed at home.

A more substantial undertaking was the next year's Mediterranean cruise, from 15 September to 12 October. He had been given the Freedom of Worcester in a grand ceremony on 12 September, which was organized by Hubert Leicester, by then mayor of the city. While marching past his father's house, Elgar stopped to salute the upstairs window from which the by-then frail old man was watching.[19] The invitation came to cruise on board HMS *Surprise* with Schuster, as a guest of Lady Charles Beresford (wife of the Commander-in-Chief of the Mediterranean Fleet). He hoped that the cruise – which would pass by the Acropolis – might stir him creatively, and he recorded all the beautiful scenery, including a 'pretty shepherd boy playing on a pipe', in his diary. Most impressive was the ancient city of Smyrna (modern İmir), whose bazaar offered a 'much finer sight than Constantinople . . . (This was my first touch with Asia & I was quite overcome . . .)'.[20] He wrote an atmospheric short piano piece, *In Smyrna*, on board ship.

---

[16] In the absence of copyright laws, composers were losing out to illegal copies of printed songs, and Elgar had joined William Boosey's Musical Defence League. The issue of copyright wasn't sorted out until 1911, when the modern laws came into force.

[17] Young, *Elgar O.M.*, p. 115.

[18] Rosa Burley and Frank Carruthers, *Edward Elgar: The Record of a Friendship* (London: Barrie and Jenkins, 1972), p. 175.

[19] W. H. Reed, *Elgar*, 2nd edn. (London: Dent, 1943; orig. edn. 1939), p. 87.

[20] All quotations Moore, *Creative Life*, pp. 466–7. As soon as he returned to London he hastened to the East End to find Eastern food.

To cure eye trouble in late 1906, a doctor recommended time in a warm climate. Elgar went to Italy from 28 December to 23 February, visiting Naples, Capri, and Rome, and meeting local musical eminences from the sacred and secular spheres, Dom Lorenzo Perosi (1872–1956) and Giovanni Sgambati (1841–1942).[21] It seemed good to return for a longer stay next year, and he sought out apartments in Rome.

He returned next year, being away from Hereford from 5 November 1907 to 29 May 1908. On such a long trip both Alice and Carice went with him. His long stay at the heart of Catholic Christianity seems to many writers finally to have murdered his faith. It certainly ended his interest in completing the third religious oratorio, *The Last Judgement*. He wrote to Schuster 'My dear Franky: Here is my Mecca & I love it *all* – Note the fact that I am pagan not Xtian at present' and to Littleton that he had decided 'definitely and finally to give up the idea' of writing it.[22] Composition of *The Kingdom*, Op. 51, the second part of the intended trilogy, had been blighted by insecurity throughout the period of its composition (1905–6). 1905 was a bad year for Elgar, during which the *Introduction and Allegro*, Op. 47, was poorly received. His faith seemed to totter, and he lost interest in his music.[23] Now, though, the end of his gigantic religious compositions had definitively come.

Did Elgar's faith weaken? His letters and public pronouncements after 1905 strongly suggest that it did. Yet he continued to attend church until his death, received the last rites from a Catholic priest (though perhaps this wasn't his choice: he was heavily sedated by then), and chose to have a Catholic burial. Perhaps he was keeping up appearances; that is the usual view. But in a closely reasoned article, Charles M. McGuire argues that our view of Elgar having a weak faith is an anachronism arising from a modern British society in which secularism is the normal behaviour; it makes us more comfortable with Elgar to smother his religiosity. McGuire writes that throughout his life Elgar remained *culturally* Catholic, and that even though that might not make much sense to an age that thinks religious belief depends entirely on religious acts (as it thinks that sexuality depends entirely on sexual acts), it was nevertheless meaningful to Elgar and comprehensible to those around him.[24] A sign

[21] Perosi was admitted to a mental hospital in 1922 and never fully recovered. Sgambati was a pupil of Liszt's and an important promoter of secular music in Italy. He owned the full score of *Die Meistersinger* that Wagner sent to Liszt in 1868. Elgar told Jaeger of the thrill of touching it.

[22] Moore, *Creative Life*, p. 520.

[23] See Kennedy, *Portrait of Elgar*, pp. 199–200.

[24] See Charles Edward McGuire, 'Measure of a Man: Catechizing Elgar's Catholic Avatars', in Byron Adams (ed.), *Elgar and His World* (Princeton: Princeton University Press, 2007). There is space in the modern mind for the idea of a non-believing Jew who nevertheless proclaims his or her Jewish identity (and we have no problem understanding Mahler's 'conversion' to Catholicism because as a Jew he could not be appointed Kapellmeister in Vienna – what does it matter to

of Elgar's continuing Catholic behaviour in 1907 was his presence at the confirmation of Carice, by now 16, on 19 May 1907.[25] The evidence of a letter to Hubert Leicester, Lady Elgar's diary, and the entry in the register at Belmore Abbey confirm the later date. Elgar and Alice were both there, and May Grafton, not Rosa Burley, was Carice's sponsor.[26]

Professor Elgar

For more than a year after the premieres on 8 March 1905 of the *Introduction and Allegro* and the third *Pomp and Circumstance* March, Elgar completed no major composition. Recent travels to Europe and America had slowed him down, and *The Kingdom* was perhaps his most stressful undertaking, but it is not insignificant that he was approaching his fiftieth birthday, and had still got nowhere with a long-promised symphony. He had also started delivering lectures as Professor of Music at Birmingham.

The lectures were almost without exception scandalous affairs, and their preparation and delivery became, for Elgar, a torment. The press railed against his frankly expressed opinions, and fellow musicians were hurt. It was poor judgement on Elgar's part to strongly criticize contemporary English composers in the first lecture on 16 March 1905 (several times repeating the word 'commonplace'),[27] and it made it difficult for him to recover. Right from the opening lines of the second lecture on 1 November, he tried without success to correct the impression of 'that much misquoted lecture'.[28]

More interesting was the following week's lecture, devoted entirely to Brahms's Third Symphony (8 November). Elgar might have affected to dislike academic musicology, but we can call his bluff: he delivered an entire *analytical* lecture on a single work, and would do so again exactly a year later, in his sixth and final lecture, on Mozart's Symphony No. 40 in G minor. Tovey, who must have been in the audience for the Brahms lecture, credited Elgar with the observation that a theme in the finale has

---

sprinkle water when there's a job at the end of it?), but not for a non-believing Catholic who remains culturally Catholic. A sense of identity has been strengthened in both groups through centuries of persecution (of Catholics, in Britain; of Jews, everywhere). Although quite understandably the more recent and vicious persecutions of the twentieth century override older memories, these should not be forgotten altogether.

[25] Not 11 June 1903, as Moore states in a passage from *Creative Life* where he builds the argument that Elgar's faith was weakening.

[26] See McGuire, 'Catechizing Elgar's Catholic Avatars', and Moore, *Creative Life*, p. 407.

[27] Edward Elgar, *A Future for English Music, and Other Lectures*, ed. Percy M. Young (London: Dobson, 1968), p. 51.

[28] Ibid., p. 79.

its root in the slow movement.[29] Although only the rough notes for this lecture have survived, it presumably had analytical depth.[30]

There is more evidence of Elgar's closeted musical intellectualism. In the fourth talk, on 'Critics', he said that audiences are not 'necessary for *the well-being of the whole* art of music', except insofar as they are informed, critical listeners. It is in that sense – and only that sense – that audiences are 'a necessary part of a living art'. Remove the act of criticism, and one is not, on Elgar's definition, a musical listener. Just listening and vaguely enjoying is not enough.[31] He wrote an analytical commentary on his own *Falstaff* several years later because he expected – *required* – listeners to engage critically with the work, and it greatly irritated him that Tovey had not got to know this essay before writing his own analysis.[32] Although Elgar might not have known of the theorists Schenker or Riemann, he was by instinct, and despite his occasional protestations, a music analyst. Few composers are, which makes him even more remarkable.

In the penultimate lecture, 'Retrospect', Elgar made some of his most interesting philosophical points about the nature of music. Already in the Brahms lecture he had laid emphasis on the value of 'absolute music', deploring listeners who '[call] up all sorts of pictures, which might or might not have existed in the composer's mind',[33] making critics feverish with disbelief. Now he put flesh on the bones. Again he was misunderstood.

> Turning to the question of absolute music: I still *look upon music* which exists without any poetic or literary basis as the true foundation of our art . . . absolute music [is] the real staple of our art. *No arguments I have yet read have altered this view.*[34]

He expresses scepticism towards those who only love vocal music (the form, he says, in which music first emerged), and traces what sounds to modern ears a very old-fashioned evolutionary view.

---

[29] Ibid., p. 101; Tovey's acknowledgement, 'To Sir Edward Elgar I owe the remark that this is the tragic outcome of the wistful theme in the middle of the slow movement', is in Donald Francis Tovey, *Essays in Musical Analysis*, vol. 1: *Symphonies* (London: Oxford University Press, 1935), p. 112.

[30] The Mozart analysis also exists only in rough notes, though Matthew Riley has recently delivered a fascinating reconstruction of it in a conference presentation. Contemporary reports show that Elgar illustrated his talk often at the piano, and perhaps therefore he spoke extempore, having sketched out only the essential analytical points in his notes.

[31] Elgar, *Future*, p. 163; italics original.

[32] 'That tiresome & tireless Tovey has written a long acc[oun]t of Falstaff, & wanted me to read it. I glanced at it & it seems all wrong: so I "quit". I sent him my own notes & he now drearily wants to print *his* with my notes to shew where he is wrong – a most misguided idea. I have said to do what you like. I wish people wd. drown themselves in ink & let me alone.' (From a letter to Carice, 1 December 1932, quoted in Elgar, *Letters of a Lifetime*, p. 458.)

[33] Quoted by Newman from memory or notes taken at the lecture, in Elgar, *Future*, p. 105.

[34] Ibid., p. 205.

> Out of these [vocal] beginnings were evolved the suite and similar collections of pieces, until we come to the Sonata and the Symphony. I hold that the Symphony without a programme is the highest development of art. *Views to the contrary are, we shall often find*, held by those to whom the joy of music came late in life or who would deny to musicians that peculiar gift, which is their own, a musical ear, or an *ear for music* . . . a love of music for its own sake.[35]

It is generally remarked, as it was at the time, that there is a tension here between Elgar's stand for 'absolute' music in his lectures but 'programme' music in his symphonies and other orchestral works.[36] The distinction, however, is false. In his modernist music, most triumphantly in *Falstaff*, Elgar found ways of transcending the distinction by bringing criticism, not just picture-painting (the thing he disliked in the minds of listeners, which was, presumably, a failing brought on by composers) into the sphere of what is commonly called 'programme' music. Elgar claimed that 'absolute' music had a higher intellectual value than *existing* 'programme' music, but that would not exclude the possibility that he could improve the situation through his own writing.

He resigned the professorship on 29 August 1908, a little over two months before the premiere of his First Symphony which, in line with the letter of his remarks at Birmingham on the relative value of absolute and programme music, he said had no programme.

Back to the future

Elgar's brother Frank sent an old chest of childhood memorabilia from the family shop in Worcester on the day Elgar reached his half-century, 2 June 1907. It reawakened memories in Elgar of the play he says (and people like to think) he put on with his siblings when they were children. He drew for the last time on old sketchbooks to produce two suites, *The Wand of Youth*, Op. 1 (a playful opus number).[37] They are charming, and his earliest-known music, the 'tune from Broadheath – 1867', crops up at

[35] Ibid., p. 207.

[36] Julian Rushton points out (Julian Rushton, 'In Search of a Symphony: Orchestral Music to 1908', in Grimley and Rushton (eds.), *The Cambridge Companion to Elgar*, pp. 139–53, at p. 148) that his view of absolute music and symphonies might have been coloured by reading Parry's article on 'Symphony' in the first edition of *Grove's Dictionary of Music and Musicians* (1878), which greatly influenced Elgar as a young man. Parry's article was still the one used for the second edition (*Grove's Dictionary of Music and Musicians*, ed. J. A. Fuller Maitland, 2nd edn., vol. 4 (London: Macmillan, 1908), pp. 763–97). In it he ranks Brahms 'the greatest representative of the highest art in the department of Symphony' (p. 795).

[37] He certainly did not just orchestrate the old tunes, as Moore claims (Moore, *Creative Life*, p. 514). Had he such boyish talent as that assertion supposes, he would never have had such a long musical apprenticeship but would have burst onto the musical scene *c.*1867 and have written a dozen great symphonies by the century's end.

the start of 'Fairies and Giants', showing itself to be the entirely everyday and conventional thing it is. Some of the music from the suites, notably the central section of 'Little Bells' from the second, was reused to good and appropriate effect in *The Starlight Express* (as I shall discuss in chapter 5). A holiday following the conclusion of the first suite ended with a train journey that Robert Anderson calls 'hilarious'. Alice's diary: 'Slow train – E. and C. had riotous games & E. fell full length along the bottom of the train! A. laughed so much she cd. not even urge him to rise before some one came down the corridor'.[38] Perhaps it was funnier if one was there. The first suite was premiered on 14 December 1907, the second on 9 September 1908.

Having shelved plans for a string quartet that began to emerge after *The Wand of Youth* in November, Elgar worked during his long overwintering in Italy in 1907–8 on the First Symphony, which swallowed the quartet's sketched themes.[39] There is no record of how far he got with composition there. He relieved what one presumes was the tension of symphonic composition by writing a few part songs. One was to Alice's text (a 'Christmas Greeting' for Sinclair's concert in Hereford), while others set words by 'Pietro d'Alba' ('White Peter'). These were actually by Elgar, but credited to Carice's white Angora rabbit, which of course was named after Beatrix Potter's Peter Rabbit (see figure 17, overleaf).[40] Elgar's admiration for the animal – he bought a book on the care of rabbits to ensure its good upkeep, and gave him a hot-water bottle at bedtime – parallels Lord Emsworth's for his pig, Empress of Blandings, in P. G. Wodehouse's novels.[41] But Emsworth never thought the Empress capable of poetic expression. Nor orchestration: Elgar wrote the creature a note to thank him for an orchestral idea in *The Wand of Youth*.

The Elgars were visited by Arthur Benson, who found Lady Elgar '*very* kind but without charm, & wholly conventional, though pathetically anxious to be *au courant* [up-to-speed] with a situation'.[42] Carice took singing lessons, but when it began to disturb Elgar's composing time Alice made her stop, as she did whenever the girl tried to develop any interests that might be audible over pin-drops.

The year 1908 began sadly with the death of William Grafton, husband of Elgar's sister Pollie (and father of May), on 13 January. It ended on the

---

[38] Robert Anderson, *Elgar* (London: Dent, 1993), p. 80.

[39] These sketches are published in Robert Anderson's edition of the chamber music for the *Elgar Complete Edition* (vol. 38, 1988). The transition between the middle movements, already present in the string quartet design, is interestingly different from its symphonic version, and worth playing at the piano.

[40] *The Tale of Peter Rabbit* had been published six years earlier, in 1902.

[41] The comparison has purchase: George Bernard Shaw offered assurances that Elgar could talk intelligently about pigs (see George Bernard Shaw, 'Sir Edward Elgar', *Music & Letters,* 1 (1920), pp. 7–11, at p. 10).

[42] Moore, *Creative Life*, p. 526.

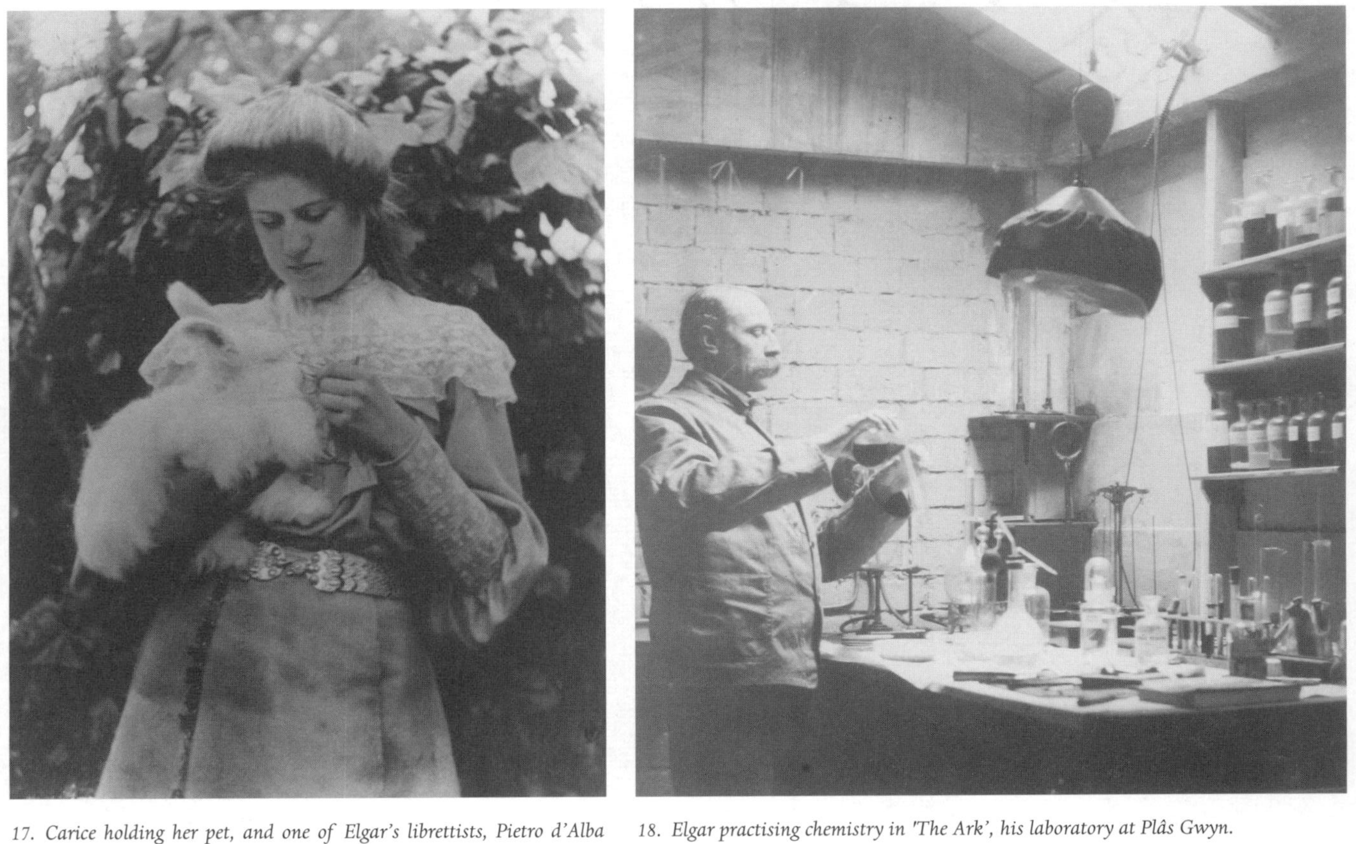

17. Carice holding her pet, and one of Elgar's librettists, Pietro d'Alba (Peter Rabbit), c.*1909–10.*

18. Elgar practising chemistry in 'The Ark', his laboratory at Plâs Gwyn.

heights, with the premiere of the First Symphony, Op. 55. The period between Elgar's return to Hereford on 29 May and the symphony's first rehearsal on 3 September was filled with its composition, and with the setting up of his laboratory, 'the Ark', in a shed at 'Plâs Gwyn' (see figure 18 opposite). The only other important development was that Jaeger was finally losing his battle with tuberculosis, which had been diagnosed in 1905.

It is not too much to say that Jaeger's musical life since beginning his close association with Elgar in 1896 had been founded on a growing desire to hear a symphony by him. This wish was granted virtually on his deathbed. He had been sent parts of the score of the First Symphony as it was written, and was moved to his core by the slow movement.

> My dear friend that is not only one of the very greatest slow movements since Beethoven, but I consider it *worthy of that master*.[43] How original!, how PURE, noble, elevating, soothing. &c &c . . . I cried happy tears of 'Wonne' over so much beauty. It's the greatest thing You have done . . . At [figure] 104 we are brought near Heaven . . .
>
> I wish I were near you that I might press & kiss your hand & say: thank you, my friend, for this great piece of music.[44]

He wrote only one more letter to Elgar, to say more about the symphony and added: 'I feel so ill to-night that I want to go to the nearest Ry Station & throw myself under a train to end my misery'.[45]

The symphony was premiered in Manchester on 3 December, under Richter, to whom it was dedicated ('To Hans Richter, Mus. Doc. / True Artist and true Friend'). Jaeger struggled out of the house to attend the London premiere four days later. Praise was resounding and unanimous. Richter considered it 'the greatest symphony of modern times, written by the greatest modern composer, *and not only in this country*',[46] and Arthur Nikisch (1855–1922), the conductor of its Leipzig premiere, felt strongly enough to write to the press.

> I consider Elgar's symphony a masterpiece of the first order, one that will soon be justly ranked on the same basis with the great symphonic models – Beethoven and Brahms . . . When Brahms produced his first symphony it was called 'Beethoven's tenth' . . . I will therefore call Elgar's symphony 'the fifth of Brahms'.[47]

---

[43] Richter thought so too: 'Ah! this is a *real* Adagio – such an Adagio as Beethove' would 'ave writ' (quoted in Reed, *Elgar*, p. 97).

[44] Letter of 26 November 1908, Elgar, *Elgar and His Publishers*, p. 715.

[45] Ibid., p. 716.

[46] Quoted in Reed, *Elgar*, p. 97.

[47] 'Occasional Notes', *The Musical Times*, 50 (1909), p. 446. Moore slightly misquotes this and gives the wrong date.

Performances in its first year were given in every part of the world then generally accessible to classical music. Aside from British concerts in London, Birmingham, Leeds, Edinburgh, Glasgow, Liverpool, Newcastle, Nottingham, Hull, Middlesbrough, Doncaster, Eastbourne, Hereford, and Norwich, foreign performances were given in New York, Chicago, Boston, Cincinnati, Pittsburgh, Louisville, Toronto, Budapest, Bonn, Munich, Frankfurt, Rome, Vienna, St Petersburg, and Sydney.[48] Altogether there were eighty-two performances in this first year, an astonishing figure which surely made it the most fêted modernist work by any composer at the time. Elgar was cross, however, to learn that he was receiving relatively small performing fees, and wrote to Henry Clayton in dudgeonous xenophobia: 'They [Queen's Hall] pay *any* foreigner 4, 5, 6, 7 or even 8 times the amount given to me & lose largely over the visitor because they say its [*sic*] good for art. It annoys me that the money they really make out of me is spent on other people'.[49] Further disappointment in 1911 led Elgar to cancel his exclusive contract with Novello. From then, they would have to compete with other publishers for the rights to each new work, something they had not done since 1904.

Elgar heard of Jaeger's death (in his late fifties) while on a two-month sojourn in Europe in summer 1909. He wrote a consoling letter to his widow, Isabella Donkersley Jaeger, the day before returning to Hereford, on 21 May: 'The news came as a great shock & I cannot realise that the end is come. I am overwhelmed with sorrow for the loss of my dearest & truest friend'.[50]

Part of the summer was spent at Julia Worthington's villa at Careggi, near Florence. There some music was written for the Second Symphony, though a plan to 'get the (1000000) frogs in the Vineyard into the score of Sym II – a fine sound' seemed doomed. Earlier in the year, while taking a cure at Llandrindod Wells, he had sent 'Peter Rabbit, esq. Mus D' a postcard, but he sent none from Florence.[51] That didn't stop the higher-degreed buck from collaborating with Elgar on a pair of songs, 'The Torch' and 'The River', published together as Op. 60. Adapted by Pietro d'Alba from East European traditional poems, they were written in 1909–10 and orchestrated in 1912. The dark tone of 'The River' was remarked upon in a letter to Frances Colvin: here is 'my friend Pietro d'Alba in his most, or *almost* most pessimistic mood. To read it one wd.

---

[48] These locations are taken from a letter regarding unpaid performance fees on 8 February 1910 (Elgar, *Elgar and His Publishers*, p. 728). The symphony was heard in still more places.

[49] Letter of 2 February 1909, ibid., p. 720.

[50] Anderson, *Elgar*, p. 90. Isabella, Jaeger's English widow, felt compelled to change the family name to Hunter after the outbreak of war in 1914.

[51] The most enthusiastic chronicler of Elgar's relationship with this rabbit is Robert Anderson; his *Elgar* has thirteen index entries for him.

think the carrot crop had failed or some other catastrophe acutely affecting the rabbit world was toward'.[52]

Elgar also set three poems by Sir Gilbert Parker (1860–1932; a human being, though a poorer poet than the coney) as Op. 59. The Canadian-born Parker was an acquaintance through the Stuart-Wortleys, and Conservative MP for Gravesend. Like Schuster, he was 'somewhat of a dandy in his dress'.[53] Elgar suppressed a sexual reference in the first stanza of the second poem he set, but the songs remain hot with yearning nostalgia for a dead love. He orchestrated them for a Jaeger memorial concert on 24 January 1910; perhaps that means something, perhaps nothing.[54] In their orchestral version they are especially touching.

A short string *Elegy* also written in 1909 was not for Jaeger but Rev. Robert Hadden, former warden of the Worshipful Company of Musicians, which still plays the work around St Cecilia's Day to commemorate members who have died during the year.[55] Elgar was still heartbroken over something in November, writing to Schuster that, being consulted concerning a cough, his doctor 'thinks it's nerves over composition – when it's only heartbreak for something or somebody else'.[56] A close friend like Schuster might have known who or what that referred to; we can speculate but never know.

In January 1910 Alice's text for the fourth *Pomp and Circumstance* March (which had been premiered on 24 August 1907) was published by Boosey. It was called 'The Kingsway', after the road in London opened in 1905 following the demolition of the characterful sixteenth-century streets north of Aldwych. Composition proceeded on the Second Symphony, Violin Concerto, and an inevitably neglected Romance for bassoon and orchestra, Op. 62, premiered under Elgar's direction on 16 February 1911.

When he started to call themes in the concerto 'Windflower' themes, after the pretty little flower *Anemone nemorosa*, he struck upon a way around the problem that two important women in his life were both named 'Alice'. Alice Stuart-Wortley would henceforth be 'Windflower'. It is significant that she, not his wife, received the pet name. The concerto themes were dedicated to her, and as they grew increasingly close, he was frank about the centrality of his present emotional involvement in his work to his relationship with her.

---

[52] Letter of 2 February 1910, quoted in ibid., p. 92.

[53] Damian Atkinson, 'Parker, Sir (Horatio) Gilbert George', *Oxford Dictionary of National Biography*, vol. 42 (Oxford: Oxford University Press, 2004); available online at www.oxforddnb.com.

[54] Julian Rushton suggests that he might have orchestrated them because the Jaeger concert would be taken up mostly with a performance of the *Variations*, and these songs were the only new thing he could produce quickly. See Julian Rushton, 'Lost Love and Unwritten Songs: Elgar's Parker Cycle, Op. 59', in J. P. E. Harper-Scott and Julian Rushton (eds.), *Elgar Studies* (Cambridge: Cambridge University Press, 2007).

[55] Anderson, *Elgar*, p. 90.

[56] Quoted in Moore, *Creative Life*, p. 558.

In the spring the Elgars spent three months away from 'Plâs Gwyn'. Alice had her mind set on a return to the capital, so they took a flat at 58 Cavendish Street, London, on 7 March, and went on a motoring holiday with Schuster, involving a trip to the Stuart-Wortleys at Tintagel. Elgar announced a death to Frances Colvin on 3 May.

> I write to tell you how very sad we are to-day: my dear old friend Peter left this life this morning quite suddenly & painlessly: Why should I tell you this! Because I want to write to somebody (– ?everybody) and say how really grieved I am & then only two people in the world would understand & you are one.[57]

Pietro d'Alba's death was followed on 7 May by that of Edward VII. The second part of this double tragedy probably affected Alice more (see above, section 2). Certainly it didn't prevent Elgar from completing the Violin Concerto, Op. 61, on 5 August. His friend, the violinist W. H. Reed, had offered practical advice on the solo part since 28 May; Elgar returned to 'Plâs Gwyn' on 18 June, and within a fortnight was ready to show the short score to Fritz Kreisler (1875–1962), who was to be the soloist at the premiere. He had wanted an Elgar concerto for five years. Although at the premiere on 10 November he appeared nervous, and suffered a lapse of concentration, the performance was a considerable success.

The Second Symphony was to be the last work completed at 'Plâs Gwyn', the home in which he had written all of his modernist music to date. Orchestration was finally wrapped up by 28 February 1911, and the premiere on 23 May would be under Elgar's baton, since he had agreed to succeed Richter as conductor of the London Symphony Orchestra. It was an enormous disappointment, with merely polite applause at the end, and subsequent performances were poorly attended. (For further discussion, see next chapter below.) If Elgar's music was associated with the Edwardian age, then it was natural that his music should be buried with the old king. Elgar wrote a *Coronation March* and the song, 'O Hearken Thou', for the crowning of George V on 22 June 1911, but didn't attend the ceremony. It might seem rather cheeky that he should stay at home only two days after it was announced that he was to receive the Order of Merit (OM) from the same man.[58]

Dwindling success

Especially after Elgar received the OM, a house even grander than 'Plâs Gwyn' seemed necessary to Alice. They moved on 1 January 1912 to

---

[57] Quoted in Anderson, *Elgar*, p. 95.

[58] The award was created by Edward VII and is held by only twenty-four people, plus the sovereign, at any one time.

42 Netherhall Gardens, Hampstead, which they called 'Severn House'. Now demolished, it was a quite vast and absurdly expensive pile which brought them closer to the centre of things in London, complete with ceaseless irritation by doorbell and phone that drove Elgar mad, and led him in financial desperation to compose one of his most controversial pieces, *The Crown of India*, Op. 66, a masque for alto and bass soloists, chorus and orchestra. It was an inauspicious start for the new Hampstead homestead.

The work's motivation was, largely, financial. There can be no grounds for suggesting that he was attracted on any deep level to writing music for a masque (by Henry Hamilton), written to commemorate George V's coronation durbar, held in Delhi in December 1911, and intended to popularize the idea that imperial Britain could impose a new capital city on India – New Delhi – at the same time suggesting that all of India *wanted* British rule. Elgar knew that music-hall entertainment of this vacuous sort sold well, as it still does, and his wife, who was imperialist to the ends of her toenails, had run up impossible living costs, which gave him no choice.

That said, he *was* politically purblind enough not to mind too much the masque's imperial tone, and doubtless found the durbar spectacle of elephants and marches-past thrilling – and no moral opprobrium need attract to a fondness for pachyderms. He said at first that 'there is far too much of the political business', but after the text was altered a little, said 'it was an inoffensive thing & some of the music is good'.[59] True enough, but more important was the money. 'When I write a big serious work e.g. *Gerontius* we have had to starve & go without fires for twelve months as a reward: this small effort allows me to buy scientific works I have yearned for & I spend my time between the Coliseum & the old book-shops . . . God bless the Music Halls!'[60] It was premiered on 11 March 1912, at the London Coliseum. The piano score was published by Enoch; the full score is now fragmentary. Even works of the last century can be lost or incomplete.

His next work was more serious but also not well received. *The Music Makers*, Op. 69, sets the opening 'Ode' from Arthur O'Shaughnessy's *Music and Moonlight* (1874). Its text is probably most familiar from the 1971 film *Willy Wonka and the Chocolate Factory*, an association which does not debase it.

> We are the music makers,
> And we are the dreamers of dreams

---

[59] Anderson, *Elgar*, p. 264, and Elgar, *Letters of a Lifetime*, p. 244.
[60] Elgar, *Edward Elgar: Letters of a Lifetime*, p. 244.

Perhaps because it had to be composed in a hurry, or perhaps because he wanted to introduce the romantic artist-subject into the work before deconstructing it (as in other modernist works), he made extensive use of pre-existing music, principally from the *Variations* and symphonies. This self-borrowing has disappointed most critics, starting with those at the premiere (conducted by Elgar on 1 October 1912), but Aidan J. Thomson's defence of the work is sensitive.[61]

Towards the end of the year Elgar sold the Gagliano violin he had bought as an investment more than 20 years earlier. The proceeds were exchanged for a billiard table he had decided he must have (see opposite). During 1913 he was either on holiday or writing *Falstaff*, which was promised for the Leeds Festival in October. In preparation he read everything he could lay his hands on, with critical materials reaching back into the eighteenth century. In Italy in February, Lady Elgar confided in a letter to Carice that she was feeling her age (mid-sixties), and they heard the news (a pattern that seemed to blight most of their holidays) of another friend's very poor health. This time it was Julia Worthington; she died on 9 June.

Elgar left Alice at home and spent a few days with Schuster in The Hut. On his return she ran excitedly to meet him in his music room, slipping and falling (though Elgar tried to catch her).[62] While he was away again for a fortnight with his sister Pollie at Stoke, Alice had an oddly overambitious conversation with a friend concerning the Nobel prize. 'Pray it may be given to E'[63] – give an haute-bourgeoise the taste of medals between her teeth and she will never be sated. He didn't get a Nobel prize, of course, or a peerage. (Britten was the first composer to manage that, before they became two-a-penny.)

Falstaff was finished early in the morning on 5 August. Elgar was up at 4.00 a.m. to complete it in time to depart for a seaside holiday in Wales later that day. During the break Elgar wrote an analysis of the work for the *Musical Times*, and dealt with proofs. Alice recorded her thoughts on the trip: 'Sorry to leave the Sea', but 'delighted to leave the disagreeable Welsh'.[64] It was evident at the premiere in Leeds on 1 October that for a work of *Falstaff*'s complexity a better conductor than Elgar would have been welcome.[65] Elgar's last early modernist work, and one of the last from any European composer, had a cold reception and hardly any repeat performances. The climate had changed.

---

[61] See Aidan J. Thomson, 'Unmaking *The Music Makers*', in Harper-Scott and Rushton (eds.), *Elgar Studies*.

[62] Moore, *Creative Life*, p. 646.

[63] Anderson, *Elgar*, p. 110.

[64] Ibid., p. 112.

[65] Kennedy, *Portrait*, p. 256.

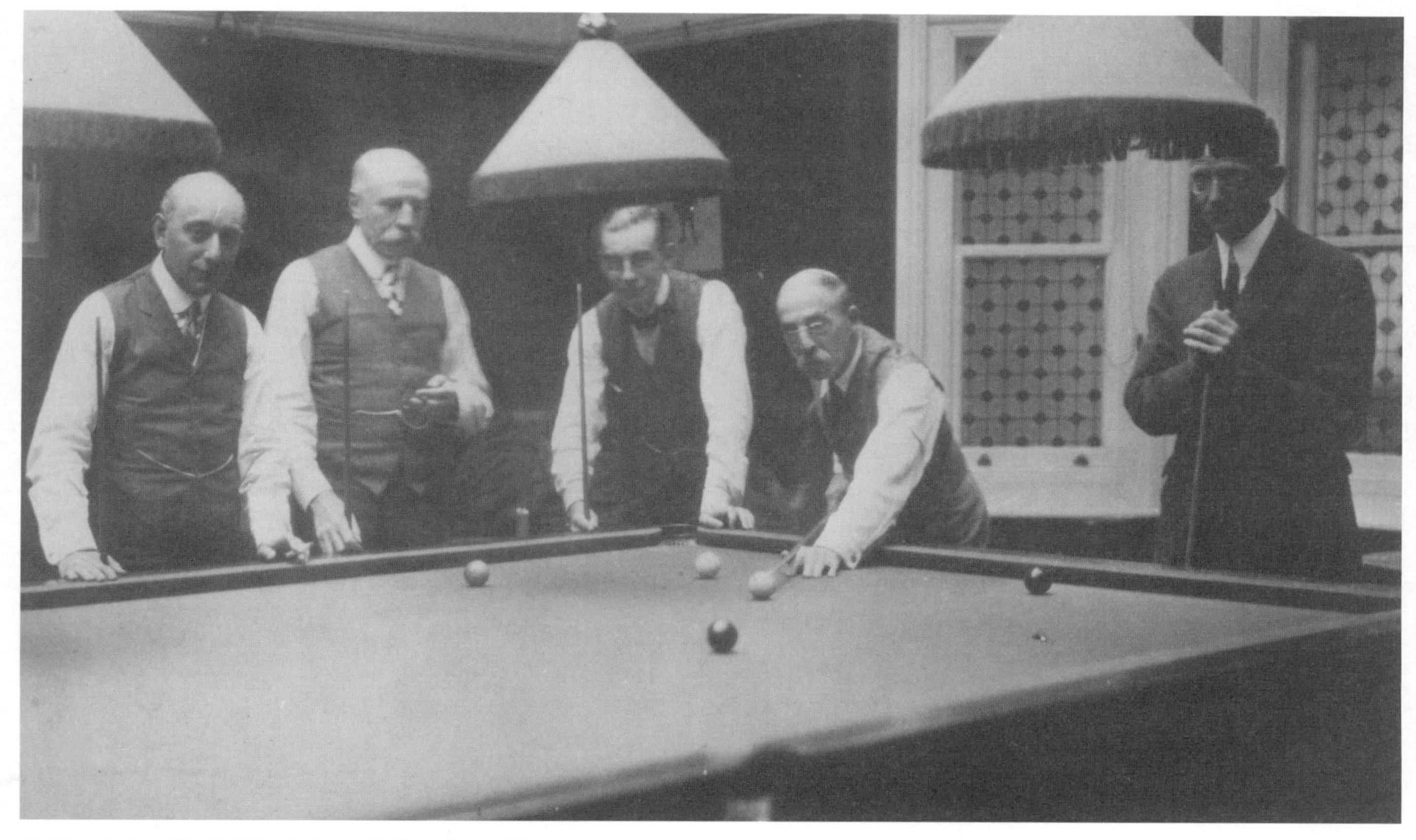

19. Elgar timing a friend's billiards shot, probably at Severn House.

FOUR

THE FIRST MODERNIST MUSIC IN ENGLAND

In the South and *Introduction and Allegro*

The music Elgar wrote between 1903 and 1914 is among the most popular and emotionally powerful of the twentieth century. Now virtually every week on BBC Radio 3 one can hear something from the symphonies and concertos, the overture *In the South*, or the *Introduction and Allegro* for strings. It would shock many listeners to be told that this music, widely considered 'late romantic', is in fact as thoroughly modern as almost anything written in that decade.

So, for an ordinary listener, how can Elgar's music be heard to be modernist? We are trained to think of musical modernism as something more 'difficult' to listen to than music like Elgar's, Strauss's, Puccini's, and so on. Even Elgar's symphonies, which present challenges of structure and length to many listeners, aren't 'difficult' in the way that Schoenberg's or Webern's music is. There is something about the quality of the sound of Elgar's music that makes it seem faintly unbelievable that Strauss could call him a 'progressivist', or that we should take the idea seriously now. Wasn't he a conservative, and doesn't that disallow modernism? That depends on whether one thinks new methods are necessary for communicating new thoughts – for instance that the only way to write a revolutionary manifesto is to use a computer. Yet older methods can often communicate modern sentiments with the same power as new ones, and one can bring about change in 2007 by writing on paper as successfully as by writing a blog.

Much of Elgar's modernism concerns his handling of tonal structure; as we've seen, this preoccupation was common to all European modernists. But unless it can be *heard*, rather than just seen on the page, appreciation of this aspect of modernism will be limited to the exclusive set of people who can understand music at an unusually technical level. Fortunately,

Elgar's modernism is audible to anyone who has been tipped off to listen in a way only slightly different from usual. It hinges largely on the order in which he presents his themes, what effect they have on the listener as they are heard, and what the listener thinks the tone of the music or the choice of theme at the end of the work communicates. That is, it is the music's *meaning*, insofar as that can be grasped from a sensitive (but not necessarily technical) listening, that makes it modernist. We shall see how this operates in discussion of the works from 1904 to 1913.

In the South, Op. 50 (1904) is Elgar's *Don Juan*. With it he became a modernist composer, just as Strauss had done 15 years earlier. The 'South' of Elgar's title is Italy: there is a sense in the overture of that country's bright sunshine (though the weather was miserable there when he wrote it), memories of its ancient history, and the imagined bucolic sweetness of its peasant life. It is an uplifting work that begins and ends in vigorous and exciting thematic material (music for the bulldog, Dan). Writing of this sort, hugely orchestrated and with virile, almost wild driving power, is typical of the modernist aesthetic, however that might be twisted or shaped by different composers for different ends. But in itself that does not make the work modernist. Furthermore, despite its bulky proportions (it lasts more than 20 minutes), it seems to have a relatively straightforward sonata-form plan. The masculine first theme gives way in due course to a feminine second idea springing from the name of a village (Moglio) Elgar visited with Carice on the Italian trip. W. H. Reed writes that he 'learnt from her afterwards that [Elgar] kept repeating this ridiculous name until at last he actually put it into his music'.[1]

It is in the development section that Elgarian modernism establishes itself. In *Cockaigne* he had experimented with inserting picturesque episodes of new material in the development section, with brass bands passing through London streets and a pair of lovers disappearing into a church. Beethoven had used this device famously in the 'Eroica' Symphony of 1803, inviting two centuries of speculation about the work's meaning. Comparison with Beethoven will help us to understand what to listen for in Elgar, who clearly alludes to the 'Eroica' in *In the South* (and to other works elsewhere: allusion and quotation are popular with modernists). If Beethoven's symphony, or at least its first movement, is about a particular hero, say Hektor (from Homer's *Iliad*) or Napoleon Bonaparte, then the gentle/sad/mysterious (hear it how you will) new tune in the development space may be read in various ways. Perhaps it represents some kind of outside agency – morality? God? Christian charity imposing itself on a pagan epic? – calling the hero to account for his bloodthirstiness. Or maybe it is a vision of the afterlife to follow the great

---

[1] W. H. Reed, *Elgar as I Knew Him*, p. 35.

hero's death. In twentieth-century psychological readings of Beethoven's 'Eroica' it has even been thought that the hero pauses on the battlefield to reflect on past victories, or is so worn out by the struggles in his own personality that he is reduced to brooding on the tangle in his sense of self.[2]

As varied as these readings are, developmental episodes invite this sort of speculation because they disturb the logical sequence of the sonata plan, which itself has a 'meaning' we can more or less grasp as follows. In simple terms, contrasting ideas are set up in the exposition (the first section, which introduces the themes), often characterized as masculine and feminine, though other opposites would do just as well. The development (which follows the exposition) traditionally explores their interrelation. This process can be conceived as an argument between two positions. In the recapitulation, a decision is reached in favour of the second idea, which appears at last in the same key as the first (as it were, arguing from the same position, or 'singing from the same hymn sheet'), and provides the climactic moment of satisfaction at the end. Introducing an episode into the development space complicates this process by bringing to bear on the argument new and unexpected angles, as if from third or fourth voices which might not exactly take sides with either of the two original ones. If the new ideas are reconciled with the main material by the end of the movement – as happens in Beethoven's symphony when the development's new tune returns in the coda as part of a subtle winding-up of various 'problems' in the music – then their total effect can be positive: they will have enriched the argument and deepened the experience the work offers. But if they just pop up and disturb the progress of the piece, perhaps by leaving an evil smell in an otherwise positive work, or a glorious vision of hope in a negative one, and are *not* ultimately integrated in such a way as to make sense, then they give us something to think on when the music has ended. We are invited to wonder whether the argument of the work has been *completed*, or has just *stopped* in mid flow. Like the character in the Monty Python argument sketch whose argument is cut short when his five minutes is up, we might want to say 'I was just getting interested!'

In the South has two such episodes in the development, the first painting a picture of the Romans through their ancient ruins: 'the massive bridge and the road still useful, and to a reflective mind awe-inspiring'.[3] The second, a beautiful pastoral episode beginning with a viola tune in C major, is, Elgar said, a *canto popolare* (popular song) sung by a shepherd in the

---

[2] A useful discussion of the most important and interesting interpretations of the first movement of the 'Eroica' is in Scott G. Burnham, *Beethoven Hero* (Princeton, NJ: Princeton University Press, 1995), pp. 4–28.

[3] Elgar's words on this section, from Percy Pitt and Alfred Kalisch, *Analytical and Descriptive Notes* for the Covent Garden premiere of the work, are quoted in Moore, *Creative Life*, p. 427.

countryside. He originally said that the tune was copied down in Italy, but later admitted that he had written it himself.[4] Its 'innocence' is a musical characteristic that Elgar would make special use of throughout the remainder of his composing life. These episodes do not return later in the work, but since they have such clear picturesque motivations this does not confuse the 'argument' of the work. On a formal level they make the sonata design more subtle and satisfying, but need not trouble us after the last note has sounded.

Things are different with the *Introduction and Allegro*, Op. 47 (1905), which, like *In the South*, is sometimes regarded as being among Elgar's least characteristic pieces. Its instrumentation, for string quartet and string orchestra, sounding very much (superficially, at least) like a baroque concerto grosso, is certainly unique in his output, and because timbre influences perception of music so profoundly, it might make the work sound somehow less Elgarian (the overt Straussian tone of *In the South* is the reason why some find that a little uncharacteristic too). But technically, and in terms of its 'meaning', the *Introduction and Allegro* is absolutely a model of Elgar's modernist style.

There is a 'popular tune' in this work too: the second main idea, which Elgar thought he heard while on holiday with Rosa Burley in Wales in 1901. He explained its provenance in a programme note for the premiere four years later, in January 1905.

> In Cardiganshire, I thought of writing a brilliant piece for string orchestra.[5] On the cliff, between the blue sea and blue sky, thinking out my theme, there came up to me the sound of singing. The songs were too far away to reach me distinctly, but one point common to all was impressed upon me, and led me to think, perhaps wrongly, that it was a real Welsh idiom – I mean the fall of a third . . . The tune may therefore be called, as is the melody in the overture 'In the South', a canto popolare, but the suggesting country is in this case Wales, and not Italy . . . The work is really a tribute to that sweet borderland where I have made my home.[6]

---

[4] Ibid., p. 430.

[5] This is not strictly true. Elgar was to conduct a concert for the new London Symphony Orchestra in March 1905, and Jaeger suggested that he write a '*brilliant* quick *String* Scherzo . . . a real bring down the House *torrent* of a thing such as Bach could write (Remember that *Cologne* Brandenburger Concerto!)': letter of 28 October 1904, quoted in ibid., p. 451. So the inspiration for the piece and its generic feel (the concerto grosso) was Jaeger's idea in 1904, not Elgar's in 1901.

[6] Quoted in Daniel M. Grimley, '"A Smiling with a Sigh": The Chamber Music and the Works for Strings', in Grimley and Rushton (eds.), *The Cambridge Companion to Elgar*, pp. 120–38, at pp. 124–5.

James Hepokoski notes that this story sets up a few important markers for the listener.[7] The 'Welsh tune', which is the emotional core of the piece and the focus of its final climax, is represented as 'authentic' – that is, of the people – as well as 'truly human' (rather than modern and mechanical). It is 'innocent' of the artifice of art: pure, unsullied, a vision of lost contentment, like Eden. And Elgar hears it from below while he broods on his vantage point on the cliff. That is, he paints himself into the place of the typical isolated romantic artist, cut off from the world but able to lead the herd to a deeper understanding of its own nature. The modernist twist is that by colouring the work with a distinctly Elgarian nostalgia he presents his insight negatively. The work is his first to end unquestionably both (a) without hope and (b) with a pasted-on 'happy' ending.

The 'Welsh tune' appears at first as if it were from another world. The work's stern, serious, opening melts away into a gently throbbing presentation of the tune, which has a sadly nostalgic, yearning tone that unmistakably places it in the category of an elegy. At the same time it mourns past innocence and presents it as a goal the modern world should strive for.[8] But ultimately the innocence of the tune remains lost: it cannot cement itself in the closing pages as hope for the future (an important phrase in connexion with a later work). It never properly cadences into the tonic (the 'home' key), and isn't allowed to bring the work to a conclusion. Only the serious tune from the opening, representing the stern modern world that has lost its innocence, can end the work. The closing bars are spirited, even cheerful, but they appear too hard after the most impassioned statement of the 'Welsh tune', which ends tantalizingly open, unfulfilled, so that one can only hear in the end a provisional conclusion of a work that could easily end more tearfully, or at least one that hides potential sobs behind a stiff upper lip. We are shown a dream of the happy place, the Eden we lost, but are, in the end, shut out from it. Detailed knowledge of the musical workings is not essential to communicate the problematic nature of this impressive work, though close study unlocks wonders.

The Kingdom, Op. 51 (1901–6), marks an advance on *The Apostles*, but the oratorio project ended here. As Wagner had done with *The Ring* cycle, whose composition spanned the years 1852 to 1874,[9] Elgar had changed musical language in the middle of his project. Wagner got diverted by *Tristan* part-way through writing the third opera in his cycle, *Siegfried*, and

---

[7] The following reading of the piece is a précis of Hepokoski's with additional reflexions. See James A. Hepokoski, 'Gaudery, Romance, and the "Welsh" Tune: *Introduction and Allegro*, Op. 47', in Harper-Scott and Rushton (eds.), *Elgar Studies*.

[8] This was a commonplace in German art of the time, which is precisely why the Germans considered Elgar progressive and admirable.

[9] It was premiered as a cycle in 1876, under Richter, Elgar's champion.

the change in style between its first two acts (written before *Tristan*) and the third (written after) is astonishing: opera-goers might be forgiven for thinking they have eaten something odd in the dinner interval. Wagner was fortunate: his new style enriched his cycle without imperilling its coherence. Elgar drew the short straw: in becoming a modernist and putting behind him the sometimes insipid neo-romanticism of *The Apostles*, he had developed a language that was ill fitted to completing a grand narrative of everlasting hope and the ongoing redemption of the Christian God. But it would be a mistake to attribute his modernist cynicism straightforwardly to the implosion of his religious worldview, even if that ever happened. The world he knew was rotting around his ears, and the stench choked many reflective artists, not just Elgar. It didn't take the death of God to show his contemporaries the inevitable approach of war with Germany, a country Elgar loved, and whose musical tradition he assimilated. *The Apostles* ends grandly, with a procession of leitmotivs, bright and loud orchestral scoring, and a final 'Alleluia!'. *The Kingdom* ends quietly, deflatedly, avoiding perfect cadences, giving little or no backing to the sense, in the earlier work, that the Kingdom of God could be established, could endure, could serve any redemptive purpose.[10] The oratorio project fizzled out in large part because it was no longer possible for Elgar to reaffirm old verities, whether religious or musical. There would no longer be anything so reassuring as a perfect cadence in Elgar. From now, any that he wrote would chill with an air of unreality.

The symphonies and Violin Concerto

Elgar's Symphony No. 1 in A flat, Op. 55 (1907–8), opens with one of the most straightforwardly 'tonal' beginnings of any symphony in the tradition. Its stately tread grows from an opening pair of timpani rolls until one can almost smell the scent of mothballs given off by a five-hundred-person procession up the aisle of Westminster Abbey. The tune is magnificent, the orchestration gorgeous and sparkling, and it has only one accidental (note outside the key) in its first few minutes. He told Newman that it was 'intended to be simple &, in intention, noble & elevating . . . the sort of ideal *call* (in the sense of persuasion, not coercion or command) & something above everyday & sordid things'.[11] It is probably the most unnervingly solid, almost conceited, opening of any symphony in the history of Western music. Unnerving because we know – this is Elgar – that the rug is about to be pulled from beneath the procession's feet. We do not have to wait long.

As soon as this astonishing introduction has seated itself on the throne of the as-yet unchallenged tonic key, the first movement's main Allegro

---

[10] This idea was suggested to me by reading Julian Rushton, 'Elgar, Empire, and Kingdom'.

[11] 4 November 1908, Elgar, *Letters of a Lifetime*, p. 200.

theme smashes onto the scene like a monster seeking blood. Fifty minutes later the symphony is still reeling from the shock. The first Allegro theme is impossible to tie down to a key, though it suggests A minor as much as anything; Elgar said (when it returns with a mildly bitonal feel at the start of the recapitulation) that it has 'a nice sub-acid feeling'.[12] Whatever it is, it is disconcertingly far from the symphony's A flat, and the majestic tone of the opening. Although a gentle 'second subject' starts on F major, it quickly loses its way in a chromatic quagmire so that not until the end of the exposition do we hear a solid presentation of a new key. This key is A minor, and the tune is a grotesque distortion both of the opening 'ideal call' and of its own 'sad & delicate' first appearance, a few minutes earlier. The first movement is, in part, a terrible war between these two principal themes. In the closing bars, after a strong reassertion of the 'ideal call', we hear the second of them again, in its quieter guise, casting a menacing shadow. The 'ideal call' has done nothing to banish the intruder.

The second movement scherzo is a blaze of colour with a twitchingly nervous third theme that Elgar told his orchestra to play 'like something we hear down by the river'.[13] Its opening rush of semiquavers in F sharp minor is mutated at the end of the movement so that, gradually slowing, it becomes almost note-for-note the theme of the slow movement which then follows without a break. Here at last the symphony finds peace, even bliss, in the tune that Jaeger said brings the listener 'near Heaven'. The raucous second principal theme of the first movement haunts this slow movement as the counterpoint to a secondary idea, now in A major. This key, the dominant (that is the second main chord) of the tonic Dmajor, closes naturally into the tonic for the concluding 'heaven tune'. Elgar wrote this originally in 1904, and over the sketch wrote 'the rest is silence'. Those are Hamlet's last words, and they seem to take on a baleful significance in a work that is also concerned with the question of whether, in a state with something rotten in it, facing the slings and arrows of outrageous fortune is worth the fight. This theme is strong tonally, relative to the other music in the symphony (stronger than the 'ideal call', because it has support from its own dominant chord), and there is hope in it. Listeners familiar with *Parsifal* or *Gerontius* (the Good Friday Music or the Angel's Farewell) will recognize in its colour and shape the promise of redemption that forms part of the neo-romantic philosophy. It also inhabits the innocent, prelapsarian world of the 'Welsh tune' from the *Introduction and Allegro*. In Mahler, moments of shimmering otherworldliness like this cut through the fetid air of his darkest music and return in triumph at the conclusion; the philosopher Theodor Adorno calls this

---

[12] Ibid., p. 203.

[13] Reed, *Elgar as I Knew Him*, p. 141.

technique 'breakthrough'.[14] But Elgar is more depressing even than Mahler. Between 1904 and 1913, hope tends to die in his music.

The 'breakthrough' doesn't conquer in the finale. Its serene D major is a tritone – the *diabolus in musica* (the devil in music) – away from the symphony's opening A flat. Furthermore, D major is flatly contradicted by the D minor that opens the finale with a final parody of the 'ideal call', a march tune that grows in power. The trajectory of the movement, which is in sonata form, is through a series of discomfiting eruptions and formal surprises towards a blistering restatement of the 'ideal call' and a big question mark at the end. The exposition ends in the 'wrong' key by refusing to leave the movement's tonic. The recapitulation starts in the 'wrong' key too, neither the movement's D minor nor the symphony's A flat, but E flat minor (which will eventually lead to A flat). It comes as no surprise that the recapitulation ends in the 'wrong' key too, this time F minor. Then everything becomes deeply ambiguous. Energy builds immensely until the 'ideal call' returns – in the symphony's tonic, A flat. Brass chords clatter through this final statement, visceral signs of weakness or panic. The uncomfortable fact is that the 'ideal call' has been weakly presented in the symphony. The only real hope in the symphony is presented by the 'heaven tune' in the slow movement. So the return here to the opening is unlikely to reassure. Once again the orchestration is splendid, the final chords a ringing restatement of A flat. Elgar said 'there is no programme [in the symphony] beyond a wide experience of human life with a great charity (love) & a *massive* hope in the future'.[15] We must wonder, though, whether the theme that had its heart ripped out of it at the start of the symphony offers us much surety in its return at the close. It would be a mistake to decide firmly whether Elgar's message is affirmative or negative: ambiguity is essential to the design. In that respect, the symphony is a typical work of its time.

Elgar inscribed the score of the Violin Concerto in B minor, Op. 61 (1909–10), with a dedication in Spanish: 'Aquí está encerrada el alma de . . . . .'. He translated it for Kilburn: 'Here, or more emphatically *In here* is enshrined or (simply) enclosed – *buried* is perhaps too definite[16] – *the soul of* . . .? the final 'de' leaves it indefinite as to sex or rather gender. Now

---

[14] See Theodor W. Adorno, *Mahler: A Musical Physiognomy*, trans. Edmund Jephcott (Chicago: University of Chicago Press, 1992; orig. edn. 1960), p. 10. Adorno's prose style is recommended to those who enjoy extreme sports.

[15] Letter to Walford Davies, 13 November 1908, quoted in Elgar, *Letters of a Lifetime*, p. 205.

[16] Although the English translation of the source for the quotation is 'interred'. It is from Alain René Le Sage's *L'histoire de Gil Blas de Santillane* (1715): the full quotation is 'Aquí está encerrada el alma del Licenciado Pedro Garcias' ('Here is interred the soul of the Licentiate Pedro Garcias'). *Gil Blas* was more popular in Elgar's time than ours, so the reference is not quite as recherché as it might seem. See Brian Trowell, 'Elgar's Use of Literature', in Raymond Monk (ed.), *Edward Elgar: Music and Literature* (Aldershot: Scolar, 1993), pp. 182–326, at pp. 244–6.

guess.'[17] Here we have an Elgarian enigma far less tedious than the first. Lady Elgar apparently confirmed Dorabella's surmise that the soul was Julia ('Pippa') Worthington.[18] Others have guessed that it might be Lady Elgar herself (which seems very doubtful), Helen Weaver, Frank Schuster's sister Adela, or, most likely of all, Alice Stuart-Wortley. All suspects have five-letter names, so the curious ellipsis of five dots doesn't offer much of a clue. Brian Trowell's solution is the sharpest. He draws attention to Elgar's turn of phrase in his question to a Spanish friend, Antonio de Navarro: 'If I want it to refer to the soul of a feminine shd. it be – de la . . .?'.[19] Why say 'a feminine' if he meant 'a female', or correct (biological) 'sex' to (grammatical) 'gender'? This 'seems to [Trowell] to show that what is missing is not a female name but a feminine noun. The obvious candidate is "la anímona" or "la anímone" (Spanish for "windflower")'.[20] The invention of Alice Stuart-Wortley's nickname at the same time as the composition of the 'Windflower' themes in this concerto proves the closeness of thought between central musical material and the identity of a woman, and so this evidence alone is enough to make it almost certain that it is her soul that the concerto 'enshrines'.

Elgar wrote the piece at a time when his contemporaries were developing new modernist models for a genre that in the nineteenth century had been dominated by diabolically virtuoso (and often vapid) showpieces, but also allowed room for the touching simplicity of mendelssohn or the high seriousness of Brahms. Sibelius's concerto, premiered in 1905, was perhaps the first to bring modernist formal procedures to bear on a still recognizably virtuoso work. Its interesting treatment of the cadenza – which comes at the end of the development rather than the recapitulation – is one way in which it foreshadows Elgar's concerto, which has one of the most remarkable cadenzas in the repertory. Its dense symphonic working is another way. Aleksandr Glazunov (1865–1936), who received the honorary D.Mus. from both Oxford and Cambridge in 1907, wrote his Violin Concerto, one of his finest works, in 1904. Max Reger (1873–1916) wrote his own in 1907–8, and it carries Brahms's motivic technique of 'developing variation' into the modernist era. Nielsen's Violin Concerto would follow a year after Elgar's in 1911. Whether Elgar heard or even knew of these works is less important than the fact that at the same time, several contemporary composers were approaching similar formal questions in the genre.

---

[17] Letter of 5 November 1910, quoted in Edward Elgar, *Letters of Edward Elgar and Other Writings*, ed. Percy M. Young (London: Bles, 1956), p. 201.

[18] Powell, *Edward Elgar*, p. 86.

[19] Quoted in Moore, *Creative Life*, p. 587.

[20] Trowell, 'Elgar's Use of Literature', p. 245. He explains why in Spanish the feminine 'anímona' does not require 'del'. The botanical name for the windflower is *anemone nemorosa*.

Elgar's treatment of the third-movement cadenza focuses the meaning of the work, which is another of Elgar's explorations of the distinction between public show and private sentiment, modern reality and past beauty or innocence.[21] Traditionally standing for the public sphere, in which the soloist shows off his or her outstanding technical ability, in Elgar's hands the cadenza becomes the most intimate part of the work. The quiet orchestral accompaniment (an innovation) seems to constrain the soloist, keeping the violin earthbound in the positive sense of being more concerned with the simply human than the superhumanity of the traditional display. In this passage we are offered glimpses, as in the *Introduction and Allegro* and First Symphony, of an idealized, perfect world. An attempted close for the whole work in D major, the relative major (the happy side, as it were) of the work's B minor, is glimpsed at figure 107, seven pages before the end. A close here would be into the key of the *Parsifal* Good Friday Music, of the Angel's Farewell from *Gerontius*, and of the First Symphony's 'heaven tune': richly suggestive, all, of redemption and return. But, typically for the modernist Elgar, this close is denied. The public sphere returns with the concerto's opening theme, and the shutting of the window that had opened onto the idyllic. If the 'Windflower' has her soul enshrined here, the happiness she offered Elgar is denied as a realistic possibility.

Symphony No. 2 in E flat, Op. 63 (1909–11), has one of the strongest literary connexions among Elgar's modernist works, but its bearing on the symphony is not easy to assess. The work carries an epigraph from the poet Shelley's *Song*, 'Rarely, rarely comest thou, / Spirit of Delight!' (see figure 20, overleaf). The word 'delight' is sometimes misrepresented as communicating the essence of the poem, or the symphony, but both are more concerned with loss. In any case there is no reason to read the poem closely alongside the symphony. Elgar had a wide interest in the arts, and in the long process of writing a symphony different works caught his attention at different times. Not until *Falstaff*, where the literary connexion is strongly focused, need we be detained too long by the attempt to discern what light literature casts on the work's 'meaning'.

Shelley at the start – Elgar associated the theme in bars 3–4 of the movement with the 'Spirit of Delight' – is joined by Tennyson in the third movement, the scherzo. There a grim passage of mechanical grinding and thrusting, which grows to an ear-splitting Mahlerian climax around figure 120, made him think, he told a friend, of lines from Tennyson's *Maud*:

---

[21] The following reading draws on Christopher Mark, 'The Later Orchestral Music (1910–34)', in Grimley and Rushton (eds.), *The Cambridge Companion to Elgar*, pp. 154–70, at pp. 155–6.

20. The opening of the Second Symphony, in short score, with Elgar's cartoon of the 'Spirit of Delight' (a typical marginal illustration in his manuscripts).

Dead, long dead,
Long dead!
And my heart is a handful of dust,
And the wheels go over my head,
And my bones are shaken with pain,
For into a shallow grave they are thrust,
Only a yard beneath the street

Elgar didn't quote the last three lines, but Brian Trowell points out their significance.[22] Until 1823 in England 'a suicide was buried on the highway with a stake driven through his body'. A once pious Roman Catholic would know the traditional high-minded English view of suicide. Elgar was known to have been suicidal a decade earlier. He told an orchestra that this critical moment in the symphony 'represent[ed] a man in a high fever. Some of you may know that dreadful beating that goes on in the brain – it seems to drive out every coherent thought'.[23] Perhaps the high fever was a reaction to the death of Edward VII in May 1910, as Elgar was finishing work on the Violin Concerto, or even a memory of the gloom following Rodewald's death in 1903, after which the magnificent music between figures 74 and 76 in the slow movement of the Second Symphony was almost certainly written. The fever could also be a symptom of the 'unnatural' desire he had for Alice Stuart-Wortley (or even for Rodewald, if that line is followed).

Elgar leaves so many autobiographical clues that one could go on indefinitely trying to piece together a satisfactory reading of them all. Perhaps there is none. More interesting, ultimately – for we are (or should be) more interested in the totality of human life than the single life of a curious man from the Midlands – is the reading that the work seems to offer of its age. Through that, we can more pungently feel its entanglement with our own situation.

If the tune of the opening bars, and others like it, stands for 'Delight', then the theme Elgar marked in the sketches as '1st sketch of Symphony No.2 – Ghost',[24] once he had filled it out with a cello countermelody, might stand for 'Decay'. It is the theme of the third-movement crisis, the work's greatest challenge. If we follow the associations of the sound of this music one stage further, we can begin to hear a social commentary developing in the music. The strong marching rhythms and seemingly

---

[22] Trowell, 'Elgar's Use of Literature', pp. 259–60.
[23] Bernard Shore, *The Orchestra Speaks* (London: Longmans, Green, 1938), p. 135. The same author remembered the instruction differently 11 years later. See Bernard Shore, *Sixteen Symphonies* (London: Longmans, Green, 1949), p. 279.
[24] See Christopher Kent, 'A View of Elgar's Methods of Composition through the Sketches of the Symphony No. 2 in E- (Op. 63)', *Proceedings of the Royal Musical Association*, 103 (1976–7), pp. 41–60, at p. 44.

boundless optimism of the 'Spirit of Delight' is redolent for many of the imperial mindset of the Edwardian ruling class. Here is Britain in its pomp, tremendous in ceremony and infinite in potential. The 'Spirit of Decay' that cuts across it could be any one of a number of things: the effects of the Liberal government, active by 1911, among them limiting the power of the House of Lords in the first Parliament Act, and otherwise causing offence to the Tory Elgar; the rise of the working classes, and the movement from women's suffrage (ditto); or, most plausibly, the growing horror engulfing Europe and threatening Western civilization in its then-present form (which scared more or less everyone). The thematic struggle that develops in this symphony is not, therefore, just one man's struggle with sexual demons or the loss of friends. It is, potentially, a discourse on the health of the world order and the consequences for humanity should it fall apart.

Elgar described the 'Spirit of Decay', in its first appearance in the development of the opening Allegro vivace e nobilmente ('Quick, lively, nobly'), in a letter to Alice Stuart-Wortley as 'the most *extraordinary* passage I have ever heard – a sort of malign influence wandering thro' the summer night in the garden'.[25] It is, eventually, in C major, the symphony's 'alternative' key centre a third below the symphony's tonic E flat. The middle movements are in C minor and C major respectively. In the case of the funereal slow movement the tonic crops up only at a few formal junctions. Towards the end of a movement mostly filled with a profound ceremonial mournfulness, the Spirit of Delight returns in an effort to effect a close (figure 87). The music has been moving away from C, the 'key of Decay', towards E flat, the 'key of Delight', but at the exact point that the theme of the Spirit of Delight returns, Elgar cadences into the 'wrong' key, C major (the movement eventually ends in C minor). Suddenly Delight seems tainted by Decay. When the third movement's crisis comes with the theme of Decay now in excoriating form, the key of Delight, E flat, has the life rattled out of it. The symphony's tonic returns for the easy-going opening of the finale – Robert Meikle compares this passage to Sunday bandstand music in the park, the musicians not quite visible behind the rhododendrons[26] – but the tone of the music is placid, not vigorous. Perhaps a contented sitting-about on the tonic, on Delight, on Edwardian splendour and the majesty of old Europe, is enough: perhaps maintaining the status quo will do. Or perhaps this finale is an acknowledgement that the old order is powerless in the face of present dangers to it, some of them (the affording of new opportunities to the lower classes and all women) evidently good to most people, others (war,

[25] Elgar, *The Windflower Letters*, p. 75.
[26] See Robert Meikle, '"The True Foundation": The Symphonies', in Monk (ed.), *Edward Elgar: Music and Literature*, pp. 45–71, at p. 55.

financial ruin) evidently bad, and still more (the collapse of empire) possible to view differently from different political positions. When the Spirit of Delight returns, back on its original key of E flat once more (at figure 168), its dying fall 'could either be a reaffirmation of a promise whispered by the spirit of an age, or the dying puff of a dream that's banished by the cold, raised finger of the dawn'.[27] At the premiere, Elgar said the audience 'sat there like a lot of stuffed pigs',[28] perhaps unsettled by its message. It still speaks a century on.

Falstaff

The 'symphonic study for orchestra, in C minor, with two Interludes in A minor',[29] *Falstaff*, Op. 68 (1913), is the summit of Elgar's achievement and one of the last masterpieces of European early modernism. In it Elgar created an amalgam of text and music that goes beyond the symphonic or tone-poem tradition. Not only characters and elements of plot (that is, a 'programme') from Shakespeare's *Henry IV* plays, but also high spots from 140 years of Shakespeare criticism make their way into the work. In this sense Elgar's choice of the word 'study' is significant: it is an act of literary criticism as well as programme music. It was also the culmination of a life-long 'bardolatry', and takes the character of Falstaff, Shakespeare's Everyman, to produce a study not only of a fat knight but, through him, of the rest of us.

The 'programme' in a work of music does not exist in the notes. It is part of an elaborate game agreed between composer and listener. The composer tips us off, and we agree to search for connexions only insofar as they fit the disclosed model. Berlioz wrote the first detailed musical programme for the premiere of his *Symphonie fantastique* (Fantastic Symphony – in the sense of being 'full of fantasy') in 1830. Liszt followed with his symphonic poems, giving 'programme music' its definition and a forward-looking philosophy. It was often distinguished from 'absolute music' (broadly, music without text or 'non-musical meaning'), and considered by some a less high ideal of musical construction. Non-programmatic symphonies of the kind that Elgar praised in his professorial lectures could be imagined as the preserve of serious intellectual composition, not the frivolous picturesqueness of the programmatic genres. In *Falstaff*, Elgar created a model of programme music capable of deepening its intellectual content by engaging with serious works of criticism, while maintaining the traditional intellectualism of the symphonic form.

---

[27] J. P. E. Harper-Scott, 'Elgar's Deconstruction of the *belle époque*: Interlace Structures and the Second Symphony', in Harper-Scott and Rushton (eds.), *Elgar Studies*. This essay gives a very detailed reading of the Second Symphony and its possible implications.
[28] Reed, *Elgar*, p. 105.
[29] The title he gives it in Edward Elgar, 'Falstaff', *Musical Times*, 54 (1913), pp. 575–9, at p. 575.

In the analytical note he wrote for the *Musical Times* before the work's premiere, he divided the structure into four named parts.

I. Falstaff and Prince Henry;
II. Eastcheap, – Gadshill, – The Boar's Head, revelry and sleep;
III. Falstaff's March, – The return through Gloucestershire, – The new King, – The hurried ride to London;
IV. King Henry V.'s progress, – The repudiation of Falstaff, and his death.[30]

In these sections Elgar unfolds the tale of two close friends (Prince Henry, or 'Hal', and a drunken, endearingly filthy-minded knight, Falstaff) whose friendship is tested when the prince becomes king – ultimately rejecting his bawdy former companions. The traditional reading of Hal's character development, and his rejection of Falstaff, was as favourable in the centuries leading up to Elgar's composition of *Falstaff* as it remains now. Hal would become Henry V, would win at Agincourt; he can be forgiven for shaking off his association with scurvy vulgarians who dislike authority, if that will purify his character. Falstaff was a buffoon and could have no place in a kingly retinue. But one critic Elgar admired (and quoted in his analytical note) strongly disagreed with this assessment. In his 1777 *Essay on the Dramatic Character of Sir John Falstaff*, Maurice Morgann argues that Falstaff is neither coward nor buffoon, and that it is required by Shakespeare's design that we should examine the roots of Falstaff's and Hal's friendship, filling in the gaps in the playwright's presentation with our own knowledge of human motivation. One reading that can result from this – a minority one, but not unreasonable, and certainly Elgar's own reading – is that Falstaff is a tragic figure, rejected by a boy he adored (and by whom he felt *he* was adored), and hurried into a mortal decline by a broken heart. Their relationship has some elements in it of the ancient Greek model of pederasty, in which mutually beneficial relationships between older and younger men were based on the younger learning from the older, and the older enjoying sex with the younger. Hal clearly learns from Falstaff, thus maintaining the teacher–pupil dynamic. Depending on one's interpretation of Falstaff's feelings for Hal, the sexual element might also be present.

Part I of Elgar's work is in the form of a symphonic exposition. There are several themes for Falstaff, all of a puckish and (from the 'purely musical' point of view) worryingly unstable nature. Prince Henry ('Hal') has one of Elgar's greatest noble themes, although – significantly – it is not here marked *nobilmente*, only *con anima* ('with animation'). From the beginning, Falstaff's themes are in C minor, the official tonic of the work, and Hal's

---

[30] Ibid., at p. 576.

are in E flat, the key that tonal tradition has established as its close companion, its 'relative major'. The friendship of the two men is thus demonstrated through simple musical association with a traditional 'friendly' tonal relationship. A third key, E minor, is used for a theme that Elgar said represents Falstaff singing 'sweet wag, when thou art king': in other words, it stands for 'kingship'. Several other themes in the work will do the same in this key.

As the work grows through part II – the development – picturesque episodes severely complicate the audible structure. For those who are interested in grasping these things, study reveals that through parts II and III Elgar merely cycles through existing material – that introduced in the exposition, or at the Boar's Head Tavern at the start of part II – and inserts picturesque material (robbery, role-play, battle) to advance the narrative.[31] As in Sibelius's Seventh Symphony (1924), all the material of separate symphonic movements is worked into a single, propulsively generated shape.[32] It keeps tension high and makes the narrative unfold with the inevitability of Greek tragedy.

After an interlude in which Falstaff recalls being page to the Duke of Norfolk – another of Elgar's ideal pictures of an innocent world – events turn towards Hal's accession to the throne. Falstaff rides through Gloucestershire (another interlude) and the accession is announced, his tune now on kingly E major, not princely E flat. Quickly Falstaff rides to Westminster to greet the new king, and part IV, the coda, begins. For the first time in the work we are given a strong presentation of C minor, the tonic that we might have expected to dominate the work. This undermining of the tonic is familiar from the symphonies, but because the tonic is also associated in this work with the main character, it has a clearer significance. The king rejects Falstaff publicly; Falstaff's C minor is flattened by kingly E minor. In the closing bars, the last music – the king's march theme, introduced in the coda – blares out in E minor, threatening to close there, but after a general pause the work ends with a single quiet bar of C (major mode provided only by violas, more or less inaudible). Falstaff ends the work, but he is dead; the chord sounds ridiculous out of context, because 'the man of stern reality [Henry V] has triumphed'.[33] The last bar is Falstaff's tombstone, but Elgar also seems to suggest that it is his own – his age's – *ours* – too.

All Elgar's modernist music had ruminated on the Wagnerian tonal legacy, and the problem of how to end a piece of music when a simple

---

[31] A detailed analysis of the work, which includes a careful mapping of the narrative onto the musical structure, can be read in J. P. E. Harper-Scott, 'Elgar's Invention of the Human: *Falstaff*, Op. 68', *19th-Century Music,* 28 (2005), pp. 230–53.

[32] There are earlier precedents for a single-movement presentation of a multi-movement plan, such as Schubert's *'Wanderer' Fantasy*, but it is the Sibelius that *Falstaff* more closely matches.

[33] Elgar, 'Analytical Note', at p. 579.

return to the tonic key might seem old-fashioned or redundant. All of his modernist music (unlike Mahler's, but like Sibelius's) returns to the tonic key, regardless of the cost. But there's the rub. The cost is enormous. By showing that the tonic is powerless in the modernist idiom, but nevertheless returning to it in conclusion, Elgar's modernist music allows us no hope. Whatever seems to have strength and purpose has neither; whatever promises protection can give none. And when Falstaff, the character in Shakespeare who shows us how to live free from the restrictions of honour, duty, or deference (a model with strong appeal for our own world), is destroyed by the aftershock of his misunderstanding, the message is still bleaker. Human freedom is an illusion. Elgar says this as consistently and forcefully as any modernist composer, in musical structures that compel attention. This alone earns him his place at the spearhead of musical early modernism, as well as in the intellectual history of the early-twentieth century.[34]

[34] For a fuller consideration of Elgar's modernism, see J. P. E. Harper-Scott, *Edward Elgar, Modernist* (Cambridge and New York: Cambridge University Press, 2006).

An un-Edwardian erotic life

Elgar's catalogue of love affairs is not long, but it is interesting. His music was more profoundly influenced by the people he loved – but was not officially attached to – than it was by either his early fiancée, Helen Weaver, or his wife. The pitiable truth about his emotional life is that although he found in Alice a deep, faithful, encouraging, and mothering love, she seems not to have satisfied him sexually.

Michael Kennedy owns a letter written in 1936 by Clare Stuart-Wortley, the daughter of 'Windflower', to Elgar's daughter, Carice Elgar Blake. It accompanied the bequest to the Elgar Birthplace of Alice Stuart-Wortley's letters to Elgar. They are the record of the most emotionally important relationship of Elgar's adult life, but Clare's explanation of them is disingenuous, and couched in the stiff propriety of an Englishwoman in 1936.

> Being the soul of honour, he felt himself under an obligation to her for giving him an impulse at a critical moment & he thought to discharge that obligation by giving her what she most liked, themes and MSS [manuscripts] . . . This I propose to write down and put with the MSS as it is the true explanation & honourable to all parties.[1]

This is almost certainly a misrepresentation – but of what? Clare Stuart-Wortley is perhaps the person who deleted or entirely removed portions of the surviving letters between Elgar and her mother.[2] Were they still readable, these excisions might have given a better idea of the nature of their relationship, but there is in any case no doubt that for his part Elgar was hopelessly in love. Physically there could be no comparison between his two Alices. Even in middle age Alice Stuart-Wortley was a beautiful woman, five years his junior; Lady Elgar was plain, and nine years older than her husband.

The most obvious intention behind Clare Stuart-Wortley's letter quoted above must have been to disguise the fact that the love between Elgar and her mother was adulterous (they were both

---

[1] Kennedy, *The Life of Elgar*, p. 117.

[2] Jerrold Northrop Moore's published collection is almost entirely of Elgar's letters to Alice Stuart-Wortley. See Elgar, *Windflower*.

21. Alice Stuart-Wortley, painted by her father, Sir John Everett Millais (1829–96).

married). Alternatively, it might have been an effort to hide the embarrassing possibility that their relationship was one-sided. We know that Elgar loved 'Windflower'; from the existing letters we cannot be sure – though it is likely – that she loved him. If his love was not so fully requited, their involvement would be doubly tragic.

Elgar and 'Windflower' met in 1902 (when she was 40, he 45), but their relationship only became serious in 1909, when he decided that she needed a different name from his wife. ('Carrie' was his first attempt – her full name was Alice Sophie Caroline – but she didn't like it.) They remained friends until the end of his life, and she died two years after him, in 1936. Their time spent together at each other's homes or on holiday is noted elsewhere in this book.

Her first and closest influence on his music was the Violin Concerto, which he routinely called 'our concerto' or 'your concerto'. She had persuaded him not to abandon its composition, during one of his periodic spells of self-doubt, on 7 February 1910. Her spur led to the composition of the first 'Windflower' theme, and her name-giving, and each year thereafter Elgar held 7 February as their 'anniversary'. On that date in 1917 he had an oddly poorly day, spending it entirely in bed or in his room, his wife's diary relates.[3] He had been suffering throat trouble, but perhaps there was a different cause for a solitary, sad day. The next morning he wrote to 'Windflower' with a fragment of his unfinished Piano Concerto.

Elgar's description of the windflower itself survives at the Birthplace. 'The little group of anemones commonly called windflowers are happily named . . . for when the east wind rasps over the ground in March and April they merely turn their backs and bow before the squall'.[4] Each spring he collected the first one he saw, pressed it, and sent it in a letter to her. Romantic involvement could not be more obvious. There is no incontrovertible evidence either to prove or disprove the suspicion that their relationship was sexually consummated. Flat denial is prudishness, confirmation prurience.

'Windflower' was his principal emotional focus while his wife was alive, but in the last few years of his own life a meeting with Vera Rebecca Hockman, a violinist with the London Symphony Orchestra, established a rival.[5] Hockman was also married, but

---

[3] Moore, *Creative Life*, p. 701.

[4] Kennedy, *The Life of Elgar*, p. 209.

[5] How much 'Windflower' knew of Vera is unknown, but it seems that Elgar did not introduce them.

separated from her husband, a rabbi. She was in her thirties and Elgar in his seventies when they met on 7 November 1931. He would remember that date, and establish it for a parallel commemoration,

> the first 'mensiversary' of our meeting.[6] From that day the seventh of every month was to be a festival because he knew he would not live long enough to celebrate the years.
>
> . . . [Elgar said] I am going to give you a little book – Longfellow's *Hyperion* – which for many years belonged to my mother; since then it has gone with me everywhere. I want you to have it because you are my mother, my child, my lover and my friend.[7]

Vera was a revelation to him, a talented musician who girlishly adored the accomplished and much older man. She did not have the social position of Lady Stuart of Wortley, but to add to their similarities, her Jewishness made her as much of an outsider as his Roman Catholicism, and they might have bonded tightly. It is tempting to think that if he had met someone like her many years before, his relationship with his wife (by now dead, of course) would have been more sorely tested. He called Vera his 'dear little wife' and spoke to her openly about 'Carice, who is so clever but is alas buried alive in a Sussex village where there is no scope for her brains and energy; but one can do nothing for her'.[8] In giving Vera his mother's copy of *Hyperion* he granted her a connexion with the first big work – *The Black Knight* – that he had written at 'Forli' 40 years earlier, when he was nearer her age. As he had done with 'Windflower', he quickly set down his feelings for Vera in a musical idea that he marked 'V. H.' It was to be the second subject of his Third Symphony. For a second time, love for a woman who was not his wife was to lead to a creative surge.

Women were not the only creative fillip for Elgar, as we have seen in earlier chapters. It is legitimate to consider that Jaeger had a more pronounced effect on Elgar's composition than his wife, and probably fair also to say that in some sense Elgar felt more passionately about Jaeger than he did about her. The question is what 'in some sense' means.

---

[6] 'Mensiversary' means 'returning every month', a monthly commemoration of their meeting. There would be 26 before Elgar's death.
[7] Moore, *Creative Life*, p. 795.
[8] Ibid.

One cannot doubt the basic insights of recent stimulating work on the nature of Elgar's male friendships.[9] Elgar was keenly aware of the abominable fate of homosexuals in Edwardian Britain; a symptom of his deeply neurotic character was an apparent unwillingness to project an undisguised image of himself; and although he was generally communicative about the potential signification of elements of his major musical works, he was communicative only up to a point. Part of the reason for disclosing ostensibly private meanings of works might have been to distract listeners from the truth. For instance, the public dedication of the Second Symphony to the memory of Edward VII appears to cover its likely real dedication – to the 'Windflower'. It is possible, as Adams suggests, that in the *Variations* and *Falstaff* he used the 'characters' in his music to give himself cover for expressing homoerotic feelings.

There is no proof that Elgar's obvious and powerfully expressed love of his male friends was based on physical attraction. Adams does not suggest that there is. Elgar's relations with women other than Alice were transparently romantic, doubtless because in those cases he was only trifling with one taboo, adultery. This openness leads naturally to the feeling that homosexuality would be out of character for him. Yet in the deviousness of his general mask-wearing, there is another sense in which it would not be out of character at all for this raging heterosexual to be hiding a pinker secret.

Elgar's sexuality was no more unambiguous than his religious faith, his views on empire, or any other part of his public persona. He built an immovable barricade between his inner self and the world. It made him appear conventional; it is for us to peer through the chinks and wonder.

---

[9] See Adams, 'The "Dark Saying"', and 'Elgar's Later Oratorios'.

FIVE

WAR AND RETREAT (1914–18)

A different modernism

The years of the First World War were among Elgar's worst – emotionally, professionally, and physically. During them his public image waned and he began to seem an irrelevance;[1] his house was burgled; he suffered much ill health, losing his tonsils and collapsing on a train; and a worrying operation on Lady Elgar prefigured darker news. There was also a war to deal with.

The year began for Elgar with a different national problem, the question of home rule for Ireland. He was one of twenty signatories to a letter to the *Times* on 3 March 1914, opposing the bill that would have established it. Another binding commitment was celebrated on 8 May, the Elgars' silver wedding anniversary. Philip Leicester, the son of Elgar's friend Hubert, noted that he was looking noticeably older these days.[2] He remained technologically youthful, though, and was recording in June: *Pomp and Circumstance* No. 1, *Salut d'amour*, and the *Bavarian Dances* (see chapter 6 for more on his recording activity).

On the morning of 29 June two news items would have leapt out at Elgar from the morning paper. The previous day, Sardanapale had won the Grand Prix de Paris by a neck, and Archduke Franz Ferdinand had been killed in Sarajevo.[3] He went to Scotland on holiday on 19 July and was unable to hear the news of the outbreak of war on 4 August. After returning to London on 14 August he wrote to Schuster, asking how God dared to kill horses (but saying men and women could go to hell). Another letter in September showed delight in his new role in the Special Constabulary in Hampstead, with an arch acceptance of an invitation to

---

[1] 'Composers commonly go out of fashion shortly after their death; Elgar achieved this in his lifetime' (Rushton, *'Enigma' Variations*, p. 3).

[2] Anderson, *Elgar*, pp. 115–16.

[3] Norman Davies, *Europe: A History* (Oxford: Oxford University Press, 1996), p. 883.

stay with him ('I have to acknowledge the receipt of your letter . . . in which you ask that a special constable shall be detailed to visit The Hut for an indefinite period') and a list of further questions or instructions, one of which was 'State what feminine society The Hut will provide for No. 0015014'.[4]

Sarajevo might not have precipitated an immediate worldwide crisis, but Elgar's relative inactivity in 1914 signified a major musical turning point. Though he was perhaps not aware of it consciously, he was beginning a search for a new style after the modernism of 1904–13 had failed commercially, and seemed to offer no answer to the musical questions that were being posed in continental Europe and – following Henry Wood's premiere of Schoenberg's *Five Orchestral Pieces* on 3 September 1912 – in Britain. Critics have traditionally attributed Elgar's creative 'turn' to the death of Lady Elgar in 1920, but we should really identify it as a response to the first performances in Britain of avant-garde music by pioneers such as Schoenberg and Stravinsky. He reacted to his change in fortune by turning to a different audience, in the theatre, and paid little further attention to the concert hall till his last years.[5]

At the same time Sibelius, partly as a response to the commercial failure of his early modernist music, and partly also because the Zeitgeist had taken an unexpected turn at the lights, was following an almost exactly parallel course.[6] Gabriel Fauré (1845–1924) also worked imaginatively with old forms and language in a direct rejection of the avant-garde; his greatest chamber works date between 1916 and 1924. Nielsen, facing a personal crisis as well as the general European one,[7] was one of the first from this generation to respond in an essentially positive way to the new musical situation. Starting with his Fourth Symphony, 'Det uudslukkelige' ('The Inextinguishable', 1914–16), he stepped up the philosophical and experimental seriousness of his earlier works; his masterpiece, the Fifth Symphony, also belongs to this later period. An even later starter than Elgar, Leoš Janáček (1854–1928), coaxed out of his pupa by the musical activity round about, was just about to start writing his most characteristic music. Elsewhere in Europe the dominant stream of mature modernism was widening. Stravinsky was setting out his stall as the century's most important composer, taking the success of *The Firebird* on to ecstasy and riot with more ballets, *Petrushka* (1910–11),

---

[4] Young, *Elgar O.M.*, p. 174.

[5] The arrival of mature musical modernism in Britain was delayed, ironically enough, by Edward VII's death, which led to the cancellation of London performances of Stravinsky's *Firebird*; Richard Buckle, *Diaghilev* (London: Weidenfeld and Nicolson, 1979), p. 167.

[6] See James A. Hepokoski, 'Sibelius', in D. Kern Holoman (ed.), *The Nineteenth-Century Symphony* (New York: Schirmer, 1997), pp. 417–49, at p. 418.

[7] He began an eight-year separation from his wife after his infidelity and illegitimate children became too much for her to bear.

and the London premiere of *The Rite of Spring* (11 July 1913). Bartók was collecting folk tunes with Kodály and he too wrote a ballet, *The Wooden Prince* (1914–17). Schoenberg moved from the expressionist Second String Quartet (1907–8), *Five Orchestral Pieces* (1909), *Erwartung* (1909), and *Pierrot lunaire* (1912) towards the serialism of the *Variations for Orchestra* (1926–8) and the Third String Quartet (1927).

So Elgar was not alone in searching for a new approach to the changing musical situation; but his answer, typically, marked him out. He turned to a quite different audience, and developed a new, less challenging style to suit them. Continuity with his modernist style comes from the emphasis – now greatly amplified – on a particular treatment of diatonicism (the 'in-a-key' feel of eighteenth- and early-nineteenth-century music). This third phase is no less 'modern' than the second, but certainly seems more backward-looking. If this was to be his 'late style', there would be ample precedent for atavism; but the other side of 'the late style' in such classic exemplars as Beethoven is that at the same time as the music looks backwards in its language, it looks forwards in its form, technique, or philosophy, perhaps in a way that bewilders contemporary audiences. In his increasingly self-conscious use of outdated musical materials, we might say that Elgar's third style was, insofar as the term makes sense or has any useful function, 'postmodern'.

This may seem an odd choice of epithet for the man with the moustache, yet if the diatonicism of parts of Elgar's music before 1914 stands out as an image of a time passing (or passed) away, its increasing dominance after 1914 should invite reflexion. The post-1914 music often *sounds* untroubled and straightforward; soothing, even blithe. Its detractors, giving it little thought, find it disappointingly silent on the suffering of Europe, or of its new musical environment. Yet still others might think that its 'silence, like a poultice, comes to heal the blows of sound';[8] perhaps the most touching example of this is the testimony of a soldier in the trenches who wrote to say that he treasured a recording of songs from *The Starlight Express*, written in 1915. 'It is the only means of bringing back to us the days that are gone, and helping one through the Ivory gate that leads to fairy land or Heaven, whatever one likes to call it.'[9] In many cases modernist complexity would be out of place in the third-phase music. Elgar's light-hearted settings of Kipling, *Fringes of the Fleet*, are one such example. But not all of the music in this phase need be 'simple', and in works that could have had room for more serious musical language we can wonder what its suppression signifies. However consoling this music may be to those desperate to take relief from whatever they can find, there is in it,

---

[8] Oliver Wendell Holmes, 'The Music-Grinders', *The Complete Poetical Works* (Cambridge: Sampson Low, 1909), p. 13.

[9] Letter from J. Lawrence Fry, a soldier at the front, 5 October 1917, in Moore, *Creative Life*, p. 695.

as everywhere in Elgar's best music, a core of darker sentiment that both saddens and disquiets.

Slaying vampires in Europe

Elgar's musical activities in 1914 looked feebler than they had done at any point in his career since the early 1890s. On 20 January he recorded *Carissima*, a short orchestral piece written for the Gramophone Company (which became 'Electric and Musical Industries', EMI, after a merger with Columbia in March 1931). It was a signal moment in the history of composer recordings. Right up to his final days on his deathbed he was sent test and final pressings of records. His only new compositions that year were remarkably small-scale, a sign of his sensitivity to the changing public attitude towards him. He wrote six part songs (or perhaps seven: the date of one is uncertain) and sketched parts of a Piano Concerto that never saw the light of day.[10] These he sent to Alice Stuart-Wortley, who played them through for him.

As a direct response to Germany's invasion of Belgium, in September Elgar finalized a new poem for 'Land of Hope and Glory' with Arthur Benson, the author of its two earlier incarnations.[11] It was published in the *Times* with the intention of bending the national song to the war effort.

> Land of Hope and Glory, Mother of the free,
> How shall we uphold thee, who are born of thee!
> Gird thee well for battle, bid thy hosts increase.
> Stand for faith and honour, strike for truth and peace.[12]

The new text didn't take off. On 10 November Elgar telephoned Tita Brands Cammaerts, the daughter of the first Angel in *Gerontius* (Marie Brema), and now wife of Émile Cammaerts, a royalist Belgian poet. The plight of Belgium in the early days of the war moved Elgar deeply, and after reading Cammaerts's poem 'Après Anvers' ('After Antwerp'; the Siege of Antwerp from 28 September to 10 October had been devastating) decided to set it for reciter and orchestra as his *Carillon*, Op. 75 ('Carillon' was the title of the English translation by Mme Cammaerts). It started a series of wartime theatre pieces, presenting Elgar with the new audience he needed, and the space to develop his new style; it was also the first of three collaborations with Cammaerts, a series written with diminishing enthusiasm.

---

[10] A performing version has been recorded, but the quantity (and quality) of material Elgar left does not encourage interest.
[11] For their interesting correspondence see Elgar, *Letters of a Lifetime*, pp. 277–83.
[12] Young, *Elgar O.M.*, p. 173.

The first poem defiantly implores Belgians to reclaim their cities, and one-up Germany by marching on Berlin. Rosa Burley suggested to Elgar that he might 'provide an illustrative prelude and entr'actes as background music for a recitation of the poem'.[13] This became the model for all three Cammaerts settings. *Carillon* is in a vigorous 3/4 time with forward-driving dotted rhythms and the carillon itself cutting across in duple time. The sound represents the ruined bell towers and churches of Flanders, and suggests that religion – of a popularly imagined, essentially nationalist sort – is Belgium's chief hope. Over the orchestra a speaker recites the poem. It was recorded early in 1915 and became immensely popular, encouraging Elgar to feel that his best contribution to the war effort would be through music. He resigned as a special constable and joined the Hampstead Volunteer Reserve in April 1915. Carice, now 24 and a gifted linguist, joined the Censorship Department in the War Office.[14]

Elgar completed his second Cammaerts setting, *Une voix dans le désert* ('A Voice in the Desert'), Op. 77, a year later. Again Mme Cammaerts was the translator of her husband's text, in which there is a strong spiritual element. A little girl sings of the day when the spring will come again, 'And then our graves will flower / Beneath the peace of God'; the image touchingly focuses the blind destructiveness of war. The orchestration is smaller than in *Carillon*, and bleaker too: on either side of the beautiful central soprano solo, 'Quand nos bourgeons se rouvriront' ('When Our Buds Reopen'), muted strings and side drum add grave world-weariness to the little girl's voice. There is no hope for victory, only rebirth after the holocaust. Its composition led to a meeting with the young conductor Thomas Beecham, whom Alice took agin, apparently for no reason other than that he drank water at tea-time.[15] (A third Cammaerts setting, *Le drapeau belge*, 'The Belgian Flag', was written under sufferance in 1916, to fulfil a publisher's contract, but not performed until the following year. It sets a drab reflexion on the symbolism of the flag's colours.)[16]

In January 1915 Sidney Colvin (1845–1927), a Fellow at Trinity College, Cambridge, whom Elgar had met at a Schuster dinner party in 1904, had tried to interest Elgar in a setting of some poems by Laurence Binyon (1869–1943).[17] Elgar sketched music for one, 'For the Fallen', now much anthologized.

---

[13] Burley and Carruthers, *Record of a Friendship*, p. 198.

[14] Moore, *Creative Life*, p. 682.

[15] Young, *Elgar O.M.*, p. 179.

[16] This third poem was translated by Lord Curzon of Kedleston, a former Viceroy of India, the undoing of whose partition of Bengal had led to the commission for *The Crown of India*.

[17] In 1913 he had written on Thomas Hardy's behalf to try to persuade Elgar to write an opera on *The Trumpet Major, The Return of the Native, A Pair of Blue Eyes*, or the *Dynasts*, but *Falstaff* was on Elgar's mind at the time, and nothing came of it. See Moore, *Creative Life*, p. 649.

> They shall not grow old, as we that are left grow old:
> Age shall not weary them, nor the years condemn.
> At the going down of the sun and in the morning
> We will remember them.

There was a problem with its completion. Cyril Rootham of St John's College, Cambridge, had already completed a setting, which was to be published by Novello. Elgar felt unable, as a matter of honour to another composer, to continue with a competing version, and wrote to apologize to Binyon, who urged Elgar with bitter disappointment to 'think of what you are witholding [*sic*] from your countrymen and women. Surely it would be wrong to let them lose this help and consolation . . . I am sure that Rootham would agree with me.' (In fact he was wrong: Rootham was furious.) Colvin wrote a still more prickly letter, Oxbridge-cocky.

> Surely, granted that the majority of [Britons] are not very sensitive to the appeal of art, you cannot in your heart fail to realise that there is a big minority passionately sensitive to it, to whom your work makes all the difference in their lives, & whom – forgive me – you have no right to rob of such a hope as you were holding out to them a month ago . . . Do the work you had promised & begun . . . do it for your country & the future & to honour and justify the gift that has been given you . . . P.S. The above is not to be answered except by deeds.[18]

Elgar did as instructed, turning attention to Binyon's 'Fourth of August', whose opening lines would give the full work its title: 'Now in thy splendour go before us, / Spirit of England, ardent-eyed'. Its penultimate verse characterized the German nation as inhuman, 'Vampire of Europe's wasted will'. Elgar said that he paused before setting this, hoping that 'some trace of manly spirit would shew itself in the direction of German affairs' before deciding on using the 'Demons' Chorus' from *Gerontius*,[19] but his words could be misleading. It was common to attribute inhumanity, bestiality, to 'the Hun', but he did not think that German culture alone was degenerate: the entire European experiment in civilization was in freefall.[20]

The Spirit of England, Op. 80 (1915–17), is a powerful work, and was well received in its time, if unfairly sidelined now. Ernest Newman said 'here in truth is the very voice of England, moved to the centre of her being in

---

[18] Letters of 27 March 1915 and 13 April 1915, in Elgar, *Letters of a Lifetime*, pp. 288–90.
[19] Moore, *Creative Life*, p. 677.
[20] Daniel Grimley makes a similar point in Daniel M. Grimley, '"Music in the Midst of Desolation": Structures of Mourning in Elgar's *The Spirit of England*', in Harper-Scott and Rushton (eds.), *Elgar Studies*.

the war as she has probably never been moved before in all her history'.[21] Though its text has elements of jingoism in it, this is not a nationalist work in any negative sense – not unless it is forbidden for a country in time of war to convince itself that it is in the right. As Daniel M. Grimley demonstrates, 'it can be understood as part of wider cultural discourse about the war in which images of mourning are of central importance'.[22] Mourning in this work is presented, as its reminiscences of *Gerontius* suggest, in a religious context even more obvious than in the Cammaerts settings. The implication is that it is through the reassuringly repetitive acts of ritual that music can heal the wounds of war.

The work was premiered in two parts: 'To Women' and 'For the Fallen' together (but under different conductors) in Leeds on 3 May 1916, and the whole piece (including the first movement, 'The Fourth of August') in Birmingham on 4 October 1917.

Elgar had met Ignacy Jan Paderewski (1860–1941), a pianist and composer in an old-fashioned Polish nationalist style, at a concert reception in 1899.[23] Paderewski turned statesman during the war (becoming prime minister of Poland briefly in 1919) and established a 'Polish Relief Fund' in response to destruction on the Eastern Front. Elgar was inveigled into writing music in support of it in April 1915. He duly produced a 'symphonic prelude', *Polonia*, Op. 76, somewhat better than an occasional piece (and streets ahead of the Cammaerts settings). The title came from a symphony of that name by Emil Młynarski, part of which was to be played in the same concert as the premiere of Elgar's work.[24] It contains a decent Elgarian A-minor march idea followed by a sub-*Pomp-and-Circumstance* trio theme (replete with immediate grand climax) and several Polish themes: two national hymns – 'z dymem Pozarow' ('With the Smoke of the Buildings') and 'Jeszcce Polska nie Zginela' ('Poland Is Not Yet Lost') – a delicious silvery orchestration of Chopin's G-minor Nocturne, and a theme from Paderewski's own *Fantaisie Polonaise* (*Polish Fantasia*). The premiere was poorly attended, perhaps owing to bad advertising, but Alice over-egged as usual: 'Enormous audience, the real *roar* there is for E. – his own roar I always calls it'.[25]

In fairyland

Ten days in summer 1915 were spent near Ravenglass in Cumbria with the Stuart-Wortleys. Elgar went alone at first but Alice arrived after a few days,

---

[21] Ernest Newman, '"The Spirit of England": Edward Elgar's New Choral Work', *Musical Times*, 57 (1916), pp. 235–9, at p. 239.
[22] Grimley, 'Structures of Mourning'.
[23] Moore, *Creative Life*, p. 268.
[24] Młynarski was conductor of the Scottish Symphony Orchestra and had visited Elgar on 13 April to commission the work.
[25] Moore, *Creative Life*, p. 683.

in time to grumble about churches ruined by 'that Hun Henry VIII'.[26] He also visited his sister Pollie several times in 1914 and 1915 at Stoke Prior, her place in the Worcestershire countryside. Back in London, on 9 November 1915 Elgar was approached by Robin Legge, music critic for the *Daily Telegraph*, to write incidental music for a theatrical adaptation by Violet Pearn of Algernon Blackwood's novel *A Prisoner in Fairyland*. It would become *The Starlight Express*, Op. 78, his biggest war-time work (see figure 23, overleaf).

The novel's story concerns a businessman, Henry Rogers, who leaves London to stay with relatives in the Jura mountains. The children there consider grown-ups like Henry to be 'wumbled', which means (more or less) that although they might think up wonderful ideas – their father is an author with writer's block, and Henry himself has visionary schemes for social improvement – these ideas get muddled on the way out because adults have lost the child's fruitfully imaginative engagement with the world. 'Wumbled' adults can be 'unwumbled' by 'coming out' of their bodies at night and wandering the skies, collecting 'stardust' with children.[27] Henry is the first to 'come out', and with the children he gradually unwumbles the rest of the adult community, including Father, who can now write down the story he has been struggling with.

For *The Starlight Express* Elgar borrowed music from the *Wand of Youth* suites, and set *The First Nowell* for the scene added for the stage version, in which the Star of Jerusalem rises as a sign that a particular child is the only hope for mankind's redemption. It is a mawkish moment, but more intellectually defensible (to those of a religious bent) than the suggestion that childhood itself is the solution. The best music comes in Act II, as adults are being drawn out of their bodies, with music in the style of the *Falstaff* interludes to accompany the process. Daddy's unwumbling is the most touching moment, with a beautiful song, 'They'll Listen to My Song', for one of the sprites (the magical creatures who help the children; each is a transformed character from their everyday life).

The music throughout is simply diatonic – self-consciously so – and either cynically modernist or postmodern, depending on one's viewpoint. It delights, as the letter from the soldier at the front quoted above attests, but this brand of nostalgia is also troubling, for we know that things were never like this, and that solutions are never so easy. Particularly not in time of war. It was premiered on 29 December 1915 and ran only until 29 January 1916. Critics disliked it ('it is preachy and pretentious. It pretends to be meant for children, but is canvassing all the while for grown-up sentiment'), and Elgar scholars feel little different (Diana McVeagh says that

[26] Anderson, *Elgar*, p. 122.
[27] It is impossible in a world so fatuously obsessed with paedophilia that the play could ever be restaged.

22. Cover for the full score of the concert overture Cockaigne.

23. Programme cover for the play The Starlight Express, *based on Algernon Blackwood's novel* A Prisoner in Fairyland, *adapted by Violet Pearn, and with music by Elgar.*

'it is pompous and it is trivial'.)[28] It was never published (the publishers wanted something as popular as *Peter Pan*, and were bound to be disappointed) and has been rarely heard since. A BBC presentation of the music with a truncated version of the play was broadcast in 1965 and again in 2004, but the music can only otherwise be easily heard in recordings of a suite Elgar made from it.[29]

In July 1916 Elgar was again at Stoke Prior,[30] and Alice Stuart-Wortley visited. A letter to her makes clear the importance of this place, or any other that could be purely *theirs*, unpolluted by association with his wife.

> I am glad you 'feel' Stoke – that is a place where I see & *hear* (yes!) you. A. has not been there since *1888* & does not care to go & no one of my friends has ever been but you. No one has seen my fields & my 'common' or my trees – only the Windflower and I found her namesakes growing there . . . Bless you.[31]

It was also a year of much ill-health; Menière's disease (progressively worsening ear trouble) had been diagnosed in 1912, possibly inaccurately,[32] and he imagined sometimes that he would lose his hearing altogether, with ruinous effect on his musical life. There were hard words written on Elgar in a *History of Music* by Stanford and Cecil Forsyth published that year: it was said that Elgar 'was lucky enough to enter the field and find the preliminary ploughing already done'. Supportive scuffling among friends now would be dwarfed towards the end of Elgar's life by reaction to a more substantial criticism by E. J. Dent (see next chapter). Good news came from outside his official family: Alice Stuart-Wortley's husband was made a baron, and she would now be styled Lady Stuart of Wortley. No matter; Elgar still called her 'Windflower'.

That autumn and winter friends dropped like flies, principal among them Richter and George Sinclair. Then in 1917 Elgar joined the ballet-writing fraternity when he was asked to score *The Sanguine Fan* (Op. 81), based on a fan design by Charles Conder, to raise money for war charities.[33] It is no *Rite of Spring*. The story depicted on the fan concerns a young boy and two girls in a wood, kneeling before a shrine to Eros (god of sex). After some tempting flirtation with Echo, a Greek nymph with a particularly cruel

---

[28] Moore, *Creative Life*, p. 693, and McVeagh, *Elgar: Life and Music*, pp. 186–7.

[29] For more on *The Starlight Express*, see J. P. E. Harper-Scott, 'Elgar's Unwumbling: The Theatre Music', in Grimley and Rushton (eds.), *The Cambridge Companion to Elgar*, pp. 171–83.

[30] An attempted visit in April was called off when he collapsed on the train and was taken to a nursing home in Oxford. See Anderson, *Elgar*, p. 126.

[31] A letter of 16 August 1917, quoted in Moore, *Creative Life*, p. 698.

[32] A doctor consulted by Moore about Elgar's symptoms said that it might have been 'chronic tonsillitis in fearful combination with worry and profound unhappiness about himself and the changing of his world' (ibid., p. 715).

[33] 'Sanguine' here means 'red'.

way of treating men, the boy curses Eros for the obvious reason, and is immediately struck dead by lightning. Elgar set the tale to a delicate minuet in eighteenth-century colours which occasionally remembers the 'Enigma' theme and Violin Concerto. The thunderstorm has little venom in his hands, and the piece ends quietly.[34] The ballet had been intended for only one performance, which was given on 20 March 1917; its success can be gauged by the fact that there was just one further performance, on 22 May.

After dallying with the idea for a year, Elgar finished setting four songs in 'a broad saltwater style'[35] on texts by Kipling, in time for a premiere on 11 June. The author had objected to his verse being set as low musical entertainment (singers dressed up in fishing boots and sou'westers) but eventually capitulated. More important during that summer was a visit to a cottage in the countryside near Petworth and Fittleworth, West Sussex, called 'Brinkwells'. Only six years after Alice had insisted they move to London, Elgar had a new home in the country. He would spend much time, and write some of his best later music, there in the next few years. During the run of *Fringes of the Fleet*, Kipling became agitated again and Elgar reluctantly withdrew the piece. 'Most of what I do is not worth much from a financial point of view, and if I do happen to write something that "goes" with the public and by which I look like benefiting financially, some perverse fate always intervenes and stops it immediately.'[36] The songs had been an enormous commercial success – Elgar's last.

Chamber music in the country

In March 1918 Elgar had a tonsillectomy, which seemed to cure the symptoms previously diagnosed as Menière's disease. Within days he sketched the first theme of what would become the Cello Concerto, one of four works, Opp. 82–5, to be written in either E minor or A minor, mostly at Brinkwells (where he was from 2 May to 27 December 1918, doing without a piano until 19 August). The first, begun in March, was the String Quartet in E minor, Op. 83, which he completed after some effort on 24 December. The Violin Sonata in E minor, Op. 82, was composed quickly between 20 August and 15 September, on which latter date the Piano Quintet in A minor, Op. 84, was begun. That would be finished on 9 February 1919, but is best discussed here.

The String Quartet was Elgar's first completed effort in the genre and the instigator of over a year of chamber-music composition (1918–19),

[34] Pan is also at hand, and Matthew Riley has fascinating things to say on Elgar's nature imagery – in which Pan features largely – in this work and others like *The Dream of Gerontius*, in Matthew Riley, 'Rustling Reeds and Lofty Pines: Elgar and the Music of Nature', *19th-Century Music*, 16 (2000), pp. 155–77.

[35] Letter to Newman, 17 June 1917, quoted in Moore, *Creative Life*, p. 706.

[36] Reed, *Elgar*, p. 121.

which might have been suggested by W. W. Cobbett's proposal that composers should aspire 'to provide a corpus of works to head an English tradition of non-Teutonic chamber music'. As Daniel M. Grimley points out, however, Elgar chose a definitely German style for these chamber works, and also nodded to Fauré, which suggests that they are better understood as broadly European than narrowly English works.[37]

The chamber works, among Elgar's most touching and satisfying, return to the familiar topics of loss, melancholy, and the failure of deflated heroism. Their difference from earlier works such as the symphonies or the *Introduction and Allegro* lies in the fact that now heroism is not presented as a realistic possibility, but kept meaningfully absent from the music. The first movement of the Violin Sonata, for instance, denies its sonata form the traditional directional, often heroic, energy of the drive to the dominant key (a fifth above the tonic). Its material dissolves flatwards, towards the subdominant (a fifth below the tonic). This technique is calculated to shut off the possibilities for building tension whose resolution could then bring a sense of achievement, even redemption. The finale also discountenances the traditional 'heroic' ending to minor-key works, the glorious final statement of an important theme in the tonic major. Here, the expectation is created that the theme will be a remembrance of the second movement, the 'Romance', but Elgar steers away from the tonic major, keeping things in the minor, creating a 'crisis in the Sonata's heroic male subject'.[38]

The String Quartet is also written in Elgar's characteristic third-phase diatonicism. It finds new things to say by using a language that has superficial resemblances to one from the previous century, but is in fact forward-looking in the sense that it is a rejection of his own most recent style. This has the effect of rethinking what the preceding style seemed so darkly to say. Though not a masterpiece, it is unjustly neglected.

The Piano Quintet opens weirdly, darkly, with music often associated with ghost stories, some of them with roots in Blackwood.[39] The first movement is a tense disagreement over whether the five instrumentalists are playing against each other (as in the opening) or together (as in the luscious 'Spanish' second theme). The coda returns comfortably to the tonic, but only with the opening music, underlining the old tension. The glorious slow movement promises more hope but builds to an

---

[37] See Brian Trowell, 'The Road to Brinkwells: The Late Chamber Music', in Lewis Foreman (ed.), *"Oh My Horses!": Elgar and the Great War* (Rickmansworth: Elgar Editions, 2001), pp. 353–62, at p. 367, and Grimley, '"A Smiling with a Sigh"', pp. 129–30. The discussion of the chamber works that follows draws heavily on Grimley's superb essay.

[38] Grimley, '"A Smiling with a Sigh"', p. 132. He says later (p. 138) that this male subject can be understood as Elgar himself.

[39] Michael Allis traces some of the connexions in Michael Allis, 'Elgar, Lytton, and the Piano Quintet, Op. 84', *Music & Letters*, 85 (2004), pp. 198–238.

anxious climax in the development, and has a slightly tentative coda. The finale's confident main theme seems assured, diatonic and strong (unlike the chromatic music that opens the work), a direct contradiction of the frequent uncertainty of the preceding music. The outcome is similar to earlier works built on a conflict between chromatic and diatonic music: the final return of the 'heroic' main finale theme comes after the most ghastly chromatic episode of the movement. Its strength is doubtful.

By the time he completed the chamber music the war had ended, but there were more troubles at home. Alice was almost 70 and had begun to suffer from ill health. He established a trust to take care of Carice in case either parent should die. Elgar had more of the old ear trouble, and a nasty boil appeared on Alice's forehead. She consulted a physician in London in October and was taken into a nursing home to have it removed, leaving a large scar. Returning to Brinkwells, a cough kept her in bed for days on end. Letters written to friends at the time modulate from concern about Alice to the more practical difficulty of nursing an ailing wife.

> It means another interruption & the future is dark as A. poor dear is not well . . . It means that if I have to live again at Hampstead composition is 'off' – not the house or the place but London – telephones etc all day and night drive me mad![40]

The uncertainty would not last long. On 29 December 1918 they returned to Severn House, 13 days after a robbery there, which had caused much distress. They would spend only one more summer together at Brinkwells.

---

[40] Letter to Schuster, 3 December 1918, quoted in Moore, *Creative Life*, p. 732.

A man in short trousers

Built into modernist music is a critique of the various cultural assumptions upon which it relies. These might be purely formal, or more broadly social. Sonata form ranges across both areas, since the genre in which it typically operates, the symphony, depends on a social context, the bourgeois concert, for its survival and propagation. In works like the Second Symphony Elgar formulates answers both to 'purely musical' and also to 'social' or 'political' questions. On one hand he engages with the traditional symphonic sonata form, questioning its message of struggle and redemption (learnt from Beethoven). On the other hand, through showing the problem of writing a traditional symphony in 1911 he asks whether the social context – indeed society more generally – is sustainable in its present form.

One aspect of his technique that holds special fascination is his treatment of diatonicism. In some cases this seems to promise a kind of Wagnerian redemption. This is diatonicism at the service of cultural conservatism and the promise of a renewed life, at one with nature and away from machines. The nostalgic element of his diatonicism points to an ahistorical, ideal world. In critiquing this tradition he suggests that such hope cannot be guaranteed.

In other cases, Elgar makes an explicit link with a different past, the universally experienced past of 'the child'. Here too he joins in a cultural tradition, but a different and slightly older one. It is the tradition of the 'Romantic Child'. The first hint given that he was entering the particular world of this symbolic infant is in a passage he quoted above the score of *Dream Children*, Op. 43 (1902).

> And while I stood gazing, both the children gradually grew fainter to my view, receding, and still receding till nothing at last but two mournful features were seen in the uttermost distance, which, without speech, strangely impressed upon me the effects of speech: 'We are not of Alice, nor of thee, nor are we children at all . . . We are nothing; less than nothing, and dreams. *We are only what might have been.*'[1]

[1] From Charles Lamb, 'Dream-Children: A Revery', which gave *Dream Children* its title. The emphasis is Elgar's.

Charles Lamb, the author of those words, was part of a Victorian literary tradition that idealized childhood as an 'innocent' state.[2] A child's wonder in the face of the world was felt to lead to a profounder understanding of the nature of things than could be experienced in adulthood. Adults are too worldly and everyday to properly hold on to the magical understanding of youth. This is the sentiment of such poems as Wordsworth's 'Ode: Intimations of Immortality from Recollections of Early Childhood':

> There was a time when meadow, grove, and stream,
> The earth, and every common sight,
> To me did seem
> Apparelled in celestial light,
> The glory and the freshness of a dream.
> It is not now as it hath been of yore . . .
> The things which I have seen I now can see no more.
> (ll. 1–9)

Adulthood is felt to be cursed with a painful loss of insight and pleasure in the perpetual newness of experience. Regaining the innocent insight of childhood is, on this view, a prize worth seeking. Literature in this tradition is familiar: J. M. Barrie's *Peter Pan*, Lewis Carroll's stories about Alice, and – more expressly for adults – Blake's *Songs of Innocence* (which laud the state of childhood innocence) and his *Songs of Experience* (which bemoan its passing).[3] The Romantic Child has remained a powerful theme in literature. Even after the pleasing grotesqueness of Roald Dahl, in which children are sometimes portrayed quite cheerfully as the causes of horrific suffering (as of the grandmother in *George's Marvellous Medicine*), the novels of writers like J. K. Rowling depend on an understanding of a child as someone untainted by the nastiness of adult life – and in Hogwarts the magic of childhood is made real.

The two short orchestral pieces called *Dream Children* establish a topic of 'childhood' in Elgar's music, rich for later development. His choice to emphasize the last words of his quotation from Lamb is telling, and an early sign that his engagement with the Romantic Child would be critical. In Elgar's hands, children are not straightforwardly beacons of hope; they are reminders of

---

[2] Michael Allis locates Elgar in this tradition with particular reference to *Dream Children* and *The Starlight Express* in Michael Allis, 'Elgar and the Art of Retrospective Narrative', *Journal of Musicological Research,* 19 (2000), pp. 298–328.
[3] Rousseau's *Émile* is a pivotal text in the transition to this way of thinking.

failure. They stand not for 'what might be' in a future utopia, but for *'what might have been'* – something that is no longer open as a possibility. Another literary infant springs to mind: Little Father Time in Hardy's *Jude the Obscure*, the boy who hangs himself and his half-siblings because (picking up on an incautious remark of their mother's) *'we are too menny'*. In Elgar childhood doesn't comfort – it warns. He might well have approved of the premise of William Golding's *Lord of the Flies*.

The case is similar in *Falstaff*. The 'dream interlude' in that work shows Falstaff as a boy, when he was page to the Duke of Norfolk. The music is in Elgar's most old-fashioned diatonic tone – he himself called the interlude 'antiquated'[4] – and the image it conjures is both nostalgic and, to those familiar with the tradition of the Romantic Child (which means almost all of us), somehow reassuring. But that is only on the surface. The interlude ends and we are returned to the drama of the piece. Falstaff is soon to be rejected by his friend, Prince Hal. By dreaming that his life is still full of promise Falstaff is showing himself to have no strong grasp on the reality of his present situation. The positive message of his childhood is a lie. Furthermore, since Falstaff is an Everyman, Shakespeare's best example of human freedom, the message is applied by extension to all of us.

Falstaff is a work with an obviously adult tone, in which images of childhood play only a relatively small (if crucial) part. In *The Starlight Express*, however, childhood is the main focus. Its story of 'unwumbling' is straightforwardly charming on one level (and saccharine on another), until one reflects on its message, which is that adult problems can only be solved by becoming a child again. Yet children grow back into adults and then presumably the cycle starts all over again. Unwumbling is therefore palliative – pain-relief, not a cure.

The problem Elgar's music of childhood broods on is actually symptomatic of a particular view of children, a view based on the assertion that children are 'innocent'. On the evidence of his music for *The Starlight Express* one can say confidently that Elgar would have shared W. H. Auden's belief that 'no boy is innocent, [and] he has no clear notion of innocence, nor does he know that to be no longer innocent, but to wish that one were, is part of the definition of an adult'.[5] The implied, rather hopeless cycle of attempts to find redemption – through a return to a state that

---

[4] Elgar, 'Analytical Note', at p. 578.

[5] W. H. Auden, 'Dingley Dell & the Fleet', *The Dyer's Hand and Other Essays* (London: Faber and Faber, 1963), pp. 407–28, at p. 409.

logically leads back to the place where the problem was identified – also ties the work in with one theme of Elgar's early modernist works. An example is the First Symphony, in which the return to the work's opening music in its final bars might seem superficially reassuring, but is on reflexion seen to be problematic. Another is the Second Symphony, where the finale's apparent failure to regain the Spirit of Delight says that return to safety is unfeasible.

Elgar's suffocation of the tradition of the Romantic Child is the murder of romanticism's last great assurance. If even children are not a model of innocent goodness, where can we look for encouragement to hope?

24. A typically sentimental visualization of the Romantic Child, taken from a Victorian postcard.

SIX

REGROUPING AND REBIRTH (1919–34)

A different country

Elgar's last 15 years began with the death of his wife and ended with Hitler's first year as Chancellor of Germany. During this period many of Elgar's composer contemporaries died: Puccini, Fauré, Stanford, and Busoni in 1924; Janáček in 1928; Nielsen in 1931; Gustav Holst (born 1874) and Frederick Delius (born 1862) both months after Elgar in 1934; Strauss would linger till 1949.

The mainstream modernists Schoenberg and Stravinsky continued to hold the world's attention, and in England, new voices began to speak. Holst and Ralph Vaughan Williams (1872–1958) had been composing in Elgar's shadow, though in a quite different spirit, for some years. Holst's *Somerset Rhapsody* (1906) and Vaughan Williams's *In the Fen Country* (1904) and three *Norfolk Rhapsodies* (1905–7) showed the influence of their folksong collecting, something that did not interest Elgar at all. Vaughan Williams had approached Elgar for lessons in orchestration in his early thirties and 'received a polite reply from Lady Elgar saying that Sir Edward was too busy to give me lessons but suggesting that I should become a pupil of Professor Bantock . . . But though Elgar would not teach me personally he could not help teaching me through his music'.[1] Holst and Vaughan Williams were close friends and musical confidants, having regular meetings that they called 'Field Days'. During these they would play, discuss, and improve each other's works.[2]

---

[1] Quoted in Michael Kennedy, *The Works of Ralph Vaughan Williams*, 2nd edn. (London: Oxford University Press, 1980; orig. edn. 1964), p. 59.

[2] This was an age of clubbable creative men in England. In Oxford, a group called 'The Coalbiters' that formed to read old Scandinavian sagas together developed eventually into 'The Inklings', a set of writers of myths and sagas in a related but modernized tradition, sharing and criticizing each other's work, as Holst and Vaughan Williams did. Their membership included C. S. Lewis and J. R. R. Tolkien.

Holst emerged as a major composer in 1919 with his orchestral masterpiece *The Planets*. With works including *Beni Mora* (1908), *The Hymn of Jesus* (1917), the neglected *Ode to Death* (1919), and the tone pictures *Egdon Heath* (1929) and *Hammersmith* (1930), he created a distinctive body of English composition. Vaughan Williams, one of the most instantly recognizable composers in twentieth-century Western music, had already made his mark in 1910 with the *Fantasia on a Theme by Thomas Tallis* and *A London Symphony* (Symphony No. 2, 1911–13); in this later period he was to move in increasingly dark directions with the Third Symphony ('Pastoral', 1921), *Sancta Civitas* (1923–5), *Flos Campi* (1925), the 'masque for dancing' *Job* (1927–30), and the catastrophic explosions of the Fourth Symphony (1934). In this emerging new British symphonic tradition Arnold Bax (1883–1953) would contribute notable examples in his first six symphonies (1922–34; the seventh and last followed in 1938–9). Meanwhile, the man who would take Elgar's place as unofficial musician laureate, William Walton (1901–83), made a significant early start in this period, with his politely scandalous *Façade* (first performed 1922), a modern–romantic Viola Concerto (1929), and *Belshazzar's Feast* (1932).[3]

A kind of honorary Englishness was bestowed on Sibelius in the 1920s, and it was his symphonies, not Elgar's, that seemed most promisingly modern to these emerging composers. The musical world was suddenly unrecognizable to those of an earlier generation. Only Schuster believed that nothing had changed, and that his soirées could continue in 1918 just as they had done in 1914. War didn't despoil them of cultural relevance as seriously as these musical developments.

Almost all of this made Elgar an alien. Though painful to him, and a change in domestic circumstances almost insuperably hard to bear, the death of Lady Elgar on 7 April 1920 did not itself end his composing career, no matter what the conventional wisdom says. The rejection of his early modernist music before the war had been a body blow; the increasing reconditeness of his 'postmodern' music – which seemed to impatient critics both old-fashioned and irrelevant – revealed him to be taking a fruitless course. The 1920s were therefore, first, a time of adjustment at home, and musically a slow but resolute motion, sustained by the comforts of theatre composition and commercial arrangements, towards a new style that death would prevent him from achieving fully. Its first monument was to have been the Third Symphony. The sketches he left behind for that work preserve some of the most consummate music

[3] Elgar attended a Worcester Three Choirs performance of the Viola Concerto in 1932 and did not like it, 'deploring that such music should be thought fit for a stringed instrument'; Michael Kennedy, *Portrait of Walton* (Oxford: Oxford University Press, 1989), p. 52.

he ever wrote, and show no evidence of a dwindling musical intellect or ambition.

Burying the dead

Elgar returned to 'Severn House' at the end of 1918 after a summer spent writing the Cello Concerto, partly at 'Brinkwells'. Lady Elgar was scarcely able to leave the house for long stretches, but she went out to post the full score of the concerto to the publisher. Post-war austerity led her to acknowledge finally on 2 September 1919 that 'Severn House' must be sold. Fourteen days later they returned to 'Brinkwells' – for what was to be Alice's last visit.

Philip Leicester, who had thought Elgar had looked suddenly older at the start of the war, felt this still more keenly now. 'His hair & moustache are now more white than grey. His face is paler. Otherwise he seems unchanged. The same low voice, rapid earnest speech, keen sense of humour, & quick movement'.[4] This increased pallor, partially concealed by a lingering vigour, was evident in the concerto.

The Cello Concerto in E minor, Op. 85, is an anatomy of melancholy. That alone explains both its long-held status as one of England's favourite pieces of classical music, and also our picture of Elgar as a gloomy romantic. Its churning, aimless, piercingly sorrowful main theme rises and falls in dynamic intensity as its instrumentation is enriched and denuded, wrapping the scarified limbs of the war-wounded around the first movement's arch form. One thing that marks this music out from what Elgar had written before is that there is no longer a vision of the happy place that is gone; now there is only loss, perpetual loss, and the heavy certainty that there could never be a past, present, or future *without* loss. Elgarian climaxes almost always fade within bars, as if the strength that created them is exhausted in the effort of the ascent. In this concerto's first movement, rare moments of passion seem to burn off the orchestra like alcohol on a wound, leaving only the self-pitying cries of the cello behind in the texture. Passages in the second and fourth movements have a quick, increasingly pompous energy, but the touching sadness of the slow movement – which ends in mid-thought with an imperfect cadence, a device Elgar might have been intending to use again in the slow movement of his Third Symphony – puts a limit on its positive effect. The return of the intense brooding of the first movement's opening at the end of the finale seals the matter. In a gesture that recalls the conclusion of the *Introduction and Allegro* or (where it is much bigger) the First Symphony, Elgar returns to grandiose display for the closing fifteen bars. Their verve is entirely conventional, and in any case

---

[4] Letter of 2 November 1919, quoted in Moore, *A Creative Life*, p. 747.

minor-key. Melancholy is all-consuming. Newman said that the concerto was 'the realisation in tone of a fine spirit's lifelong wistful brooding upon the loveliness of earth'.[5] He gleaned that through probably the worst premiere of a work of Elgar, in a hall that was not full (27 October 1919). Three months later Elgar conducted a recording of the work with the cellist Beatrice Harrison, the first of his concerto recordings with young artists. (The second was of the Violin Concerto with Yehudi Menuhin in 1933.)

In January 1920 the first issue of a new academic periodical, *Music & Letters*, presented a sterling defence of Elgar by George Bernard Shaw, which placed him at the highest point of European composition.

> Elgar is carrying on Beethoven's business. The names are up on the shop front for everyone to read. ELGAR late BEETHOVEN & CO., . . . Symphonies, Overtures, Chamber Music, Bagatelles.
>
> . . . You can rave about Stravinsky without the slightest risk of being classed as a lunatic by the next generation . . . But if you say that Elgar's Cockaigne overture contains every classic quality of a concert overture with every lyric and dramatic quality of the overture to Die Meistersinger you are . . . damning yourself to all critical posterity by a *gaffe* that will make your grandson blush for you.
>
> Personally, I am prepared to take the risk. What do I care about my grandson? give me Cockaigne.
>
> . . . If I were a king, or a Minister of Fine Arts, I would give Elgar an annuity of a thousand a year on condition that he produced a symphony every eighteen months.[6]

It was now only a few months before her death, but Alice wrote to thank Shaw for the article. He would later start an unlikely friendship with Elgar – he a socialist atheist, Elgar a spiritual Tory – and produce through insistent nagging a symphonic commission not wholly unlike the one he whimsically outlined in his article.

Also in January Elgar wrote a revision, with less chromaticism (and less interest), of 'For the Fallen' (called *With Proud Thanksgiving*) for the dedication of the Cenotaph on Whitehall. Elgar's previous commission related to work by its architect, Sir Edwin Lutyens (1869–1944), was *The Crown of India*. Then imperial New Delhi, largely the work of Lutyens, was to become the capital for British rule, and the masque was on an appropriately large scale. Now, less was needed of Elgar, and in the event this short work wasn't even used for the dedication, but was performed in a fully rescored version at a Royal Choral Society jubilee concert in 1921.

---

[5] Quoted in ibid.

[6] George Bernard Shaw, 'Sir Edward Elgar', *Music & Letters*, 1 (1920), pp. 7–11, at pp. 6 and 9.

In late March Alice's health became a serious concern. Elgar kept a diary of her last days; it makes pitiful reading.

> March 26 . . . Alice very ill – retaining nothing . . .
> March 27 . . . A. better – less pain during day. E. to Savile [Club] lunch (only went to soothe A.) Home to tea. A. not so well . . .
> March 28 . . . A. *very unwell*. Dr. Rose came. A. awake during most of the night. alas! . . .
> April 6. My darling – in great distress – cd. not understand her words – very, very, very painful. Dr. Rose called early – nurse arrived midday – Dr. Larkin (specialist) with Dr. Rose – bad report.
> April 7. My darling sinking. Father Valentine gave extreme unction . . . Sinking all day & died in my arms at 6.10 p.m.[7]

She had had undiagnosed cancer, very advanced. Elgar was inconsolable; Rosa Burley told him 'to pull himself together'.[8] She also said that she was effectively Carice's mother now, and the affront made Elgar immediately and forever stop talking to her, notwithstanding that he had been her friend as long as he had been Alice's husband. Lady Elgar was buried in the cemetery by St Wulstan's Church at Little Malvern on 10 April. As a cruelly delayed consequence of Elgar's original low social standing in their eyes, part of Alice's money reverted now to her '*awful aunts*', shutting Carice off from inheritance. Elgar told Schuster 'I feel just now rather evil that a noble (& almost brilliant) woman like my Carice should be penalised by a wretched lot of old incompetents simply because I was – well – I'.[9] Newman wrote with condolences. Alice had disliked him because of his views on the oratorios, but now Elgar became much closer to him and his daughter.

Carice had recently met and fallen in love with an older man, Samuel Blake, a farmer in Surrey. He proposed to her on 23 March 1921 and she accepted, subject to Elgar's approval (which was immediate). She was married on 16 January 1922, and Elgar was finally alone.

'Severn House', put on the market by Lady Elgar, would not sell; nobody wanted a house of such a size. After a gloomy summer at 'Brinkwells', Elgar had the young violinist Jascha Heifetz (1901–87) to tea at 'Severn House'. Heifetz was to play the Elgar concerto at a Philharmonic concert. Elgar enjoyed the performance but told Lady Stuart that it was 'not exactly our own Concerto . . . there is nothing in it all somehow & I am sad'.[10] He eventually decided to sell the house at

---

[7] Moore, *Creative Life*, p. 752.
[8] Burley and Carruthers, *The Record of a Friendship*, p. 202.
[9] Moore, *Creative Life*, pp. 754–5.
[10] Ibid., p. 758.

auction in autumn 1921 (it fetched £6,500), and moved into a ground-floor flat at 37 St James's Place, just off Pall Mall.

Other activity was bitty: he wrote letters to the *Times Literary Supplement*, played with his microscopes, and opened the His Master's Voice record shop on Oxford Street in London. His return to music was small-scale: orchestrations of Bach's Fantasy and Fugue, BWV 537, as his Op. 86. The fugue was orchestrated first, and premiered on 27 October 1921; the fantasia followed, after Strauss (who met Elgar this year, during his first post-war trip to Britain) refused the challenge of orchestrating it.

Elgar's first worthy commission came in January 1923, when Laurence Binyon (of *Spirit of England*) asked for music for his play *Arthur*, based on Thomas Malory's *Le morte d'Arthur*. At first Elgar was resistant. 'I *want* to do it but since my dear wife's death I have *done nothing* & fear my music has vanished.'[11] Yet this request from a former collaborator offered a gentle way out of his morbid semi-retirement. He initially wrote 120 pages of music for the play, and added more for a battle scene during its run.[12] (It was not unusual, in the days before film, for theatres to have small orchestras performing live music, and for respectable composers to write for them.)

The play makes nine scenes out of two of Malory's eight parts (these were 'The Book of Sir Launcelot and Queen Guinevere' and 'The most Piteous Tale of the Morte Arthur saunz Guerdon'). Binyon wanted an overture and short pieces between scenes, which should establish the mood for what follows. For the music Elgar returned to the chivalric tone of *Froissart* and other early works. Some of the best of it was reused in the early 1930s for two unfinished works, his Third Symphony and opera *The Spanish Lady*. Arthur's 'chivalry' theme went into the symphony's finale, and some of the banquet music from Scene iv ended up in its second movement. *The Spanish Lady* inherited Guinevere's theme for its overture and Act II Scene ii.

The music for Scene viii of *Arthur* is among the most successful. The final stage direction called for 'a wide distance of moonlit water, over which glides a barge, bearing King Arthur, and the three queens sorrowing over him, to the island of Avalon'. To the accompaniment of convent bells Arthur is sent to the next world over gentle waters – an image not unlike that at the end of *Gerontius*. Perhaps it was useful, still soon after his wife's death, for Elgar to write music that sent a Christian soul on its way; perhaps it was simply directionless moping in long-dead chivalrous

---

[11] Edward Elgar, *Letters of a Lifetime*, p. 370.

[12] For a comprehensive account of the *Arthur* music see Robert Anderson, '"Fyrst the Noble Arthur"', in Monk (ed.), *Music and Literature*, pp. 164–81, and see his *Elgar and Chivalry* (Rickmansworth: Elgar Editions, 2002), pp. 386–71, for further detail on Binyon's adaptation of Malory.

ideas. The play was premiered on 12 March 1923 to good reviews, but its score is no longer extant.

On 31 March he began a six-month lease of a house in the Worcestershire countryside at Kempsey. Lady Stuart was on his mind, as always after Alice's death ('I hope you are well – this seems far away – far away'), and he wrote an anonymous letter on 'the Vernal Anemonies: a beautiful native' to the *Daily Telegraph*, sending 'Windflower' the cutting.[13] He sent two part songs to Novello and was offered 50 guineas – half of his asking price.[14] Worcestershire was a lonely place, not only without Lady Elgar or Lady Stuart but also without his London friends. He told 'Windflower' 'I have been to *12* theatres since I returned . . . I am so desperately lonely & turn in to see anything'. He was trying not to be old-fashioned, he said, but added, 'I am only old-fashioned in loving you'.[15] Life would have been almost wholly routine that year, except for an extraordinary trip in November, 1,000 miles up the Amazon to Manaus in Brazil at the age of 66. But the trip didn't seem to reignite any creative energies (see figure 25, overleaf).

Though little is known of this journey for certain, James Hamilton-Paterson's novel *Gerontius* is a fictional account of it, and also incidentally an insightful (and funny) portrait of Elgar at this time of life. He has Elgar write a journal on board the *Hildebrand*, ultimately thrown overboard. His fictional entry reflecting on the nature of his art and the role of the artist in a decaying world is keenly observed.

> I suppose there's good reason for despair. The 'massive hope in the future' did after all refer as much to my own career as to anything more general since the concerns of Humanity at large seemed less pressing . . . But now after the best part of a generation has been reduced to bonemeal what do we see all around but ineffable mediocrity . . . Oh Edward what a stupid doltish ass you've been to waste your life on the idea that art – in its small way – can make the least difference to things.[16]

On 28 April 1924 Elgar received a coveted honour when he became Master of the King's Musick, officially musician laureate at last. He had given the king – who was thinking of abolishing the post – the idea through a private secretary.[17] His only musical work that year had been the production of an *Empire March* and songs for the 'Pageant of Empire'

---

[13] His description is quoted in the preceding inter-chapter.
[14] Privately the publishers found the music 'rather *cheap* for Elgar – *cheap* without being sufficiently *interesting*' (Moore, *Creative Life*, p. 766).
[15] Quoted in Michael Kennedy, *Portrait of Elgar*, p. 300.
[16] James Hamilton-Paterson, *Gerontius* (London: Vintage, 1990), pp. 183–4.
[17] A letter to Lady Stuart explains the machinations; see Moore, *Creative Life*, pp. 769–70.

25. Elgar and companions eating aboard the HMS Hildebrand, *on an Amazon cruise, 1923.*

26. Elgar as conductor, 1933.

to open the British Empire Exhibition at Wembley, and *The Daily Sketch* (a right-wing tabloid newspaper that was later absorbed into *The Daily Mail*) asked 'What is Elgar doing? – When is Sir Edward Elgar going to write another concerto, or another symphony – or any other important work? . . . He is our greatest composer and we want him to'.[18]

Multimedia man

The answer is that Sir Edward Elgar was doing two things. First, though he did not immediately know it, he was finding a new audience for his existing music, and so opening up the possibility of returning to serious composition in the future. Second, he was finding ways to preserve his music, and his interpretation of it, for posterity. In short, he was in the recording studio and on the airwaves.

Elgar's music was first broadcast on the eight-month-old BBC on 8 July 1923; it was the overture *Cockaigne*. The live relay from the British Empire Exhibition eight months later was heard by more than ten million people. Elgar conducted 'Land of Hope and Glory', the *Imperial March*, the National Anthem, and Parry's *Jerusalem* – in his own orchestration, the one still used at the Last Night of the Proms, much to the irritation of Parry connoisseurs who wish the composer's own version could be used. In all, Elgar conducted 28 times for BBC radio, several times giving concerts exclusively of his own music. He conducted a seventieth-birthday concert for the BBC on 2 June 1927, and the corporation organized three Elgar Celebration Concerts at the end of his seventy-fifth year in November and December 1932. By then he was too fragile to conduct.[19] Elgar could not fail to see that although his work might not fare as well as it had done in concert programmes, he had a large and enthusiastic audience on the radio. The richer middle classes, who lived near concert halls and could afford tickets, might have abandoned him to an extent, but the less well-off – yet still culturally aspirational – part of the public that listened to concerts on radio could still be reached. This would be remembered in 1932, when the Third Symphony commission was mooted.

Elgar's recording career was longer and more accessible to us than his career on radio.[20] He recorded intermittently in the old, acoustic system from 1914 to 1925, when the change to the electrical system vastly expanded the potential for recording symphonic works. Rather than surrounding a recording horn with a few instrumentalists, as was the

---

[18] Quoted in ibid., p. 770.

[19] This information on Elgar and the BBC is drawn from Jenny Doctor, 'Broadcasting's Ally: Elgar and the BBC', in Grimley and Rushton (eds.), *The Cambridge Companion to Elgar*, pp. 195–203. As her title suggests, she argues that Elgar was an ally to the BBC in its first decade, helping it to establish a deeply respectable image. Not since his heyday in the 1900s had an organization worn him as a lucky charm.

[20] Material in the following paragraphs is taken from Timothy Day, 'Elgar and Recording', ibid., pp. 184–94.

case with the early acoustic method, full orchestras could now be seated before a microphone in their normal arrangement, and a reasonably faithful recording obtained.

A huge market was growing for classical music, which is reflected by the founding of *The Gramophone* magazine by Compton Mackenzie (1883–1972) in 1923.[21] Elgar recorded his Second Symphony acoustically in 1924, and then again electrically in 1925. Both recordings sold at a profit. The enthusiasm of record-buyers for large orchestral works, when the technology permitted only four-and-a-half minutes to be recorded on each side of the shellac disc, makes today's situation seem lamentable by comparison.

Elgar's conducting technique had never been excellent, but he was able through strength of personality to take an orchestra with him. In front of the recording horn or microphone he had no fear. The performances he left behind, now available on CD, are almost all energetic, and played so much faster than expected that one wonders – as with other composer recordings – whether he was half-embarrassed to be conducting his own music. Their style was studied by Georg Solti for his recordings of the Elgar symphonies in the 1970s, and their influence can be felt also in recordings by conductors as different as Adrian Boult (who was a friend of Elgar's in his youth) and Colin Davis (in his recent recording of *Gerontius*).

More deaths and endings

Elgar had been a member of the Athenaeum since 1903; the election of Ramsay MacDonald as the first Labour prime minister in 1924 – which came with an *ex officio* membership for the Scot – caused Elgar to resign his membership.[22] He would later decide not to allow excerpts from *Falstaff* to accompany performances of *Henry IV* at the Shakespeare Memorial Theatre (now the Royal Shakespeare Theatre) because the architecture was 'an insult to human intelligence'.[23] Like all Tories, his instinctive response to change was to think it must be wrong, and that it could probably be shown to be immoral if the mind was bent to it for long enough.

Change at Schuster's, for instance, caused offence. Coolness began in 1920, when Schuster introduced a boy 'as his *nephew* – are we all mad!'. But Elgar seems to have been more affronted when he saw an unmarried heterosexual couple with Schuster 'sitting in the back of a smart car . . . driving with an *odd looking* – I hate to say it – *"bit of fluff"*!! in flamboyant

---

[21] Mackenzie, born in West Hartlepool but spiritually a Scot, was another Edwardian artist – the author of novels which caused mild outrage owing to their frankly sexual content – who found in the broadcast media a new outlet.

[22] Kennedy, *Portrait*, p. 332.

[23] Robert Anderson, *Elgar* (London: Dent, 1993), p. 168. The theatre is currently being redesigned along lines he might have liked better.

pink on the front seat . . . they did not see me & I was glad for I shd. have been thoroughly ashamed'.[24] The couple were Leslie 'Anzy' Wylde, a New Zealand soldier who lost a leg at Gallipoli, and his fiancée Wendela. They became increasingly influential at The Hut, and took it over around 1926, renaming it 'The Long White Cloud' (the Maori name for New Zealand).[25] It was their influence that cooled Elgar's feelings for Schuster, but growing ill-feeling was not mutual: six months after giving a seventieth-anniversary concert of Elgar's rarely heard chamber works, Schuster died on 27 December 1927, leaving a generous bequest 'To my friend, Sir Edward Elgar O.M. who has saved my country from the reproach of having produced no composer worthy to rank with the Great Masters, the sum of £7,000' – probably around a quarter of a million in today's money.[26]

Another old friend, Kilburn, died in 1924, and Elgar's sister Lucy Pipe followed him on 23 October 1925, the first family death in Elgar's generation since Joe had died in childhood.[27] Elgar's health was no better or worse than before (nor was his hypochondria), but just before Christmas that year he went into hospital (South Bank Nursing Home in Worcester) for a three-week stay to have haemorrhoids removed. Afflicted by baleful visions as he was taken away, his parting words to Carice were to 'be sure the cows in the field don't get into the garden'.[28]

Charles Stuart of Wortley died on 24 April 1926, but there was no outward sign that a greater closeness developed thereafter between Elgar and 'Windflower' – indeed for the last four full years of his life (1929–33) he wrote noticeably fewer letters to her. Straight after her husband's death, and after noting the emotional test of conducting the *Variations* and First Symphony without Charles Stuart's presence, letters to her return to an *idée fixe* of his later years, his desire for a peerage. 'I should like to know if "it" is entirely dead – my birthday (70) next June is to be "recognised" by concerts in the musical world & I do not want this or these & shall *squash* them unless the other thing turns up'.[29] It did not come – instead Elgar got 'the wretched *K.C.V.O.* (!!!) Which awful thing I must accept!'[30] – but his seventieth birthday concerts proceeded anyway. Among them was a performance of *Gerontius* that Elgar conducted on 26 February at the Albert Hall, which was partly recorded.

---

[24] Kennedy, *Portrait*, pp. 290 and 301.

[25] Kennedy, *The Life of Elgar*, pp. 174–6.

[26] Moore, *Creative Life*, p. 776. Death duties consumed only 10%, a quarter of what they would take now, but G. B. Shaw said 'I grudge Churchill [then Chancellor of the Exchequer] his share' (Kennedy, *Portrait*, p. 313).

[27] His brother Frank would die on 7 June 1928.

[28] Kennedy, *Portrait*, p. 302.

[29] Moore, *Creative Life*, p. 774.

[30] Letter of 26 November 1926, ibid. As Knight Commander of the Victorian Order Elgar was able for the first time to use postnominal knightly letters. In 1933 he was promoted within the order to GCVO, Knight Grand Cross of the Victorian Order.

He spent the end of 1927 at Battenhall Manor, just outside Worcester, writing to 'Windflower' that it was 'a real Yule-loggy house',[31] and he moved in spring to Tiddington House, on the Avon near Stratford. He fished and wrote a little theatre music, a minuet for Bertram P. Matthews, on the subject of Beau Brummell (whose name the play's title misspelt as *Beau Brummel*). The music was drawn from old sketchbooks; the play opened on 5 November 1928.

New possibilities

To most biographers it has seemed that activity in every sphere wound down in the years after Alice's death. Elgar composed little, saw less of friends, received fewer honours (though they still kept coming), and was heard – or rather *seen* – less in concerts. Yet exposure on radio and in recordings increased, and with the formation or development of three new friendships in his last five years, the possibility of renewed creative effort and personal engagement with people (rather than the dogs that cluttered his house) became newly available.

The first friendship – not entirely new, but now become closer – was with George Bernard Shaw. The two men attended the Shakespeare Festival in Stratford (before the building of the new theatre) as soon as Elgar moved there in 1928. For several reasons it is astonishing that Shaw should, around this time, send Elgar an advance copy of his *The Intelligent Woman's Guide to Socialism and Capitalism*.[32] Elgar read it with interest. When Shaw completed his play *The Apple Cart* he taunted Elgar. 'Lazy! I've not only begun a new play but finished it . . . Your turn now. Clap it with a symphony'.[33] Elgar didn't, but made a speech at the Shaw Exhibition on 17 August in Malvern, where the play opened. His suggestion that 'Bernard Shaw knows more about music than I do' was typical of the affected musical ignorance of his later years. Shaw's response was adoring.

> Although I am rather a conceited man and I feel I could carry my head high compared with any other artist in England, I am quite sincerely and genuinely humble in the presence of Sir Edward Elgar. I recognise a greater art than my own, and a greater man than I could hope to be.[34]

Elgar dedicated his *Severn Suite* (a brass band piece) to him in 1930; Shaw said 'it will secure my immortality when all my plays are dead and damned and forgotten'. The friendship continued to bear creative fruit with the

---

[31] Moore, *Creative Life*, p. 776.
[32] Anderson, *Elgar*, p. 161.
[33] Moore, *Creative Life*, p. 781.
[34] Both quotations in *Worcester Daily Times*, 19 August 1929, quoted in ibid.

completion of the fifth *Pomp and Circumstance* March, premiered on 18 September. (Elgar wrangled with his publisher over the advance royalties, lifting his usual *Pomp and Circumstance* cheque from £50 to £75.)[35] In the same year he wrote a *Nursery Suite* for small orchestra, four short orchestral movements dedicated to the Duchess of York and the Princesses Margaret and Elizabeth (who would become Queen Elizabeth II). The friendship, and even more the media-spread regrowth of his fame, was encouraging serious musical effort once more. The revision of his 1889 Piano Sonatina, also in 1930, provided further evidence that the traditional forms were returning to his mind for the first time since the Cello Concerto.

The second special friendship of his last years gave a good end to a mixed year, 1931. In May that year Basil Maine had approached Elgar about his proposed two-volume study of the composer (biography and works-study). This was welcome news after the winter, during which a storm had broken over an article by the Cambridge professor Edward J. Dent in Guido Adler's *Handbuch der Musikgeschichte* (Handbook of Music History). The article – no more than a short paragraph in the entry 'Engländer' (Englishmen) – says that Elgar was 'a self-taught man, who had little of the literary culture of Parry and Stanford', that 'for English ears Elgar's music is too emotional and not quite free from vulgarity'.[36] The defensive response was immediate. A furious letter, signed by Philip Heseltine (Peter Warlock), Cammaerts, John Ireland, E. J. Moeran, William Walton, and Bernard Shaw, among others, was sent to several English and German newspapers. 'At the present time the works of Elgar, so far from being distasteful to English ears, are held in the highest honour by the majority of English musicians and the musical public in general'.[37]

Most Elgar biographers have stuck to the line that Dent's comments were an insult, but Brian Trowell is more moderate and thoughtful. As he notes, for a 1924 publication (it appeared in the first edition, not the 1930 second edition, as Moore suggests) Dent must have written the article around 1921, when he was a jobbing music critic, not Professor at Cambridge. Dent might have said that Elgar's music was too emotional 'for English ears' without meaning that he agreed with the view, and although the remark about 'literary culture' sounds acid, a better translation of 'literarischen Bildung' would be 'literary education' (Dent avoids the loaded 'Kultur', 'culture'), which is factually correct: Elgar's literary education came from his mother, not Eton and Cambridge. Dent was, in any case, a

---

35 Edward Elgar, *Elgar and His Publishers*, pp. 870–73.

36 The full German text and a translation are given in Brian Trowell, 'Elgar's Use of Literature', in Monk (ed.), *Music and Literature*, pp. 182–326, at pp. 286–7. The translation given here – the one Elgar knew – is from Maine, *Elgar, His Life and Works*, vol. 2, pp. 277–8.

37 Maine, *Elgar, His Life and Works*, vol. 1, p. 256. A full list of signatories is given in Moore, *Creative Life*, p. 790.

lifelong Labour voter, part of whose work was to give the underprivileged better access to the arts. He would never throw mud at an originally underprivileged man like Elgar.[38]

Elgar suffered from a strangely lingering nettle-rash in March 1931, and a familiar sciatica, but the Dent furore and illness were partly offset by the creation of Elgar as the first Baronet of Broadheath on 3 June (the day after his seventy-fourth birthday). Better yet, when it began on 7 November, his latest – and last – close female friendship was absorbing enough to take his mind off most sufferings, real or imagined. We saw in the last inter-chapter how close Elgar was to Vera Hockman. As well as increasing the creative urgency of his last years (perhaps a sublimated sexual urge), his relationship with her was the cause of the apparent lessening of his affection for Lady Stuart. Like the 'Windflower', Vera would inspire ideas – always the important secondary themes – for 'absolute' music.

Elgar was on a £500 annual recording contract with HMV, but on the death in 1930 of wealthy Leeds businessman Henry Embleton, who had championed his choral works for years, he had to return a nine-year-old loan of £500 for the completion of the third oratorio in the *Apostles* series. He had bought a new house, too, his last: the two-hundred-year-old 'Marl Bank' at Worcester, which he had admired since 1917.[39] The Third Symphony began to take off after his encounter with Vera, and by September 1932 Elgar was saying that he had 'written' it. What he meant by that is uncertain, but efforts to complete it were stepped up after Shaw's intervention with the BBC in late 1932.

> In 1823 the London Philharmonic Society . . . offer[ed] Beethoven £50 for the MS of a symphony. He accepted, and sent . . . the Ninth Symphony . . .
>
> This is by far the most creditable incident in English history.
>
> Now the only composer today who is comparable to Beethoven is Elgar . . .
>
> Well, why should not the BBC, with its millions, do for Elgar what the old Philharmonic did for Beethoven? You could bring the Third Symphony into existence and obtain the performing right for the BBC for, say, ten years, for a few thousand pounds.[40]

The proposal was too attractive for the BBC to turn down, and Elgar accepted their resulting offer of four quarterly payments of £250.

---

[38] For further discussion see Trowell, 'Elgar's Use of Literature', pp. 182–6. Trowell goes on to show, in this definitive essay, how impressively wide Elgar's literary culture was despite his lack of a university education.

[39] He was filmed there with his dogs Marco and Mina, by the Novello director Harold Brooke. The clips are now available on DVD.

[40] Quoted in J. C. W. Reith, *Into the Wind* (London: Hodder & Stoughton, 1949), p. 163.

Elgar was already working on another big project, his first opera, *The Spanish Lady* (on Ben Jonson's *The Devil is an Ass*). An oddly satirical choice of subject, he hoped it would 'out-Meistersinger the Meistersinger'.[41] Relatively few sketches survive, and there is little to suggest that his hope would have been fulfilled, but it was remarkable that he should have turned to two such enormous works half way through his eighth decade, when in the time since Alice's death he had written so little, and nothing (yet) of lasting significance.[42] The opera might have been substandard, but the Third Symphony promised not only to add a work of value equal to his other symphonic music, but even possibly to turn in a quite unexpected direction, so far as his music's message is concerned.

Fred Gaisberg (1873–1951), the American recording expert at The Gramophone Company who had overseen most of Elgar's recordings, gave eager encouragement. The two became warm friends – the third important new relationship of Elgar's last years – and together visited Delius, by then very sick, in Paris in 1933. Elgar flew there, shrugging off an understandable concern over this new technology (see figure 27, overleaf). He described the sensation of flight to Delius.

> The rising from the ground was a little difficult; you cannot tell exactly how you are going to stand it. When once you have reached the heights it is very different. There is a delightful feeling of elation in sailing through gold and silver clouds . . . I should have liked to stay there forever. The descent is like our old age – peaceful, even serene.[43]

It was also Gaisberg who organized the Menuhin–Elgar recording of the Violin Concerto in 1933. On hearing Elgar play passages from the symphony, Gaisberg said it was 'youthful and fresh – 100% Elgar without a trace of decay',[44] but the work was not to be completed.

On 30 January 1933, Hitler took power in Germany. Elgar was tortured. 'I am in a maze regarding events in Germany – what are they doing? In

---

[41] Anderson, *Elgar*, p. 273.

[42] Aside from the works already mentioned, his only compositions in these years were arrangements – of Handel's Second Chandos Anthem (1923), Chopin's Funeral March from the B flat Minor Piano Sonata, and an orchestration of his own *Severn Suite* (both 1932); songs and choral music – 'The Wanderer' and 'Zut! Zut! Zut!' (1923), 'The Herald' and 'The Prince of Sleep' (1925), 'I Sing the Birth' (1928), 'Goodmorrow' (1929, based on an early hymn tune), 'It Isnae Me' (1930), 'So Many True Princesses That Have Gone' (1932), and three unison songs for children on Mackay (1932–3); some occasional pieces – a Memorial Chime for carillon, written for the Loughborough War Memorial (1923), and a Civic Fanfare for Hereford (1927); as well as two piano pieces – *Serenade* and *Adieu* (1932); one for oboe – *Soliloquy* (1930); and the dainty orchestral portrait of his dog, *Mina* (1933).

[43] Quoted in Moore, *Creative Life*, p. 813.

[44] Quoted in ibid., p. 816.

27. Elgar boarding a plane for his first flight, to visit Delius in Paris in 1933.

28. Elgar (carrying an early iPod) at the Marconi studio, 1930.

this morning's paper it is said that the greatest conductor Bruno Walter &, stranger still, Einstein are ostracised: are we all mad? The Jews have always been my best & kindest friends – the pain of these news is unbearable & I do not know what it really means.'[45]

In autumn 1933 an operation on an intestinal obstruction revealed that what Elgar had considered sciatica was instead a malignant, inoperable tumour. His doctor Arthur Thomson said 'After all his years of worrying over imagined troubles, he displayed magnificent courage in the face of great adversity . . . He told me that he had no faith whatever in an afterlife: "I believe there is nothing but complete oblivion".'[46]

On 20 November W. H. Reed received a telegram from Carice: 'Father unconscious, sinking rapidly'. He took the first train to Worcester, and heard from Elgar's lips words that would guarantee that any completion of the symphony would be controversial, seeming to confirm his anxiety about the oblivion he and his work were soon to enter. His words came slowly, with difficulty.

> I want you . . . to do something for me . . . the symphony all bits and pieces . . . no one would understand . . . no one . . . no one [. . .]
>
> Don't let anyone tinker with it . . . no one could understand . . . no one must tinker with it.[47]

He even suggested to Reed that the sketches might be burnt, though ultimately they were preserved. Death did not come quickly; he had three more months to tinker himself, though he was too unwell to do much work. Gaisberg rigged up his sick-room to the Abbey Road studios in London, and Elgar oversaw new recordings of his music, including the Woodland Interlude from *Caractacus* and his dog piece, *Mina* (see figure 29, overleaf). He offered criticisms and asked for the Interlude to be played again. But his thoughts were turned to death. He wanted to be cremated and scattered at the confluence of the rivers Teme and Severn, until Carice persuaded him to be buried next to Alice at Little Malvern. He wrote his own addition to the headstone: 'In memory also of the above-named Edward Elgar / Died – '.[48] On the morning of 23 February 1934 he died peacefully in his sleep.

Post mortem

The thought that 'tinkering' with the Third Symphony would be an offence to Elgar's memory has haunted the work, but Anthony Payne's completion

---

[45] Letter to Adela Schuster, 17 March 1933, quoted in Elgar, *Letters of Edward Elgar*, ed. Percy M. Young (London: Bles, 1956), p. 316.
[46] Quoted in Moore, *Creative Life*, p. 818.
[47] Reed, *Elgar as I Knew Him*, pp. 113 and 114.
[48] Moore, *Creative Life*, p. 823.

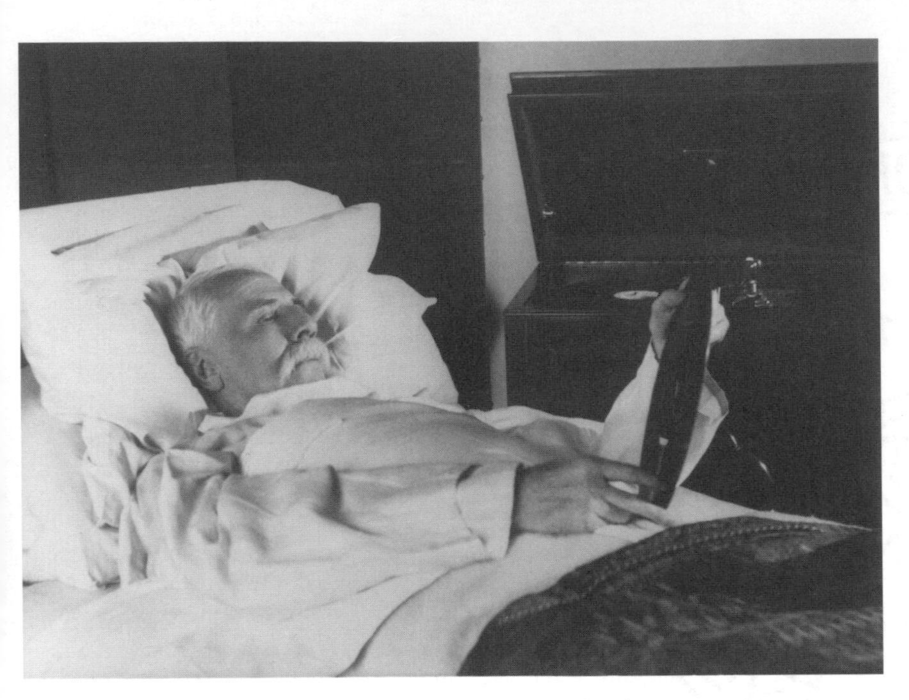

29. Elgar with a recording of his own music, on his deathbed at Marl Bank, Worcester, 1933.

30. The old-style £20 note featuring Elgar and the West face of Worcester Cathedral (Bank of England, Series E revision, printed from 22 June 1999 to 12 March 2007 – Elgar's sesquicentenary year; he has been replaced on the Series F £20 note by Adam Smith, and will eventually be withdrawn from circulation).

of it in 1997 cannot be dismissed. It is a work of extraordinary imagination, making use of over three hundred pages of existing sketches. Before Payne's work, the material leapt from the page (many of the sketches were published as an appendix to Reed's *Elgar as I Knew Him*), but Payne's completion lends them a coherence that one cannot imagine Elgar significantly bettering. Was he wrong to do it? Was the desire not to 'tinker' with it Elgar's last wish? Not really.

Elgar's first reaction on hearing that he was going to die was nobler than his piteous words to Reed. 'If I can't complete the Third Symphony, somebody will complete it – or write a better one – in fifty or five hundred years. Viewed from the point where I am now, on the brink of eternity, that's a mere moment in time.'[49] The neurotic desperation of his 'no one must tinker with it' is no more or less Elgarian than the bold, visionary statement made in the face of the news of swiftly approaching death. To say that either was his final thought on the matter would be to ignore this essential and long-established paradox in his character. So there was never a clear bar to Payne's completion, except in the mind of the ultra-sententious, and it would be idiocy to refuse on principle to listen to a work so intellectually engaging and emotionally moving.

As well as being a great work of art, the Elgar–Payne Third Symphony is a significant work of Elgar criticism, and in one respect at least it is typical of the prevailing view of Elgar in the late 1990s. One of the finest moments in Payne's completion is in the work's finale. After the crisis of a 'wrong-key' recapitulation on E minor instead of C minor (which recalls similar moments in the first two symphonies), the main secondary idea – as always in Elgar's sonata-form designs, the core of the movement and its promise of hope – returns, combined magically with a theme from the development, to close with a sense of achievement into the tonic C at bar 288. This is entirely Payne's doing, a touch of genius. The coda that follows is rich with the ambiguous Elgarian nostalgia familiar from his principal orchestral works, but the treatment of the secondary idea here says something distinctively new.

Elgar never resolved a secondary tonal area satisfactorily back into the tonic in a major orchestral work, and Elgar scholarship today would tend towards a more ambiguous conclusion than Payne presents – which is the same as saying that a composer persuaded by today's scholarship might have handled the moment differently. As we have seen, it was Elgar's refusal to do so that ensured his music could be at times destabilizingly ambivalent about the efficacy of hope. Payne's rendering of the supreme moment of Elgar's last symphony offers for the first time in Elgar's oeuvre a genuinely strong reason to believe that the repose of the final bars, and the modest hope they afford, could be relied upon. Elgar did not

[49] Ibid., p. 819.

write these bars himself, but so compelling is Payne's argument that it is difficult to believe, despite precedent, that Elgar *wouldn't* have ended this way, and that had he lived to complete the symphony modern scholarship would have a 'problem work' to deal with. The fact we can never know his final plan for the piece does not disappoint.

It would be romantic to think of Elgar accomplishing in his final work what in a lifetime's composition he appears to discountenance: the possibility of a happy ending. Perhaps that was indeed his intention, had he completed the Third Symphony. So it is in some way fitting that a composing life spent balancing ambiguities in equal poise was cut short – tragically short, we might say – before a potential final ambiguity could be resolved. As with Mahler, whose Tenth Symphony was left incomplete at his death, Elgar's passing was, in musical terms, a final artistic statement, a *coup de grâce* that resurrected the philosophy of his great works of the 1900s, and chiselled onto his tombstone the legend 'Edward Elgar, modernist'.

31. Sir Edward is incommoded by poultry.

Bibliography

Adams, Byron, 'The "Dark Saying" of the Enigma: Homoeroticism and the Elgarian Paradox', *19th-Century Music,* 23 (2000), pp. 218–35.

———, 'Elgar's Later Oratorios: Roman Catholicism, Decadence and the Wagnerian Dialectic of Shame and Grace', in Daniel M. Grimley and Julian Rushton (eds.), *The Cambridge Companion to Elgar* (Cambridge: Cambridge University Press, 2004), pp. 81–105.

Adorno, Theodor W., *Mahler: A Musical Physiognomy*, trans. Edmund Jephcott (Chicago: University of Chicago Press, 1992; orig. edn. 1960).

Alder, Mary Beatrice, 'Memories of a Pupil', in *An Elgar Companion*, ed. Christopher Redwood (Ashbourne, Derbyshire: Sequoia, 1982), p. 148.

Allis, Michael, 'Elgar and the Art of Retrospective Narrative', *Journal of Musicological Research,* 19 (2000), pp. 298–328.

———, 'Elgar, Lytton, and the Piano Quintet, Op. 84', *Music & Letters,* 85 (2004), pp. 198–238.

Anderson, Robert, *Elgar* (London: Dent, and New York: Schirmer Books/ Maxwell Macmillan International, 1993).

———, *Elgar and Chivalry* (Rickmansworth: Elgar Editions, 2002).

———, 'Elgar and His Publishers', in Daniel M. Grimley and Julian Rushton (eds.), *The Cambridge Companion to Elgar* (Cambridge: Cambridge University Press, 2004), pp. 24–31.

———, '"Fyrst the Noble Arthur"', in Raymond Monk (ed.), *Elgar Studies* (Aldershot: Scolar, 1990), pp. 164–81.

———, 'Gertrude Walker: An Elgarian Friendship', *Musical Times,* 125 (1984), pp. 698.

Attfield, John, *Chemistry: General, Medical, and Pharmaceutical*, 6th edn. (London: Van Voorst, 1875).

Auden, W. H., 'Dingley Dell & the Fleet', *The Dyer's Hand and Other Essays* (London: Faber and Faber, 1963), pp. 407–28.

Buckle, Richard, *Diaghilev* (London: Weidenfeld and Nicolson, 1979).

Buckley, Robert J., *Sir Edward Elgar* (London: Bodley Head, 1905).

Burley, Rosa, and Frank Carruthers, *Edward Elgar: The Record of a Friendship* (London: Barrie and Jenkins, 1972).

Burnham, Scott G., *Beethoven Hero* (Princeton, NJ: Princeton University Press, 1995).

Butt, John, 'Roman Catholicism and Being Musically English: Elgar's Church and Organ Music', in Daniel M. Grimley and Julian Rushton (eds.), *The Cambridge Companion to Elgar* (Cambridge: Cambridge University Press, 2004), pp. 106–19.

Dahlhaus, Carl, *Between Romanticism and Modernism: Four Studies in the Music of the Later Nineteenth Century*, trans. Mary Whittall and Arnold Whittall (Berkeley: University of California Press, 1980; orig. edn. 1974).

Davies, Norman, *Europe: A History* (Oxford: Oxford University Press, 1996).

Day, Timothy, 'Elgar and Recording', in Grimley and Rushton (eds.), *The Cambridge Companion to Elgar*, ibid., pp. 184–94.

Dennison, Peter, 'Elgar's Musical Apprenticeship', in Raymond Monk (ed.), *Elgar Studies* (Aldershot: Scolar, 1990), pp. 1–35.

Doctor, Jenny, 'Broadcasting's Ally: Elgar and the BBC', in Grimley and Rushton (eds.), *The Cambridge Companion to Elgar*, pp. 195–203.
Elgar, Edward, *Edward Elgar: Letters of a Lifetime*, ed. Jerrold Northrop Moore (Oxford: Clarendon Press, and New York: Oxford University Press, 1990).
———, *Elgar and His Publishers: Letters of a Creative Life*, ed. Jerrold Northrop Moore (Oxford: Clarendon Press, and New York: Oxford University Press, 1987).
———, 'Falstaff', *Musical Times,* 54 (1913), pp. 575–9.
———, *A Future for English Music, and Other Lectures*, ed. Percy M. Young (London: Dobson, 1968).
———, *Letters of Edward Elgar and Other Writings*, ed. Percy M. Young (London: Bles, 1956).
———, *The Windflower Letters: Correspondence with Alice Caroline Stuart Wortley and Her Family*, ed. Jerrold Northrop Moore (Oxford: Clarendon Press, and New York: Oxford University Press, 1989).
Foreman, Lewis (ed.), *"Oh My Horses!": Elgar and the Great War* (Rickmansworth: Elgar Editions, 2001).
Greening, Michael, *A Family Story: The Greenings and Some of Their Relatives (Including the Elgars)* (Leicester: Matador, 2006).
Grimley, Daniel M., ' "Music in the Midst of Desolation": Structures of Mourning in Elgar's *The Spirit of England*', in Harper-Scott and Rushton (eds.), *Elgar Studies*.
———, ' "A Smiling with a Sigh": The Chamber Music and the Works for Strings', in Daniel M. Grimley and Julian Rushton (eds.), *The Cambridge Companion to Elgar* (Cambridge: Cambridge University Press, 2004), pp. 120–38.
———, and Julian Rushton (eds.), *The Cambridge Companion to Elgar* (Cambridge: Cambridge University Press, 2004).
Hamilton-Paterson, James, *Gerontius* (London: Vintage, 1990).
Harper-Scott, J. P. E., 'Elgar's Unwumbling: The Theatre Music', in Daniel M. Grimley and Julian Rushton (eds.), *The Cambridge Companion to Elgar* (Cambridge: Cambridge University Press, 2004), pp. 171–83.
———, *Edward Elgar, Modernist* (Cambridge and New York: Cambridge University Press, 2006).
———, 'Elgar's Deconstruction of the *belle époque*: Interlace Structures and the Second Symphony', in J. P. E. Harper-Scott and Julian Rushton (eds.), *Elgar Studies* (Cambridge: Cambridge University Press, 2007).
———, 'Elgar's Invention of the Human: *Falstaff*, Op. 68', *19th-Century Music,* 28 (2005), pp. 230–53.
Hepokoski, James A., 'Gaudery, Romance, and the "Welsh" Tune: *Introduction and Allegro*, Op. 47', in J. P. E. Harper-Scott and Julian Rushton (eds.), *Elgar Studies* (Cambridge: Cambridge University Press, 2007).
———, 'Sibelius', in D. Kern Holoman (ed.), *The Nineteenth-Century Symphony* (New York: Schirmer, 1997), pp. 417–49.
Holloway, Robin, 'The Early Choral Works', in Daniel M. Grimley and Julian Rushton (eds.), *The Cambridge Companion to Elgar* (Cambridge: Cambridge University Press, 2004), pp. 63–80.
Jaeger, A. J., *The Dream of Gerontius: Analytical and Descriptive Notes* (London: Novello, 1900).

Kennedy, Michael, *The Life of Elgar* (Cambridge: Cambridge University Press, 2004).

———, *Portrait of Elgar*, 3rd edn. (Oxford: Oxford University Press, 1987; orig. edn. 1968).

———, *The Works of Ralph Vaughan Williams*, 2nd edn. (London: Oxford University Press, 1980; orig. edn. 1964).

Kent, Christopher, 'A View of Elgar's Methods of Composition through the Sketches of the Symphony No. 2 in E- (Op. 63)', *Proceedings of the Royal Musical Association*, 103 (1976–7), pp. 41–60.

Leach, Elizabeth Eva, *Sung Birds: Music, Poetry, and Nature in the Later Middle Ages* (Ithaca, NY: Cornell University Press, 2007).

Lee, Sidney (ed.), 'Roberts, Sir Henry Gee', *Dictionary of National Biography* (London: Smith, Elder & Co., 1896).

Maine, Basil, *Elgar, His Life and Works*, 2 vols (London: G. Bell, 1933; reprinted, Bath: Chivers, 1973).

Mark, Christopher, 'The Later Orchestral Music (1910–34)', in Daniel M. Grimley and Julian Rushton (eds.), *The Cambridge Companion to Elgar* (Cambridge: Cambridge University Press, 2004), pp. 154–70.

McGuire, Charles Edward, 'Elgar, Judas, and the Theology of Betrayal', *19th-Century Music*, 23 (2000), pp. 236–72.

———, *Elgar's Oratorios: The Creation of an Epic Narrative* (Aldershot: Ashgate, 2002), pp. 3–9.

———, 'Measure of a Man: Catechizing Elgar's Catholic Avatars', in Byron Adams (ed.), *Elgar and His World* (Princeton: Princeton University Press, 2007).

McVeagh, Diana M., *Edward Elgar: His Life and Music* (London: Dent, 1955; reprinted, Westport, CT: Hyperion Press, 1979).

———, 'Mrs Edward Elgar', *Musical Times*, 125 (1984), pp. 76–8.

Meikle, Robert, '"The True Foundation": The Symphonies', in Monk (ed.), *Edward Elgar: Music and Literature* (Aldershot: Scolar, 1993), pp. 45–71.

Mitchell, William R., *Elgar in the Yorkshire Dales* (Giggleswick: W. R. Mitchell, 1987).

Monk, Raymond (ed.), *Edward Elgar: Music and Literature* (Aldershot: Scolar, 1993).

———, *Elgar Studies* (Aldershot: Scolar, 1990).

Moore, Jerrold Northrop, *Edward Elgar: A Creative Life* (Oxford: Oxford University Press, 1984).

———, *Elgar: Child of Dreams* (London: Faber and Faber, 2004).

Newman, Ernest, '"The Spirit of England": Edward Elgar's New Choral Work', *Musical Times*, 57 (1916), pp. 235–9.

———, *Elgar*, 3rd edn. (London: Bodley Head, 1922; orig. edn. 1906).

Parry, Sir Hubert, 'Symphony', in *Grove's Dictionary of Music and Musicians*, 2nd edn., ed. J. A. Fuller Maitland, vol. 4 (London: Macmillan, 1908), pp. 763–97.

Porter, Bernard, *The Absent-Minded Imperialists: Empire, Society, and Culture in Britain* (Oxford: Oxford University Press, 2004).

Powell, Dora, *Edward Elgar: Memories of a Variation* (London: Remploy, 1979; orig. edn. 1937).

Rainbow, Bernarr, 'Tonic Sol-Fa', in Stanley Sadie and John Tyrrell (eds.), *The New Grove Dictionary of Music and Musicians*, 2nd edn. (London: Macmillan, and New York: Grove, 2001).

Reed, W. H., *Elgar*, 2nd edn. (London: Dent, 1943; orig. edn. 1939), pp. 10–11.

———, *Elgar as I Knew Him* (London: Gollancz, 1973; orig. edn. 1936).

Reith, J. C. W., *Into the Wind* (London: Hodder & Stoughton, 1949).

Richards, Jeffrey, *Imperialism and Music: Britain, 1876–1953* (Manchester: Manchester University Press, 2001).

Riley, Matthew, 'Rustling Reeds and Lofty Pines: Elgar and the Music of Nature', *19th-Century Music,* 16 (2000), pp. 155–77.

Rushton, Julian, *Elgar: 'Enigma' Variations* (Cambridge: Cambridge University Press, 1999).

———, 'In Search of a Symphony: Orchestral Music to 1908', in Daniel M. Grimley and Julian Rushton (eds.), *The Cambridge Companion to Elgar* (Cambridge: Cambridge University Press, 2004), pp. 139–53.

———, *Mozart: An Extraordinary Life* (London: Associated Board of the Royal Schools of Music, 2005).

———, 'The A. T. Shaw Lecture 2006: Elgar, Kingdom, and Empire', *Elgar Society Journal*, 14/6 (2006), pp. 15–26.

———, 'Lost Love and Unwritten Songs: Elgar's Parker Cycle, Op. 59', in J. P. E. Harper-Scott and Julian Rushton (eds.), *Elgar Studies* (Cambridge: Cambridge University Press, 2007).

Said, Edward W., *Orientalism* (London: Routledge & Kegan Paul, and New York: Pantheon, 1978).

Sams, Eric, 'Elgar's Cipher Letter to Dorabella', *Musical Times,* 111 (1970), pp. 151–4 and Anderson, *Elgar*, p. 156.

———, 'Variations on an Original Theme (Enigma)', *Musical Times,* 111 (1970), pp. 258–62.

———, 'Elgar's Enigmas: A Past Script and a Post Script', *Musical Times,* 111 (1970), pp. 692–4.

Shaw, George Bernard, 'Sir Edward Elgar', *Music & Letters,* 1 (1920), pp. 7–11.

Shiel, Alison I., 'Charles Sanford Terry in the Elgar Diaries', *Elgar Society Journal,* 12 (2002), pp. 193–201.

Shore, Bernard, *The Orchestra Speaks* (London: Longmans, Green, 1938).

———, *Sixteen Symphonies* (London: Longmans Green, 1949).

Sitwell, Osbert, *Laughter in the Next Room* (Boston: Little, Brown, 1948, and London: Macmillan, 1949).

Thomson, Aidan J., 'Elgar in German Criticism', in Daniel M. Grimley and Julian Rushton (eds.), *The Cambridge Companion to Elgar* (Cambridge: Cambridge University Press, 2004), pp. 204–13.

———, 'Elgar and Chivalry', *19th-Century Music,* 28 (2005), pp. 254–75.

———, 'Unmaking *the Music Makers*', in J. P. E. Harper-Scott and Julian Rushton (eds.), *Elgar Studies* (Cambridge: Cambridge University Press, 2007).

Tovey, Donald Francis, *Essays in Musical Analysis*, vol. 1: *Symphonies* (London: Oxford University Press, 1935).

Trowell, Brian, 'Elgar's Use of Literature', in Raymond Monk (ed.), *Edward Elgar: Music and Literature* (Aldershot: Scolar, 1993), pp. 182–326.

———, 'The Road to Brinkwells: The Late Chamber Music', in Lewis Foreman (ed.), *"Oh My Horses!": Elgar and the Great War* (Rickmansworth: Elgar Editions, 2001), pp. 353–62.

Young, Percy M., *Elgar, O.M.: A Study of a Musician*, 2nd edn. (London: Purnell Book Services, 1973; orig. edn. 1955).

Index